Econometric Society Monographs No. 6

Disequilibrium foundations of equilibrium economics

Econometric Society Monographs

The Econometric Society is an international society for the advancement of economic theory in relation to statistics and mathematics. The Econometric Society Monograph Series is designed to promote the publication of original research contributions of high quality in mathematical economics and theoretical and applied econometrics.

Other titles in the series:

Werner Hildenbrand, Editor *Advances in economic theory*

Werner Hildenbrand, Editor *Advances in econometrics*

G. S. Maddala *Limited-dependent and qualitative variables in econometrics*

Gerard Debreu *Mathematical economics*

Jean-Michel Grandmont *Money and value*

Franklin M. Fisher *Disequilibrium foundations of equilibrium economics*

Bezalel Peleg *Game theoretic analysis of voting in committees*

Roger Bowden and Darrell Turkington *Instrumental variables*

Andreu Mas-Colell *The theory of general economic equilibrium*

James J. Heckman and Burton Singer *Longitudinal analysis of labor market data*

Cheng Hsiao *Analysis of panel data*

Truman F. Bewley, Editor *Advances in economic theory–Fifth World Congress*

Truman F. Bewley, Editor *Advances in econometrics–Fifth World Congress* (Volume I)

Truman F. Bewley, Editor *Advances in econometrics–Fifth World Congress* (Volume II)

Hervé Moulin *Axioms of cooperative decision making*

Disequilibrium foundations of equilibrium economics

FRANKLIN M. FISHER
Massachusetts Institute of Technology

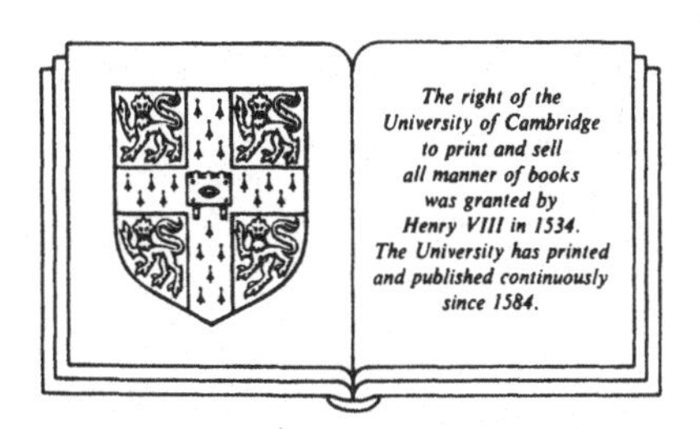

CAMBRIDGE UNIVERSITY PRESS
Cambridge
New York New Rochelle
Melbourne Sydney

CAMBRIDGE UNIVERSITY PRESS
Cambridge, New York, Melbourne, Madrid, Cape Town,
Singapore, São Paulo, Delhi, Tokyo, Mexico City

Cambridge University Press
The Edinburgh Building, Cambridge CB2 8RU, UK

Published in the United States of America by Cambridge University Press, New York

www.cambridge.org
Information on this title: www.cambridge.org/9780521378567

First published 1983
Reprinted 1985
First paperback edition 1989

A catalogue record for this publication is available from the British Library

Library of Congress Cataloguing in Publication Data
Fisher, Franklin M.
Disequilibrium foundations of equilibrium
economics.
(Econometric Society monographs in pure theory;
no. 6)
Includes bibliographical references and index.
I. Equilibrium (Economics) I. Title. II. Series.
HB145.F55 1983 339.5 82-25105
ISBN 0-521-24264-9 hard covers
ISBN 0-521-37856-7 paperback

ISBN 978-0-521-24264-6 Hardback
ISBN 978-0-521-37856-7 Paperback

For Ellen

Contents

* Contains technical material and may be omitted without loss of continuity.

Acknowledgments

This book was written during my tenure as a John Simon Guggenheim Memorial Fellow in 1981–2. It was begun and later revised during visits to the Institute for Mathematical Studies in the Social Sciences at Stanford, but was largely written while visiting Harvard University. It reflects, however, many years of teaching and writing about these subjects at my home institution, M.I.T.

I am indebted to a number of people for discussions on this subject; some of them are thanked in my earlier papers, upon which the present work is based, and I trust I may be forgiven for not repeating those acknowledgments here. I do wish, however, to thank those who helped directly with this book, while absolving them of responsibility. Richard Ericson, Andrei Schleifer, and Suzanne Scotchmer regularly attended my lectures while I was writing the book and provided a most encouraging sense of excitement as well as a number of very insightful discussions. Fernando M. C. B. Saldanha and Robert M. Solow read the manuscript and gave me very helpful comments.

Frank Hahn also read and commented extensively on the book. It was he who suggested that I write it – a suggestion that I was extremely pleased to accept and that I trust he does not now regret. My intellectual debt to him is very great and is evident throughout the work.

Franklin M. Fisher

Cambridge, Mass.
August 1982

CHAPTER 1

Introduction: Disequilibrium analysis and the theory of value

1.1 Introduction

Economists, particularly economic theorists, are most often concerned with the analysis of positions of equilibrium. This is most obviously true in microeconomics, where general equilibrium theory stands as the most complex achievement of rigorous analysis; but it is becoming true of macroeconomics as well, where it has become increasingly popular in rational expectations models to assume that markets always clear.

Less attention is given to disequilibrium. In microeconomics, the subject of the stability of general equilibrium is in poor repute. Too many economists (including economic theorists, who should know better) apparently believe that stability theory means *tâtonnement* – a branch of the subject that died in 1960 and was long ago superseded.[1] They regard it as overformal and empty of results, save under the most extreme ad hoc restrictions, and without much relation to the rich and complex world of real economies.

For macrotheorists the concentration on equilibrium manifests itself in other ways. Aside from the rational-expectations–market-clearing position already mentioned, one currently fashionable branch of the subject investigates fixed-price, quantity-constrained equilibria. Such investigations can be very fruitful, but they are not truly disequilibrium investigations, although they are sometimes misnamed as such. They are analyses of equilibria that are non-Walrasian. The question of whether

[1] I review the stability literature in Chapter 2.

and how the system gets to such an equilibrium is not solved by showing that such points exist.

Yet disequilibrium theory and, in particular, stability theory are of basic importance to economists. The proposition that the equilibria of economic models are not only stable but that convergence to a neighborhood of equilibrium is achieved relatively quickly[2] turns out to be a necessary foundation for the equilibrium analysis of economic theory. If stability theory is unsatisfactory, then that foundation is lacking. The proper conclusion is then either that the foundation must be soundly laid or that the structure based upon it must be drastically altered.

The object of this book is to begin to lay such a foundation. Since the necessary first step is an adequate theory of stability, it is in this area that efforts are largely concentrated. These efforts turn out to be moderately successful; in the model of Part II I am able to show that an economy with rational agents acting on perceived arbitrage opportunities is in fact driven to equilibrium if new opportunities are not continually perceived to arise. I argue that this is the most one can possibly hope for as a basis for a general stability result. It is only a basis, however; the question of just what processes are characterized by such perceptions then becomes central.

The results are not limited to this stability theorem, however. By building a full model of disequilibrium behavior we obtain considerable insight into a number of areas. These include the nature of fixed-price, quantity-constrained equilibria, the role of money, the behavior of arbitraging agents, and the function of the stock market. Although much of what is said is not new, the provision of a full-dress disequilibrium model may help to put these matters in perspective and to provide a framework for answering the many important questions beyond stability that remain open.

The plan of the book is as follows. In the remainder of the present chapter, I discuss the importance of disequilibrium theory and the reasons for a general rather than a partial treatment. Part I considers the existing literature on the stability of general equilibrium (not just tâtonnement!), its successes, its failings, and its methods. That consideration sets the stage for the full-scale model of Part II, which seeks to analyze the disequilibrium behavior of an economy with arbitraging agents.

The matters discussed in this book are of considerable interest to the general economic theorist. I have therefore kept technical matters separate. The nontechnical reader, by omitting those chapters and sections

[2] Throughout this book, the term *speed of convergence* refers to this.

marked with an asterisk should be able to follow the material without loss of continuity, although, inevitably, with some loss of precision. The technical reader, on the other hand, should read the unstarred as well as the starred sections, for the material is not always repeated.

1.2 The importance of disequilibrium analysis

As already stated, microeconomic theory is primarily about positions of equilibrium. The plans of agents (usually derived from the solution of individual optimization problems) are taken together, and certain variables - usually prices - are assumed to take on values that make those plans mutually consistent. Comparative static analysis then proceeds to compare equilibria corresponding to different values of underlying parameters.

In all this, very little is said about the dynamics of the process that leads an equilibrium to be established in the first place or by which the system adjusts to a new equilibrium when the old one is displaced by a parameter shift. Attention is centered on the equilibria themselves (with some awkward problems when they are not unique), and points of non-equilibrium are discussed by showing that the system cannot remain at such points.

But showing that disequilibrium points will not be maintained is necessary but very far from sufficient to justify analyzing only equilibria. The view that equilibria are the points of interest must logically rest on two underlying properties about the dynamics of what happens out of equilibrium. First, the system must be *stable*; that is, it must converge to some equilibrium. Second, such convergence must take place relatively quickly. If the predictions of comparative statics are to be interesting in a world in which conditions change, convergence to equilibrium must be sufficiently rapid that the system, reacting to a given parameter shift, gets close to the predicted new equilibrium before parameters shift once more. If this is not the case, and, a fortiori, if the system is unstable so that convergence *never* takes place, then what will matter will be the "transient" behavior of the system as it reacts to disequilibrium. Of course, it will then be a misnomer to call such behavior "transient," for it will never disappear.

A little more detail may help to bring the point home and may also serve to show that the problem is not limited to microeconomics. Consider models of rational expectations. In such models, analysis generally proceeds by finding positions of rational expectations equilibrium if they exist. At all other points, agents in the model will have arbitrage opportunities; one or another group will be able systematically to improve its position. The possibility of such arbitrage (plus the assumption that agents are smart enough to take advantage of it) is enough to show that points that are not rational expectations equilibria cannot be points at which the system remains; the process of arbitrage will drive the system away from such points. Yet this, by itself, is not enough to justify analyzing the properties of rational expectations equilibria as though such equilibria were all that mattered. The fact that arbitrage will drive the system away from points that are *not* rational expectations equilibria does not mean that arbitrage will force the system to converge to points that *are* rational expectations equilibria. The latter proposition is one of stability and it requires a separate proof. Without such a proof - and, indeed, without a proof that such convergence is relatively rapid - there is no foundation for the practice of analyzing only the equilibrium points of a system which may spend most or all of its time far from such points and which has little or no tendency to approach them. To sum up, the standard treatment of economic theory as an equilibrium subject is very incomplete without a stability proof (and an analysis of adjustment speeds). This may or may not make disequilibrium theory directly useful as a tool in the study of real-world economic phenomena, but it makes it indispensable as a basis for those tools which are typically employed in such study. (As we shall see, disequilibrium considerations also lead to further insights as to how those tools should be applied.)

The basic issue with regard to stability can be illustrated by considering a remark made to me long ago by an extremely prominent economist. He stated that the study of stability of general equilibrium is unimportant first, because it is obvious that the economy is stable and second, because if it isn't stable we are all wasting our time.

Consider first the question of whether it is obvious that the actual economy is stable. Instability need not mean explosion but rather a lack of a tendency to converge to a particular equilibrium. Are real-world economies stable? It is hard to know. Certainly it is not the case that relative prices are constant; they change all the time. It is evident that many or all such changes are caused by exogenous shocks (changes in tastes, technological change, population growth, and so forth) - although the matter of which if any of such changes are properly considered exogenous may be delicate. Yet it is not immediately obvious that *all* that is happening is convergence to new equilibria; still less is it obvious that such convergence is instantaneous or so rapid that the transient disequilibrium behavior of the system responding to such shocks is unimportant.

The more perceptive part of the above-cited remark is the second half, that if the economy is not stable many, if not most economists have been wasting their time. The truth behind this lies in the possible lack of applicability of equilibrium tools and equilibrium theory to the analysis of a system which may not be close to equilibrium at all. In such a case, however, the study of disequilibrium, if not stability, becomes the main business of economists.

However, the remark misses a point of major importance. Even if the economy is stable *and* even if it converges to equilibrium quite rapidly, this does not make the study of stability theory a matter of little importance. Quite the contrary. Without a stability theory there is no guarantee that the theoretical models used to study the economy will have the stability property which the use of equilibrium tools assumes about the economy. Put succinctly, the question is not merely whether the economy is stable but whether the models we use are stable. If the equilibrium analysis of economic theory is incompatible with stability, then there is something wrong with that analysis whether or not the economy is stable (and particularly if it is stable). If such equilibrium analysis is consistent with stability only under additional assumptions, then the study of those assumptions is surely an important matter and may yield insights about equilibrium itself.[3]

If some but not all equilibria can be the limits of stable adjustment processes this is a matter of great importance. If the equilibrium approached depends on the adjustment process, this needs to be studied. Finally, even if it were to turn out that any equilibrium was necessarily stable and that nothing further needed to be assumed to buttress the use of equilibrium tools, the proof of such a fact would be of considerable importance; it is not a matter to be taken on faith.

In brief, the question of what, if any, disequilibrium stories have equilibrium endings like those assumed ab initio by economic theorists is a question of paramount interest for such theorists especially if the world is stable.

1.3 An alternative possibility: Always-clearing markets

There is, however, another view of these matters according to which equilibrium analysis apparently needs no justification. This view, most closely associated with Lucas,[4] states that markets should always be thought of as being in equilibrium in the following sense:

Supply and demand in any particular market depend on price. Hence a market can only fail to clear because the price involved is "wrong." To fix ideas, suppose that demand could exceed supply. Then price is too low. Buyers unable to purchase will make offers at higher prices, and this

[3] In one sense, this is Samuelson's Correspondence Principle (Samuelson, 1947).
[4] See, for example, Lucas (1975, 1976, 1977).

will continue until either they obtain their desired purchases or the price has risen high enough that they no longer wish to purchase, which comes to the same thing.

Similarly, where supply might exceed demand, as in the labor market in times of unemployment, workers (suppliers) will lower the wage at which they are willing to work - simultaneously lowering the amount they are willing to work at the offered wage - until they can work as much as they want to at such wages. This includes the possibility that the wage drops low enough that they are content not to work at all.

The process just described, apart from the question of its realism, is a dynamic adjustment process. Is is essentially a tâtonnement process in which unsatisfied buyers or sellers attempt to recontract for goods or factors by changing prices. Yet the central feature of analyses based on this view is not a consideration of that adjustment process at all. Rather it is the position that all markets are best viewed as constantly in short-run equilibrium with price offers *instantly* adjusted to the equilibrium point. The movement of actual market prices is then to be analyzed as a sequence of such temporary equilibria.

But the view that markets clear instantaneously in this manner begs the question of stability. If we take the process of price offers as a dynamic one taking place in real time, then it is not obvious without a stability proof that such a process converges at all, let alone quickly enough to warrant treating all markets as perpetually clearing. Indeed, as the analysis of tâtonnement (reviewed below) suggests, stability is far from certain where we take full account (as we must) of the effects that changing prices in one market have on excess demand or supply in other markets. Only if we suppose that agents somehow leap instantly to market-clearing price offers can we avoid such stability considerations.

Can we suppose that agents in fact do so leap? There are two possibilities depending on what view we take of the nature of the prices offered by individual agents. The first possibility is that agents understand the full state of affairs in all markets simultaneously, including the effects of price in each market on all other markets. They calculate market-clearing prices and name the general equilibrium prices as their offers. Plainly this is absurd. It imputes to agents an omniscience and calculating ability that go far beyond the sensible rational expectations position that agents will act upon arbitrage opportunities. Moreover, even if we suppose that agents have complete and costless information and calculating abilities, it does not follow that it is individually optimal for each agent to move instantly to the equilibrium prices. If there are profits to be earned in disequilibrium some agents may find it worthwhile to try to earn them. (To appeal to the frequent possibility that equilibria have the Nash property of being optimal for each agent given the actions of the others merely begs this question. Why should any agent believe that all other agents will jump to equilibrium positions or that they will have similar beliefs?) Only a complete focus on equilibrium can make the disequilibrium and stability question disappear in this way. Indeed, one might add that having gone so far we might as well go the whole distance and suppose that agents move instantaneously to a position of long-run equilibrium, leaving no need to consider short-run equilibria at all.

The second possibility is to *define* equilibrium in such a way that it is always present. Of course it is possible to do this; any outcome can be considered an equilibrium in the sense that agents do what they do instead of doing something else. But such a treatment does not get us very far; the study of what happens when the optimizing plans of different agents are not compatible simply gets renamed as a study of moving equilibria rather than of disequilibrium. Either way it is important to study.

Disequilibrium questions cannot be avoided. If "equilibrium" is to have any substantive meaning, one must be willing to countenance the possibility of encountering disequilibrium states. Once that is recognized, the stability question becomes of central importance particularly for those who wish to analyze the system as though it were always in equilibrium. A stability proof is the basic underpinning for such a position.

1.4 Why study the stability of general equilibrium?

The conclusion that the widespread use of equilibrium analysis in economic theory requires a study of stability applies with perhaps greatest force to models of general equilibrium. This is so for the following reason. As long as we are merely analyzing positions of equilibrium, partial analysis can sometimes be regarded as a logical simplification. Imagine, for example, that we seek the price that clears a particular market with all outside prices assumed fixed. Assuming a general equilibrium exists, one such vector of fixed outside prices will be that vector which, together with the market-clearing price we seek, generates a general equilibrium. In that sense, partial equilibrium is consistent with general equilibrium and supposing outside prices fixed may be a helpful simplification.

When we come to comparative statics, the situation is rather trickier, because the levels at which outside prices must be fixed to assure compatibility with general equilibrium may very well depend on the parameter the effect of whose shift is being analyzed. This will occur even if only because such general equilibrium prices depend on the level of the market-clearing price in the particular market under analysis. Nevertheless, such partial analysis can provide insights into the most proximate effects of shifts that directly affect a particular market.

When we come to dynamics, however, it is harder to justify a partial treatment, particularly if we are interested in providing the kind of stability underpinning for equilibrium analysis which I have argued is needed. Consider the following. Convergence of a partial dynamic model in which only a subset of markets and prices is allowed to adjust is neither necessary nor sufficient for convergence of a full general model with all markets and prices adjusting. Suppose then that a particular partial model does converge to equilibrium but the general one in which it is embedded fails to do so. In such a case, the convergence of the partial model - however interesting it may be - provides no truly satisfactory justification for equilibrium analysis. This is because such positions of equilibrium will not in fact be reached unless other variables are artificially held fixed or other effects ignored, something which is not possible in the real economy. Suppose, on the other hand, that a particular partial model fails to converge but that the general one in which it is embedded turns out to be stable. Then the lack of convergence of the partial model - however interesting it may be - does not prevent us from analyzing its equilibria, since the convergence of the general model assures us that the partial model, as part of the general one, will get to equilibrium. It is true that the nature of that equilibrium will generally depend on the behavior of the general model and on the effects which adjustments outside the partial model have on affairs inside it and vice versa. This, however, is no different from the logical problems already mentioned which occur in comparative statics analysis in partial models.

To put one example of this succinctly: If we wish to show that rational agents, availing themselves of arbitrage opportunities, will drive the system to equilibrium, we must do so without artificially restricting the set of arbitrage opportunities which agents see. This means that we cannot hold some prices constant and ignore the effects of arbitrage in some markets on opportunities outside them.

There are, of course, other reasons for being interested in the stability of general equilibrium at least as a first topic in the attempt to provide the necessary foundation for equilibrium analysis. For one thing it (perhaps surprisingly) turns out to be easier in some senses to analyze stability in general models than in all but the simplest partial ones. This is partly because of the generality of the model, which keeps one from having to analyze various special cases and partly because of the general relationships - chiefly Walras' Law - which hold in full but not in partial models. The literature (reviewed in the next chapter), it is true, has not always taken full advantage of these things, but, over time, they have come to be increasingly well understood. Plainly, if general equilibrium stability is tractable, it is the natural place to begin.

More important than this, however, is the central role which general equilibrium plays in economic analysis. Much of what economists have to say about the results of competition, the usefulness or lack thereof of governmental intervention, and the role of the price system is based on propositions about general equilibrium. These are the propositions rigorously formulated in modern times as the central theorems of welfare economics concerning the relations between Pareto optima and competitive equilibria. These propositions, which may be the single most important set of ideas that economists have to convey to laypeople, implicitly assume that general competitive equilibrium is stable and, indeed, that convergence takes place relatively quickly. If this were not so, welfare comparisons of equilibria would be largely irrelevant since what would matter would be comparison of the relatively "transient" behavior of alternative systems including alternative forms of market organization.

The importance of the stability of general equilibrium is not restricted to microeconomic analysis, however. The central question which Keynes sought to answer in *The General Theory of Employment, Interest and Money* (Keynes, 1936) was that of whether (and how) an economy could get stuck at an underemployment equilibrium. To show this, it is not enough to show that such an equilibrium exists, we must also show that it has at least local stability properties so that an economy that gets close enough to such a point will not escape from it without an exogenous change in circumstances. This problem, however, can be treated rigorously only as a problem in the stability of general equilibrium. The fact that Keynes and later macroeconomists did not so address it (had Keynes done so the *General Theory* might never have been written), but chose instead to use illuminating but fundamentally heuristic tools should not be allowed to obscure this. Like most questions in economic theory - micro or macro - the question of underemployment equilibrium has a general setting in back of it and, like all equilibrium questions, it involves a stability analysis to justify it.

1.5 Toward a satisfactory dynamic theory

I now briefly consider the features that a proper theory of disequilibrium adjustment should have if it is to provide a satisfactory underpinning for the use of general equilibrium tools, that is, if we are to show under what conditions the rational behavior of individual agents drives an economy to equilibrium. There already emerge from such considerations some lessons for the use of equilibrium tools. The themes sounded here recur with more development in later chapters.

The first thing to say about a satisfactory theory has already been indicated. Such a theory must involve dynamics with adjustment to disequilibrium over time modeled. It will not do to attempt to buttress equilibrium analysis by assuming disequilibrium away. Further, while the analysis of temporary equilibria or of quantity-constrained, fixed-price equilibria,[5] may be both interesting and important, no satisfactory theory can stop without explaining how such points are reached and why they are maintained, if indeed they are.

Clearly, as in any dynamic model, the most satisfactory situation would be one in which the equations of motion of the system permitted an explicit solution with the values of all the variables given as specific, known functions of time. In such a circumstance, not only would the question of stability be settled, but so would the pressing question of convergence speed, which could be directly computed. Further, the transient behavior of the system would be known explicitly. If convergence speed turned out to be low, we could then discard comparative statics for an explicit comparative dynamics. If convergence speed turned out to be high, an explicit closed-form solution would let us decide to which of several equilibria a newly disturbed system would tend - a point often overlooked and quite beyond the power of comparative statics.[6] More fundamentally, the path-dependent nature of the ultimate equilibrium (discussed below) would cease to be a problem if the path were known.

Unfortunately, such a closed-form solution is far too much to hope for. At the level of generality appropriate to a theory which seeks to provide the disequilibrium foundation for general equilibrium analysis, it would be inappropriate to assume specific functional forms for the equations denoting the behavior of agents. With such forms, the obtaining of an explicit solution would be laborious and almost certainly a problem in numerical analysis. Without them it is literally impossible. Whether or not econometric estimation can ever reach the point where satisfactory prediction of the behavior of all prices, supplies, and demands can be obtained for a particular economy, it can never substitute for a satisfactory theory of economies in general.

We must thus work with the kinds of restrictions on functional forms which are generated by theory. These must be grounded in the theory of

[5] There is a very large literature on these topics. Drazen (1980) presents a survey.
[6] See Arrow and Hahn (1971) for a discussion of such difficulties.

the behavior of individual agents, the firm and the household. This has (at least) two consequences.

First, we know from the work of Sonnenschein and others[7] that the theory of individual equilibrium behavior does not much restrict the nature of aggregate excess demand functions. Beyond Walras' Law, homogeneity of degree zero in prices, and continuity properties, nothing more can be said as a general matter. Hence, stability theories which require further special assumptions on excess demand functions will be special theories. While such special assumptions would be of vital interest if they turned out to be *necessary* for stability, they are of somewhat limited interest if they are merely sufficient. While it is possible that such sufficient conditions will turn out to be empirically justified, the cases presently known to be sufficient are not such as to offer much hope in this direction.

Second – a point perhaps more fundamental for this discussion – it is a mistake to ground disequilibrium theory in the *equilibrium* behavior of agents. Rather, the theory of the household and the firm must be reformulated and extended where necessary to allow agents to perceive that the economy is not in equilibrium and to act on that perception. Without this, we cannot hope to provide a theory of what happens when arbitrage opportunities appear, for the essence of the appearance of such opportunities is that agents see and act on them. A theory that wishes to show how such actions cause the disappearance of these opportunities and a restoration of equilibrium cannot content itself either with supposing that they never exist or with assuming that agents do not see them.

Proper analysis of the disequilibrium behavior of agents, however, will require some reformulation of the theories of the individual firm and household. This is because the standard equilibrium approach to microeconomics is reflected in these theories. Agents in the standard theory react to given prices and take no account either of the fact that prices may change or of the possibility that they may not be able to complete their own transactions.[8] So long as the plans which agents make are compatible, this presents no difficulty; in equilibrium the equilibrium assumptions of agents are fulfilled. If we are to deal with disequilibrium, however, this will not be the case, and we must start at the level of individual agents.

This necessary approach leads to one problem of substantial difficulty

[7] See Sonnenschein (1972, 1973), Debreu (1974), and Mantel (1976).

[8] I do not mean to suggest that there has been no work on these matters. The fixed-price, quantity-constrained equilibrium literature referred to above is an obvious example.

and to certain enlightening consequences. The difficulty has already been referred to and will arise again. It turns out to be fairly easy to describe how optimizing agents set their quantity demands in response to their price (and constraint) expectations. It is not easy to reformulate the theory of individual behavior to explain the movement of prices, however. This is so for an obvious reason. The equilibrium theory of individual competitive behavior on which we shall build is one in which prices are taken as given and quantities optimally set. This can readily be extended to take price expectations as given. But, as Koopmans (1957) among others has remarked, in a world in which all prices are taken as given, how do prices ever change? This is a question of great importance to which there is no really satisfactory answer despite the very general results later in this book in terms of stability; I shall return to this matter later.

The necessary grounding of disequilibrium theory in the optimizing behavior of individual agents has consequences beyond stability theory (the immediate subject of this book). It also has implications for the study of the speed with which convergence is attained. This is a necessary part of any disequilibrium theory since, if equilibrium analysis is to be justified, one must show not only stability but also rapid convergence, while if rapid convergence is not attained the study of transient behavior rather than of equilibria becomes of paramount importance. A general stability proof merely shows asymptotic convergence to equilibrium but says nothing about how close to equilibrium the system gets in finite time. Without a closed-form solution it is hard to see how to get much further.

To amplify this, consider the possibility that, having proved stability, one could merely assume that speeds of adjustment were high and then conclude that convergence speed was not a problem. This turns out not to be a simple matter.

The first reason for this is technical. There exist dynamic systems whose stability depends on adjustment speeds not being too high.[9] Although this is generally not true of differential equation models, the representation of actual adjustments in differential rather than difference equation form may simply be a convenient idealization.

This is related to a far more fundamental point. A convergence theory that is to provide a satisfactory underpinning for equilibrium analysis must be a theory in which the adjustments to disequilibrium made by agents are made optimally. But in such a model, this includes the optimal speeds at which to react to changes. Hence we are not free simply to assume that such speeds are high; rather they will be determined endog-

[9] See, for example, Theocharis (1960) and Fisher (1961).

enously. Moreover, other speeds will be controlled by natural forces such as gestation times. Those speeds cannot simply be assumed as high as would be convenient.

On the other hand, certain of the adjustment speeds involved in the model will be determined by the way in which markets are organized. For example, the speed at which trade takes place out of equilibrium does not merely depend on how quickly agents adjust their demands but also on how easy it is for them to find other agents with whom to trade. It is possible that easy communication between agents leads to swifter convergence than does difficult communication.

This is by no means guaranteed, however. The fact (discussed below) that the equilibria reached are dependent on the adjustment process itself means that a change in such speeds of adjustment changes the equilibrium that is reached from given initial conditions. It is therefore not totally obvious that convergence must take place faster at higher adjustment speeds than at low ones.

The study of problems such as these would form part of a complete theory of comparative dynamics, but this is beyond the state of the art at present and certainly beyond the scope of this book. The present work is about stability and says nothing directly about convergence speeds. Indirectly it does say something, for the proof that optimal individual action (under appropriate assumptions) produces stability is itself a proof that such stability holds for all ranges of adjustment speeds for things beyond the control of agents *and* for the optimal adjustment speeds of things within their control. At least for the latter class of adjustments, the difficulty that stability may depend on the particular lag structure or adjustment process assumed does not arise. Much work remains to be done, however.

Returning to our main topic of stability, the fact that any satisfactory theory must be grounded in the theory of individual behavior has further consequences for some current work and for the way in which we view certain forms of analysis. To begin with, the stability problem is not satisfactorily solved by showing that there exist some adjustment processes which converge. However interesting certain adjustment processes may be, unless there is reason to believe that they arise from the optimizing behavior of agents, they cannot be regarded as providing more than a computational algorithm for finding equilibria.[10] Indeed, the situation here is worse than that involved in the ad hoc specialization of excess demand functions to achieve a stability proof. We know that such

[10] I take this view of the otherwise interesting work of Smale (1976a), on global Newton methods. In terms of the present problem, such work merely shows that *some* convergent processes exist.

specialization *can* obtain under special circumstances. We often do not know that particular convergent processes are *ever* consistent with a sensible story about the behavior of individual agents.

1.6 Path dependence, hysteresis, and comparative statics

The study of stability theory also casts a somewhat negative light on the usefulness of computational algorithms for the calculation of points of general equilibria even on their own grounds. Such algorithms as that of Scarf (1973) provide a method for finding general equilibrium points given (among other things) the endowments of the agents. In a real economy, however, trading, as well as production and consumption, goes on out of equilibrium. It follows that, in the course of convergence to equilibrium (assuming that occurs), endowments change. In turn this changes the set of equilibria. Put more succinctly, the set of equilibria is path dependent - it depends not merely on the initial state but on the dynamic adjustment process. Indeed, in the most general case with production and consumption, there is even a hysteresis effect, with equilibria dependent not only on the current state of the system through endowments but also on the past history of how the system developed. But even path dependence alone makes the calculation of equilibria corresponding to the initial state of the system essentially irrelevant. What matters is the equilibrium that the economy will reach from given initial conditions, not the equilibrium that it would have been in, given initial endowments, had prices happened to be just right.

A simple example for the case of only disequilibrium trade may help to clarify these matters. Consider a two-person exchange economy, with both persons (I and II) price-takers. The Edgeworth–Bowley box diagram for such an economy is drawn in Figure 1.6.1. The initial endowment point is $\bar{X}$. Corresponding to this is an equilibrium point A (assumed unique). If, starting at $\bar{X}$, prices happen to be the right equilibrium prices, shown by the solid line, then the two agents will trade until they get to A. But if initial prices do not happen to be "correct" in this sense - and, out of equilibrium, there is no reason to suppose that they will be "correct" - this need not happen at all. Suppose instead that initial prices happen to be as shown by the dashed line in the figure. Then trade will take place until the agents reach B (approximately). If prices then shift to those shown by the dotted line, trade will take place again until C is reached. It is true that C is a competitive equilibrium, but it is not the equilibrium point, A, which, in a static sense, corresponds to the initial endowment $\bar{X}$. In this example, it is the equilibrium point which corresponds statically to B, the new endowment point achieved through

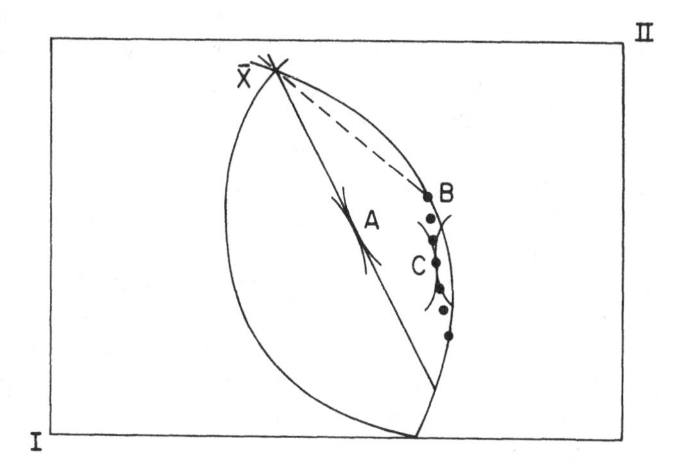

Figure 1.6.1.

trade in the first step. In more general models, there will be more than two steps (indeed, there can be continuous change) and the situation will be more complex; however, the point should now be clear. An algorithm that predicts that the economy with endowment $\bar{X}$ will get to A will simply be wrong.

A theory which hopes to provide a foundation for equlibrium economics cannot avoid these matters. This is particularly true since, as discussed in Chapter 2, the analysis of convergence *without* disequilibrium trade - tâtonnement - shows that such systems are *not* generally stable. Hence it is a mistake to believe that one can deal with path dependency by assuming such trade to be negligible.

The consequences of the path-dependent nature of equilibrium and of hysteresis reach farther than the pointlessness of static algorithms, however. Such effects imply that, however useful comparative static analysis may be at the level of the individual agent, it is unlikely to provide more than illuminating heuristic insights when applied to general or even to partial equilibrium situations. Comparative static analysis will show us how the equilibrium corresponding to a particular set of circumstances changes when a particular parameter shifts. However, the displaced equilibrium will not be that to which the disturbed system converges (assuming stability). Rather, the very process of convergence, of adjustment to the displacement, will itself further change the equilibrium. Whether or not the ultimate equilibrium will be close to the one predicted by comparative statics or even whether the ultimate effects of the displacement will be in the predicted direction is not a question that lends itself to a general answer. The answer depends on the effects of the parameter shift on the adjustment path of the system, on comparative dynamics rather than on comparative statics.[11] Unfortunately, a satisfactory analysis of comparative dynamics lies in the future. It is not satisfactory, however, to beg the question and assert that path-dependent or hysteresis effects may be small. What is required is a *proof* that they are small, and this we do not have, particularly since rapid price adjustment alone does not generally lead to stability.

These matters may be put in perhaps a more striking way. The theory of value is not satisfactory without a description of the adjustment processes that are applicable to the economy and of the way in which individual agents adjust to disequilibrium. In this sense, stability analysis is of far more than merely technical interest. It is the first step in a reformulation of the theory of value.[12]

[11] This point was made to me independently by Fernando Saldanha. Note that even apart from path dependence, comparative dynamics would be required to decide which of several nonunique equilibria the system will go to when equilibrium is displaced. Nonuniqueness, of course, is the rule rather than the exception. See Arrow and Hahn (1971).

[12] I am indebted to Hugo Sonnenschein for emphasizing this to me.

PART I

Methods and problems of the general equilibrium stability literature

CHAPTER 2

The development of the stability literature

2.1 Introduction

It cannot be pretended that the theory of stability developed historically with an eye to the considerations discussed in the previous chapter. Nevertheless, that discussion provides a useful vantage point from which to view the development of the subject. In turn, such a review allows us naturally to build an understanding of the steps which lead to ever more satisfactory stability models.

In my view, there have been four major developments in the history of modern stability analysis. These are (1) the realization that the subject was one which had to be studied in a context with a formal dynamic structure; (2) the realization that global, rather than simply local, results could be obtained; (3) the introduction of non-tâtonnement processes; and (4) closely related to this, the insight that attention paid to specifying the disequilibrium processes involved could lead to far more satisfactory results than could be obtained by restricting the excess demand functions. In some ways, the analyses resulting from each of these steps made increasing use of the economic underpinnings of the stability problem (largely, but not exclusively, Walras' Law) and led to correspondingly more and more satisfactory results.

2.2 Tâtonnement: Local stability

The history of modern stability analysis begins with Samuelson (1941, 1947) who, in considering what Hicks (1939) had called "perfect

Much of this chapter is taken from my Frank W. Paish Lecture, Fisher (1976b). Hahn (1982), Arrow and Hahn (1971), and Negishi (1962) give other surveys of the literature. The discussion given here does not pretend to be a complete survey.

stability'' observed that the subject could only be rigorously studied in a framework specifying the equations of motion of the system when not in equilibrium. He proposed as a formalization of Walras' idea of ''tâtonnement'' a set of price adjustment equations that formed the basis for nearly all later work.

I write those equations in an anachronistically general form as:

$$\dot{P}_i = F^i[Z_i(\mathbf{P})] \quad \text{unless } P_i = 0 \text{ and } Z_i(\mathbf{P}) < 0 \\ \text{in which case } \dot{P}_i = 0 \tag{2.2.1}$$

Here, P_i is the price of the ith commodity, Z_i is the total excess demand for that commodity, taken as a continuous function of the prices, and $F^i(\cdot)$ is a continuous, sign-preserving function, bounded away from zero except as Z_i goes to zero.[1] A dot over a variable denotes a time derivative; and vectors are printed in boldface.

In other words, the price of the ith commodity adjusts in the same direction as excess demand for that commodity, the exact adjustment being a continuous function of excess demand (and therefore of price). The exception to this occurs where such a rule would require that a good which is already free and in excess supply be given a negative price, whereupon the price is simply left at zero.

This formulation, which (either for relative or absolute prices) forms at least part of practically all later work, already raises some technical and some economically substantive problems. The first of these is easy to overlook. It is the assumption that excess demands can be taken as continuous functions of the prices (given endowments, technologies, and so forth). The problem is that there are plausible circumstances in which excess demands *cannot* be taken as functions of the prices, let alone continuous ones. If there are constant returns to scale, for example, a continuous increase in the price of the product, other prices constant, will cause firms to go from wishing to produce zero to wishing to produce an indeterminate amount to wishing to produce an infinite amount. Such cases are ruled out. One need not be a fanatic believer in the universality of constant returns to scale to be troubled by a formulation that cannot handle constant returns even on bounded regions. Yet the assumption that excess demands are continuous functions of prices is essential if we are to use the kind of mathematics which is embodied in (2.2.1), not only

[1] It is possible to generalize this formulation by also allowing $\dot{P}_i$ to depend on prices directly (as in Hahn (1962a), for example), or – in more complex models – on all the state variables of the system while maintaining the properties of $F^i(\cdot)$ as a function of Z_i set out in the text. There is no need to discuss such generalizations explicitly, however.

because it is hard to see what kind of adjustment process is reasonable in the absence of such a functional relationship but also because the very existence of solutions to (2.2.1) depends on such continuity.[2]

Thus we encounter important problems even in the building blocks from which the price-adjustment equation is constructed. When we come to that equation itself, we encounter another problem of even greater importance. Whose behavior does the equation represent? It seems very plausible, to be sure, that price should adjust upward when demand exceeds supply and downward in the opposite case, but just how does this happen? To state it once again, in a world in which all participants take prices as given, who changes the price?[3] Indeed, in the center of a subject which deals with individual behavior how does there arise a behavior equation (not an identity) based solely on aggregates? The familiar story, which goes with (2.2.1), of the auctioneer who adjusts prices until demand equals supply is at best an inconvenient fiction.

The model in Part II of the present book does away with (2.2.1) and replaces it with individual price adjustment - a matter which brings its own problems. I shall return to those problems below. For the present, I add three remarks concerning the difficulty with (2.2.1).

First, the difficulty arises directly with the price-adjustment equation used. It has nothing directly to do with the question of whether or not trade, consumption, or production takes place out of equilibrium.

Second, the difficulty arises because, despite having an excellent theory of static behavior, we know very little about how individuals do or ought to behave when equilibrium is not present; hence, the resort to an aggregate equation.

Finally, despite this fact, we have already made an implicit assumption about disequilibrium behavior in the formulation of (2.2.1) that will have to be considered explicitly later on. It is one which is relatively harmless in the unrealistic world of no trading out of equilibrium but very irksome otherwise. Implicit in the assumption that excess demand influences price is the assumption that individuals take action to make their excess demands effective. This involves the assumption that they *can* take such

[2] Fortunately, a somewhat related technical problem involving the continuity of the adjustment process has been successfully handled. Claude Henry (1973a,b) has shown that the violation of Lipschitz Conditions involved in restricting prices to the positive orthant will still (under reasonable conditions) allow the existence of a solution to (2.2.1) which is continuous in the initial conditions, a matter which had previously to be taken on faith. See also Champsaur, Drèze, and Henry (1977). Constant returns can probably also be handled with differential correspondences, but this has yet to be done.

[3] This important issue was raised by Koopmans (1957), among others.

action which, as we shall later see, implies that they have something of value which they can and do sell so as to have something to offer when they buy. It also involves, however, the assumption that they *do* take such actions and take them now, so that, even though the excess demand involved may be for a good dated in the far future, 1990 toothpaste, for example, individuals who will want that good in the far future begin *immediately* to attempt to acquire it.[4]

I shall refer to this as the "Present Action Postulate." It is implicit in the entire stability literature, although seldom explicitly stated. Perhaps this is because it need not be faced explicitly as long as we remain in a world in which the adjustment of prices to equilibrium can be safely supposed to take place before the dates on any commodities (future or otherwise) come due and *all* acquisitions must be made before any are needed for consumption or production – the Arrow–Debreu world in which all markets and trades occur at the beginning of time and never again.[5] Elegant as such a model is, however, it is not truly satisfactory when applied to real economies developing over time.

Note that, even if we were to adopt a more individualistic and plausible price-adjustment equation than (2.2.1), the problems involved in the Present Action Postulate would still present themselves. Stability analyses that take off from the economics of individual behavior by way of deriving unsatisfied or excess demands must concern themselves with the questions of when and how the participants attempt to exercise those demands. This can only be done in a satisfactory way by allowing agents themselves to care about such timing, which involves letting them be conscious of change. Otherwise, when agents are assumed to set their demands believing they are in equilibrium, it is hard to see how to escape from the assumption that they attempt to exercise those demands when they occur, even though this involves implausible behavior with regard to future commodities.

As indicated, however, this last set of problems can be swept under the rug if one is willing to separate the time in which adjustment takes place from that in which commodities are dated and consumption and production occur. This is essentially guaranteed if we suppose that no trade (let alone consumption and production) takes place before equilibrium is reached; so let us now return to a consideration of the historical development in which the assumption of no disequilibrium trade played an important role. It is, in fact, the latter assumption and not just the price-

[4] Or that individuals who will want to sell that good in the future begin immediately to attempt to sell it. The problems involved are particularly nasty as to firms, as I shall later discuss.

[5] See Debreu (1959) for the classic elegant treatment.

adjustment process (2.2.1) that characterizes the processes known as tâtonnement in the literature.

The early literature, beginning with Samuelson,[6] was primarily concerned with the local stability of the tâtonnement process. This followed Samuelson's observation that local stability properties could be studied by approximating the right-hand side of (2.2.1) linearly and considering the question of when the eigenvalues of the resulting matrix (essentially the Jacobian matrix of the excess demand functions) could be shown to have negative real parts. These discussions made little or no use of Walras' Law, but rather considered the excess demand functions as if they were pretty well unrestricted. Partly as a result of this and partly because of what now seems the rather peculiar origin of the subject - the relations between what Hicks (1939) had called "perfect stability" and the local stability of the truly dynamic equation (2.2.1) - these investigations did not really get very far. They ended up in the rather unfinished place of showing that, provided all commodities were gross substitutes,[7] the local stability of (2.2.1) was equivalent to the not very revealing condition that Hicks had found to be necessary and sufficient for his "perfect stability," namely, that the principal minors of the Jacobian of the excess demand functions alternate in sign.

Such a result was obviously only a very partial one. This was so even in the narrow terms of the relations between Hicks' concept and dynamic stability where it remained for a much later paper of McFadden (1968) to elucidate the matter in terms of relative speeds of adjustment. Even more partial was the result in terms of stability analysis on its own grounds, since the alternation of the principal minors is not particularly interpretable in any natural way. Such a result is best thought of as a lemma rather than as a theorem, and, accordingly, we should not be surprised to find that by the end of the 1950s Hahn (1958) and Negishi (1958) had independently proved (using Walras' Law and the homogeneity of degree zero of the excess demand functions, respectively) that the assumption of gross substitutes itself implied the alternation of the principal minors and hence that, under the gross substitutes assumption, the tâtonnement process was invariably locally stable.[8]

[6] Samuelson (1941, 1947) and including especially Metzler (1945).

[7] That is, that a rise in the price of any one good increases the demand for every other, including income effects. For an analysis of what utility functions generate individual demand functions with this property, see Fisher (1972a).

[8] Other sufficient conditions for the alternation of the principal minors are known. It is equivalent to what Arrow and Hahn (1971) call the "Gale Property" (GP), a sufficient condition for the uniqueness of equilibrium, given endowments.

2.3 Tâtonnement: Global stability

These papers, however, were superseded by the results of a pair of groundbreaking papers by Arrow and Hurwicz (1958) and Arrow, Block, and Hurwicz (1959) which contained a demonstration of the fundamental point that global rather than local stability results might be available (and, indeed, might be easier to obtain than local ones). Among the specific stability results was that of the global stability of tâtonnement under the gross substitutes assumption.

This breakthrough rested on the use of a mathematical device known as Lyapounov's Second Method. Since practically all the work that followed has been based on that device and since my later discussion requires some understanding of it, I shall digress at this point, give some not very rigorous definitions, and discuss Lyapounov's Second Method and the role it plays in analyses of stability.[9] More rigorous definitions and proofs are given in the Appendix.

A *rest point* of an adjustment process such as (2.2.1) is a point at which the process does not move. In the models we shall be considering, rest points are in one-to-one correspondence with points that are in some sense also economic equilibria (although not always Walrasian equilibria when we come to Part II); dynamic adjustment processes whose rest points do not have this property are not interesting for our purpose. (Thus, for example, the rest points of (2.2.1) are readily seen to be precisely the points at which all excess demands are nonpositive and negative excess demands correspond to free goods.) The properties of economic equilibria are often exploited in stability proofs.

A rest point is said to be *globally stable* if the system converges to it from every set of initial conditions. This, of course, is a very strong property. In particular, if there is more than one rest point, then no particular rest point can be globally stable in this sense since if the process begins at some other rest point it will never leave it. We know, however, that uniqueness of general equilibrium requires extremely strong assumptions, even when there is no trading out of equilibrium so that endowments do not change. A fortiori, this is true of more reasonable models where the equilibrium set is path dependent. Thus, since rest points and economic equilibria are in one-to-one correspondence in interesting models, it is unreasonable to require rest points to be globally stable. Instead, we need a somewhat weaker notion of global stability.

[9] Lyapounov (1907). The curious may wish to know that his First Method (for proving stability) was to solve the differential equations being studied, an alternative that is never available at the level of generality involved in general equilibrium analysis.

That notion is provided by the idea of the global stability of an *adjustment process.* An adjustment process, such as (2.2.1), is said to be globally stable if, for any set of initial conditions, there is a rest point to which the system converges. The difference, of course, is that it doesn't have to be the same rest point for all initial conditions. If there is a unique rest point (as there is in the gross substitutes case), then the two notions of global stability coincide.

Finally, it is useful to distinguish this from the definition of the *quasi-stability* of an adjustment process.[10] For convenience of language, let us suppose that the variables involved are prices only, as in (2.2.1). Starting with any initial condition, consider an infinite sequence of prices. Such a sequence may not have a limit (unless prices converge), but it may nevertheless have one or more limit points (roughly, points to smaller and smaller neighborhoods of which the sequence keeps returning). If every limit point of every such sequence is a rest point of the adjustment process, then that process is said to be quasi-stable.

Obviously, the quasi-stability and the global stability of an adjustment process are closely related. It is not hard to show that if an adjustment process is quasi-stable and the variables involved remain in a compact set,[11] then the variables converge to the *set* of rest points - but not necessarily to a particular rest point. Under these conditions, the process will also be globally stable and converge to a particular rest point provided either of two things is true. They are, first, that every rest point is locally isolated (which includes uniqueness as a special case), or, second, that any sequence starting from a given set of initial conditions has only one limit point.[12]

Accordingly, modern stability proofs tend to be in three parts. First (and usually hardest) is a proof of quasi-stability. (This is where Lyapounov's Second Method comes in.) Second is a compactness argument that often (but not always) amounts to an argument that the variables remain bounded. Third is either a demonstration of local uniqueness of rest points or a demonstration that all limit points (starting from the same initial conditions) are the same.[13]

[10] So named by Uzawa (1961).

[11] Some authors include compactness as part of the definition of quasi-stability but I find this inconvenient.

[12] Indeed, given compactness, global stability would follow from uniqueness of the limit point without a proof of quasi-stability. In practice, however, uniqueness of the limit point is generally established by first proving quasi-stability and then exploiting the properties of economic equilibrium.

[13] The work of Debreu (1970) has shown that, for appropriate differentiability assumptions, local isolation of equilibria is true almost everywhere in the appropriate space of economies. Hence the last step in the stability argument

I shall have occasion to mention the latter two steps in my later discussion and they will arise in later chapters. For the present, however, the principal focus will be on the first step: the proof of quasi-stability and the use of Lyapounov's Second Method.

Continue to think in terms of prices. Lyapounov's result is as follows. Suppose that we can find a function, $V(\mathbf{P})$, continuous in the prices, bounded below, and monotonically decreasing through time except at rest points. Then the adjustment process is quasi-stable. Lyapounov's Second Method consists of finding such functions $V(\mathbf{P})$. This is not a simple task and it forms the heart of most stability investigations. As time has gone on, such Lyapounov functions have tended to go from geometrically interpretable measures of the distance from equilibrium to economically more interesting functions such as (as we shall see) the sum of the utilities which households would expect to get if their mutually inconsistent plans could be realised.

Let us now return to the tâtonnement literature. Arrow, Hurwicz, and Block were essentially able to prove that the adjustment process (2.2.1) is globally stable provided that one is willing to place very severe restrictions on the excess demand functions. One such restriction - that of the gross substitutes assumption - has already been mentioned. Somewhat surprisingly, it turns out that this, as well as most of the other cases successfully investigated in the papers under discussion, are special cases of the assumption that the *aggregate* excess demand functions satisfy the Weak Axiom of Revealed Preference (at least in comparisons between equilibrium and other points), an axiom which makes excellent sense in terms of individual behavior but which there is no good reason to impose on aggregate demand functions.[14]

Despite this, because all the special cases they investigated turned out to imply global stability, Arrow, Hurwicz, and Block ventured to conjecture that the tâtonnement process was always globally stable, given only the restriction that the excess demand functions be consistent with underlying economic considerations such as Walras' Law. Not surprisingly, this rather wishful conjecture was soon exploded when Scarf (1960) provided a counterexample.

We now know that such counterexamples are in no sense special. Sonnenschein (1972, 1973), Debreu (1974), and Mantel (1976) have

might be made in this way for non-path-dependent cases. In practice, however, more direct results have generally been available.

14 This is because of income effects. It is worth remarking that it is easy to see that at least local stability would be guaranteed if there were no income effects in view of the negative semidefiniteness of the substitution matrix. See Arrow and Hahn (1971) for a more extended discussion.

shown that the underlying economic derivation of the aggregate excess demand functions does not imply any restrictions beyond homogeneity of degree zero and Walras' Law, thus eliminating any last forlorn hope that stability for tâtonnement processes might be aided by general rather than very special restrictions on the excess demand functions. Indeed, this is true even for local stability since negative semidefiniteness of the Jacobian of the aggregate excess demand functions is not implied by Walras' Law and homogeneity of degree zero.

Returning to the historical development as of 1960, tâtonnement stability was in an awkward corner. The process was not invariably stable; interesting necessary conditions for stability were clearly not to be had; and sufficient conditions for stability appeared to involve wildly restrictive conditions on individual (or aggregate) demand functions. Despite the fact that two other major developments were taking place at about the same time and would lead to far more fruitful results, it is not surprising that the flurry of interest in the stability of general equilibrium more or less died out at about this time.

2.4 Trading processes: Pure exchange

Both of the new developments had in common the fact that, unlike the work just discussed, which can be thought of as largely drawing implications for stability by considering properties that are just as true in equilibrium as out of it, they were based on further specification of the disequilibrium adjustment processes themselves.

One such development was the abandonment of the tâtonnement assumption of no trading out of equilibrium which had wound up in a dead end and the introduction of what are rather inelegantly called "non-tâtonnement" processes. Since that is not a very informative name, I shall refer to them as "trading processes."

It is important to remember that, while this stage of development permits trading out of equilibrium, most of the work to be discussed does not permit consumption or production to take place until equilibrium has been reached. One must think of participants as swapping titles to commodity stocks while prices (and, of course, possessions) adjust. Only after the music stops do people go home and enjoy what they have. Such a model is obviously most suited to pure exchange with no firms. Although a step in the right direction, this model clearly calls out for extension both to firms and to models that permit production and consumption to take place during adjustment.

For the moment, however, let us put such extensions aside and restrict our attention to the case of pure trading processes and pure exchange. At this level, a rather surprising result occurs. Since we have added to the price adjustment process (2.2.1) some set of equations describing how individual stocks of commodities change hands, we might expect that we have made proofs of stability harder than in the tâtonnement case, since the system is now more complicated than before. This turns out not to be true, however, provided we stay with pure exchange and are willing to make the reasonable assumption that nobody can change his wealth by trading at constant prices. That latter assumption might be called one of "No Swindling," for it amounts to saying that one cannot get anything by trading except by giving up something of equal value.

If one is willing to make that assumption, then it turns out that in essentially every case in which tâtonnement is known to be stable, exchange trading processes are also.[15] The basic reason for this lies in Lyapounov's Second Method. Suppose we have a Lyapounov function that depends on prices and on aggregate excess demands. The time derivative of that function in a trading process differs from the corresponding time derivative in tâtonnement by terms which depend on those parts of the time derivatives of the aggregate excess demand functions that come from the changes in individual commodity stocks induced by trading with prices fixed. In the absence of quantity constraints, however, an individual's demand for any commodity is affected by changes in his holdings at constant prices only insofar as these changes affect his wealth, and, by the No Swindling assumption, his wealth is not affected. The change in an individual's *excess* demand for a commodity brought about in this way is therefore merely the negative of the change in his actual holdings of that commodity. Since, in pure exchange, the aggregate stock of any commodity is fixed, there are no such effects on *aggregate* excess demand. Hence the time derivative of any such Lyapounov function is the same in tâtonnement as in exchange trading processes, so that if such a function was decreasing out of equilibrium in the former case, it is still doing so in the latter.

Unfortunately, this rather pleasant and general result does not take us very far. The difficulty with the tâtonnement results which might be said partially to have prompted the study of trading processes in the first place is that tâtonnement can be shown to be stable only under very restrictive conditions. So it is not a great help to know that those same restrictions will generally ensure the stability of general exchange trading processes too. Something more is needed.

That something more is provided by the fourth of the major developments which have marked the history of the subject, the perception that

[15] Note that the following argument depends on the retention of (2.2.1) as the price-adjustment equation in both tâtonnement and trading processes.

attention must be given to disequilibrium behavior and that relatively reasonable restrictions on the adjustment processes themselves could lead to stability proofs involving essentially no restrictions on utility or production functions. While that insight was closely and naturally associated with the development of the trading process literature, it is logically separate from that development. Credit for it (although they never enunciated it quite this way) belongs to Uzawa and to Hahn. (Indeed, one might say that it was Hahn (1962a) who saw it most clearly, since he gave a tâtonnement example in which the specification of (2.2.1) was restricted and quasi-stability apparently proved under quite general circumstances.)[16]

The result of this insight was the development of two special trading processes: the Edgeworth Process (so named because it was discovered by Uzawa, 1962) and the Hahn Process (so named by Negishi, 1962). I believe that the Hahn Process is the more interesting and fruitful by far, and most of the developments discussed in the remainder of this chapter and in the rest of this book are based on it at least indirectly. Let me then take a little time to discuss the Edgeworth Process, which is at least of some historical importance.

The central assumption of the Edgeworth Process[17] is that trade will take place if and only if there is some group of people who can all be made better off by trading among themselves at the current prices. With some complications, due to the fact that at some nonequilibrium prices no such Pareto-superior move may be possible until prices change, this leads to the use of the negative of the sum of actually achieved individual utilities as a Lyapounov function and hence to quasi-stability.

Unfortunately, this powerful and appealing result is not so helpful as it first appears. This is so for more than one reason.

First, while it seems innocuous to assume that individuals will not trade unless they can better themselves by so doing (but see below), it is not nearly so simple to assume that trade actually will take place whenever such a situation arises. This is because of the possiblity that the only coalitions that can better themselves by mutual trade consist of very large numbers of people. Thus it is possible that there is no mutually advantageous bilateral or trilateral or quadrilateral trade and that the only mutually advantageous trade involves a very complicated swapping of

[16] The fact that Hahn's result turned out to be incorrect as stated (Kagawa and Kuga, 1980) in no way detracts from the importance of the basic insight.

[17] The principal works are Uzawa (1962) and Hahn (1962b). See also Arrow and Hahn (1971) and Smale (1976b). Saldanha (1982) extends the analysis to include firms (but not production) along the lines reported below for the Hahn Process.

commodities among millions of people. To require, as the Edgeworth Process does, that such a trade must take place is to put very heavy requirements on the dissemination of information and to assume away the costs of coalition formation.[18]

Note that the addition of money to an Edgeworth Process world does not help. Indeed, the Edgeworth Process is incompatible with money as a means of exchange. Trades that take place for money instead of as direct barter transactions do so because the seller accepts money in the expectation of later being able to buy something he wants, not because the acceptance of money itself gives a direct utility gain. Yet the driving force of the Edgeworth Process is the assumption that *every* transaction increases the utilities which would be achieved if there were no later transactions to follow.

Second, the Edgeworth Process does not appear to lend itself readily to the important extension of allowing production and consumption to take place out of equilibrium. A crucial feature of disequilibrium consumption, for example, is surely that individuals take irreversible actions which they would not have taken had they correctly anticipated the future. This means that utilities turn out to be lower than anticipated. It is not easy to see how this phenomenon can be accommodated in a model whose central result relies on the increase of utilities out of equilibrium, although whether that can actually be done remains an open question.

Third, the assumption that individuals only trade when they gain by so doing is not so innocuous as it appears. The quasi-stability of the Edgeworth Process rests on the non-decrease of the utilities which households would actually achieve if trading stops (and of the profits which firms would achieve in Saldanha's (1982) interesting extension). This makes it crucial that agents only trade when such utilities (or profits) will increase by doing so. In a true disequilibrium world, however, agents trade even when there is no direct utility (or profit) gain from so doing because they wish to take advantage of arbitrage opportunities, speculating on their ability later to retrade at more advantageous prices. It is not plain that the Edgeworth Process can be adapted to handle this; for even if one redefines the utilities involved to reflect the expected gains from speculation,

[18] The parallel to the theory of the core is obvious. David Schmeidler has shown (in an unpublished communication) that if there is any mutually advantageous trade there is one involving at most the same number of participants as there are commodities. Although interesting, such a result does not really get out of the difficulty, especially when commodities at different dates are counted as different commodities. Madden (1978) shows that if every agent always has a positive stock of every commodity, then the existence of any Pareto-improving trade implies the existence of a Pareto-improving bilateral trade. The positive endowment assumption is too restrictive for this result to be of much interest, however.

the monotonic increase of these utilities will be interrupted when speculations go sour and the next leg of a series of transactions cannot be completed. Yet a crucial aim of stability theory must be to examine the question of whether arbitrage drives a competitive economy to equilibrium.

It happens that the Hahn Process is strong on exactly the points where the Edgeworth Process is weak. It requires much less information than does the Edgeworth Process, and it is particularly suited to accommodating irreversible mistakes. In addition, it lends itself easily to the introduction of firms and of money and its central assumption is almost compelled when we start considering individuals as adjusting prices. Finally, an extension of it readily permits arbitrage. Accordingly, I now turn to an examination of the Hahn Process.

2.5 The Hahn Process

Because an understanding of simple Hahn Process models is an aid to understanding the much more complex model of Part II, I supplement the verbal discussion of the next two sections by an extended, but more technical, presentation in the next chapter.

The central assumption of the Hahn Process[19] is as follows. At any one time, *after* trade has taken place, there may of course be either unsatisfied demand or unsatisfied supply for some commodity, say, apples. However, we suppose that markets are sufficiently well organized that there are not both. In other words, there may be people who wish to sell apples at the current prices and cannot or there may be people who wish to buy apples at the current prices and cannot, but there are not, after trade, simultaneously both unsatisfied sellers and unsatisfied buyers. Markets are sufficiently well organized that willing buyers and willing sellers can and do come together and consummate a trade very quickly relative to the rate at which the disequilibrium adjustment equations operate (in the idealized abstraction, such deals are to be thought of as consummated instantaneously or outside of time). This requirement, while severe, seems to be a moderately reasonable one on information flows in a competitive economy; it is much less severe than the corresponding requirement in the Edgeworth Process.

Given this assumption, it follows that any individual who has a nonzero excess demand for a particular commodity finds that the aggregate excess demand for that commodity is of the same sign. Since prices adjust in the direction of aggregate excess demand, he finds that, outside of equilibrium, the things he wishes to buy and cannot buy are getting more expensive, while the things he wishes to sell and cannot sell are

[19] The original published paper is Hahn and Negishi (1962).

getting cheaper unless they are already free. Accordingly, he finds himself getting worse and worse off in the sense that his *target* utility, the utility which he expects to get if he can complete all his transactions, is going down. Accordingly, the sum of such target utilities (which it is trivial to assume bounded below)[20] will serve as a Lyapounov function and quasi-stability can be proved.

Note the different roles played by utilities in the Edgeworth and Hahn Processes. In the Edgeworth Process, the utilities actually achieved by individuals (that is, the utilities they would attain if they now stopped trading) rise while trading is going on. In the Hahn Process, target utilities – the utilities which they would achieve if they could complete their transactions – fall out of equilibrium. One way of looking at it is to say that in disequilibrium plans are not all compatible and that, in the Hahn Process, the adjustment is such that people have to lower their expectations until equilibrium is reached and everyone can in fact attain the utility he anticipates.

One can go on from this to prove the global stability of the Hahn Process in pure exchange by establishing the boundedness of prices in one of the ways described below, or by simply assuming it, and then showing that all limit points of any sequence starting from a given set of initial conditions are the same. The latter point is proved rather nicely by using strict quasi-concavity of the utility functions[21] in the following way.

Since any agent's target utility never increases and is bounded below, it must approach a limit, and that limit must be the same at all limit points. Hence, at any two limit points of the process, the limiting endowments of any given agent must lie on the same indifference curve. By quasi-stability, every limit point is an equilibrium and, by the Hahn Process assumption, aggregate excess demand zero implies that all agents have zero excess demand. Hence the endowment for any agent at any limit point must be supported by the corresponding prices at that limit point. Ignore free goods for simplicity. Call two separate limit points A and B. Then, by strict quasi-concavity, the limiting endowments at B must cost more than

[20] Such boundedness would not be trivial if cardinal utility functions were involved, but that is not the case here. Thus, a utility function in the form $u = \sum_{i=1}^{n} \beta_i \log x_i$, $\beta_i \geqslant 0$, where x_i denotes consumption of the ith good cannot be assumed bounded below without assuming that the process of adjustment keeps the x_i positive and bounded away from zero. However, in an ordinal context such as the present one, there is no need to use this function instead of the ordinally equivalent $u^* \equiv e^u = \prod_{i=1}^{n} x_i^{\beta_i}$, which is bounded below by zero for nonnegative x_i. The exponential transformation is always available, making boundedness a harmless assumption.

[21] Arrow and Hahn (1971) were the first to do this in their somewhat more satisfactory version discussed below.

those at A at the prices which obtain at A, unless those endowments are the same. Summing over all agents, the *total* endowment of the economy at B must cost more than the *total* endowment of the economy at A when both are valued in the prices of A, unless all agents have the same endowments at both A and B. Strict inequality cannot occur, however, since, by pure exchange, the total endowment of the economy is the same at both A and B. With some minor complication to take care of free goods and with an assumption that guarantees that a unique set of relative prices corresponds to any equilibrium, the global stability theorem is established.

So far, so good. Unfortunately, there are problems with this simple version. Thus, suppose that there are at least three commodities, say, apples, bananas, and carrots (the need for at least three arises from Walras' Law). Suppose that, at current prices, apples and bananas are both in aggregate excess supply. There may be an individual who would like to buy bananas but has nothing to offer for them but apples. If he is one of the unlucky ones who cannot find a buyer for his apples, then, regardless of how easily he can find a willing banana seller, no trade will be consummated, for he can offer that seller nothing the seller regards as having value. Out of equilibrium this can occur even if apples have a positive price. No amount of efficiency in market organization will get around this and the Hahn Process depends on its not occurring.

This possibility, which depends on the need to sell before you can buy, was first recognized by Clower (1965) among economic theorists working in a somewhat different context. It is well known to historians, however, that economies which rely on the Hahn Process can run into this difficulty. As the ancient document has it[22]:

> Simple Simon met a pieman going to the fair.
> Said Simple Simon to the pieman, 'Let me taste your ware.'
> Said the pieman to Simple Simon, 'Show me first your penny.'
> Said Simple Simon to the pieman, 'Indeed, I haven't any.'

It was not enough for Simple Simon and the pieman to be able to find each other. Trade still did not take place.

Note, however, that the Simple Simon economy already had in it one feature that distinguishes it from the models I have so far discussed: the use of one commodity as the sole medium of exchange. No doubt reflecting on this, Arrow and Hahn (1971) were able not so much to solve as to isolate the Simple Simon problem by constructing a rather more satisfactory version of the Hahn Process model in which one commodity (which they happened to call "money") serves as the only such medium. In that version, "target" excess demands – the excess demands that would

[22] M. Goose (n.d.).

obtain without a money constraint – are distinguished from "active" excess demands – the excess demands which are expressed by actual offers to buy or sell, offers to buy requiring money to back them up. It is aggregate *active* excess demands which then influence prices in (2.2.1). It is natural to take the Hahn Process assumption as applying to active demands since it then really does become merely one of market organization. Arrow and Hahn were able to show the global stability of the resulting Hahn Process, *provided that nobody ever runs out of money* and that every individual who has money actively tries to satisfy some nonzero fraction of every nonzero target excess demand that he has.

The Positive Cash assumption is, of course, very strong; moreover, it appears indispensable and it is hard to know how to ensure that it holds[23] in models such as the one under discussion, although, as we shall see, it becomes more palatable when we start to let individuals rather than auctioneers control prices. It is the first manifestation of the more general disequilibrium problem of the possible inability to carry out *any* part of a current plan. We shall have to deal with this in the context of allowing agents to be aware of disequilibrium and its dangers.

The Arrow and Hahn treatment also points up other difficulties that are common to the entire literature but that now begin to surface more explicitly. While I have already referred to some of them, it is useful to mention them in the present context.

The first such difficulty concerns what I called the Present Action Postulate. Households in this model must act *now* to make some nonzero part of every nonzero target excess demand an active excess demand. Money must *now* be allocated to an attempt to buy a nonzero amount of every commodity that the household does not have enough of, even though the household may already have a large amount of that commodity and relatively little of another one that it also wants to buy. Note that it would be harder to get away with this if the household were simultaneously consuming its existing commodity stocks.

The Present Action Postulate seems as innocuous as it does in this context, however, mainly because we have already implicitly swallowed the camel of assuming that the household believes its transactions will be consummated before consumption time comes and is therefore indifferent about the order in which it attempts to complete them. This is a part of assuming that the household really does not notice that the economy is out of equilibrium, that it formulates its demands on the assumption that prices will not change, and that it rather stupidly does not

[23] For some discussion of this, see Arrow and Hahn (1971). See also Fisher (1972b).

notice what is really going on. Such problems are the natural consequence of having a good equilibrium theory and not knowing much about individual reactions to disequilibrium.

The Arrow and Hahn introduction of money also brings forward another set of problems. In this model (and this remains true even when the model is extended to allow production and consumption out of equilibrium), trade actually ceases at equilibrium. In other words, equilibrium does not involve a situation in which agents find that they are able to go on trading as planned at prices they expected, but rather a situation in which all trades have already taken place and the only remaining activities are the carrying out of consumption plans by households and the meeting of already paid-for commitments by firms. Such a phenomenon, of course, is not restricted to this stability model. The equilibrium reached is the post-trade equilibrium of the familiar Arrow–Debreu model in which all markets open (and close) at the beginning of time; however, the cessation of trade property is nonetheless not attractive. Particularly if one is interested in justifying the use of equilibrium tools through stability analysis, it is disconcerting to find that convergence to equilibrium means not merely an exhaustion of arbitrage opportunities but a total cessation of trade. In equilibrium agents will, it is true, be just indifferent at the margin between trading and not trading, but this is not the same as a cessation of all trading opportunities.

Now, money as such makes its appearance in the present model as a medium of exchange: All transactions take place for money. This gives agents a reason for holding money while they are still making transactions. However, since equilibrium in this model involves an exhaustion of trading opportunities; once equilibrium is reached, all money that will ever change hands has already done so. Hence, without further assumptions, no agent will have a reason to hold money in equilibrium. To make matters worse, agents always believe that the system is already in equilibrium so that all they need to do is to complete their current transactions. They believe such completion to be possible and, in effect, only an instant away. Hence there is no reason for agents ever to plan to hold money. Even though money is needed for transaction purposes, agents can plan to finance purchases out of the proceeds of sales as they occur.

All this is very awkward. It makes the Positive Cash Assumption that agents never run out of money quite artificial. Further, it makes money quite unsuitable as a numéraire good since nobody wants to hold it in equilibrium. Hence Arrow and Hahn follow the usual unsatisfactory practice of assuming that money enters the utility function – in effect, that it is an ordinary good which just happens to be used as the medium of exchange.[24] Plainly, the problem arises in part from the naivete of agents and the nature of equilibrium in these models. In the model of Part II, the transactions demand for money does not disappear in equilibrium and we are partly able to avoid such awkward devices, although it is necessary to make money an interest-bearing asset (but with the same interest rate as any other asset in equilibrium so that the fact that agents hold money is nontrivial).

Despite these problems, the Arrow–Hahn introduction of money as a sole medium of exchange is a considerable step forward. It clarifies and isolates the Simple Simon problem in the Positive Cash assumption; it begins to bring forward the problems just discussed; it has a modicum of realism, if not of monetary theory; and it is probably indispensable for the introduction of firms into trading processes.

This last point is true for the following reason. Without the introduction of money, firms would value their holdings the same whether or not they sold them. A firm which produced a large stock of toothpaste, for example, would feel it was doing well in terms of profits if toothpaste had a high price. There would be nothing (absent further assumptions) to make it interested in selling the toothpaste as opposed to holding it[25] and therefore no reason why the presence of that stock of toothpaste should affect the price any more than the presence of target demands that are not active. Requiring firms to keep score in money which is needed by themselves and especially their owners to back up demands assures that firms actively participate in the market process.

As it happens, the Hahn Process model can be fairly readily extended to accommodate firms (but not yet production). To this I now turn.

2.6 Firms (but no production) in the Hahn Process[26]

The obvious first question that occurs when one seeks to introduce firms into a model which permits trading but no other economic activity to take place before equilibrium is reached is that of what it is that firms are to trade. In pure exchange, the stocks of commodities are fixed and one can think of households swapping titles to various amounts of them; with firms in the picture, however, one has to think of the transforma-

[24] This problem in general equilibrium theory was first pointed out by Patinkin who also suggested the introduction of money into the utility function. See, in particular, Patinkin (1949, 1950) and, generally, Patinkin (1965).

[25] The possibility that the firm might distribute its toothpaste as dividends to its shareholders who would then sell it themselves is awkward at best. The firm ought not to be managed so as to distribute dividends which its owners do not want.

[26] This discussion is based on Fisher (1974).

tion of inputs into outputs as at least envisioned by the participants in the economy, even if we do not allow that transformation to take place during the adjustment process.

The answer is to think of firms as trading in commitments to buy inputs and sell outputs. Each firm has access to a convex production technology which describes the efficient ways in which inputs can be turned into outputs. While trading is going on, the firm contracts for inputs and commits itself to deliver outputs. Payment for all such contracts and commitments is made when they are signed, but delivery and production do not take place until equilibrium is reached. The firm trades in such commitments at current prices, seeking to maximize profits while ending up in a technologically feasible position. Since, out of equilibrium, a firm may not be able to complete all the transactions it attempts, it will sometimes be the case that the firm finds it has committed itself to sell outputs without in fact having contracted for the inputs that would enable it to do so. In that case, it must go back on the market and either acquire the needed inputs or buy up output commitments, whichever is more profitable at the ruling (presumably changed) prices. Similarly, a firm that has overacquired input commitments will wish either to sell them off again or to sell further output commitments, whichever is more profitable.

Firms in this model pay out some or all (but not more than) their actually realized cash profits as dividends to their owners, although they may (and sometimes must) keep some retained earnings for transactions purposes so long as equilibrium has not been reached (the Positive Cash assumption). Since everyone continues to believe that all transactions will be completed at current prices, however, households maximize their utilities and formulate their *target* excess demands on the basis not of received dividends but of the expected total earnings of the firms they own. Dividends only matter in providing some of the cash that backs up target demands and makes them active. Indeed, it is easy to see that Walras' Law only holds in terms of target demands and target profits and not in terms of active demands and actual profits. It is also easy to show that Walras' Law requires that all profits be paid out to owners in equilibrium, so that any apparent tension in these matters, important as it is, is a disequilibrium one.

The fact that firms and owners may have different liquidity needs out of equilibrium raises another set of issues, however. One might suppose that the fact that all agents - firms and households - share the same (stupid) expectations as to prices and hence as to profits would mean that there is no point in a stock market. (Indeed, in the model under discussion, there is no such market; households simply own but do not trade shares in firms.) The tension over intertemporal liquidity needs which can arise out of equilibrium leads to a reason for trading in shares even if profit expectations are all the same, however. Owners may wish to sell shares to gain liquidity if they do not like a firm's dividend policy. Such matters as these, however, are beyond the scope of the present discussion, although they will arise again in the more satisfactory model of Part II. This is because the model being discussed does not truly allow agents to realize that liquidity can be a serious problem. Agents always believe that prices will not change; consumption and production do not take place until equilibrium; hence agents must view the liquidity constraint as a temporary inconvenience affecting only the extent to which they can complete desired acquisitions sooner rather than later at the same prices. Nevertheless, the serious economics of disequilibrium are beginning to appear just below the surface of the model.

Putting such matters aside, what about stability in such a Hahn Process model? A crucial feature of firms that differentiates them from households is that their maximand, profits, involves prices as well as quantities directly. Nevertheless, it remains true of the firm, as of the household, that everything that it wishes to buy but has not yet bought is getting more expensive while every nonfree good that it would like to sell is getting cheaper. Accordingly, target profits are going down out of equilibrium.

Given this fact, one can go on to consider the target utility of the household. So far as its trading is concerned, it too is caught in the same Hahn Process trap of wanting to buy goods whose prices are going up and wanting to sell goods whose prices are going down. The only way it can be getting better off (in terms of target utility) is for the firms it owns to be becoming more profitable. We have just seen, however, that firms become less rather than more profitable, and accordingly it is still the case, as it was in pure exchange, that the target utilities of households are falling out of equilibrium. This means that one can once again take the sum of target utilities as a Lyapounov function and establish quasi-stability.

A full proof of the global stability of the adjustment process, however, requires two more steps, as remarked above: first, a proof of compactness; and second, a proof either that all limit points are locally isolated or that, given the initial conditions, all limit points are the same. I have rather slighted the compactness step in my earlier discussion, and it now seems appropriate to spend a little time on it since the introduction of firms begins to make it rather more complicated.

Since we have so far been working in a finite-dimensional space, compactness is basically an issue of boundedness, for, if we can show that the variables remain in a bounded set, there is no harm in taking them to lie in its closure. The basic variables here are the prices and the stocks or commitments of the commodities held by individual households and individual firms.

The problems involved in assuring that relative or absolute prices remain bounded are basically unaffected by the introduction of firms and, indeed, are the same for trading processes as they are for tâtonnement. (This is largely because the same price-adjustment process (2.2.1) is used in both cases.) Aside from the alternative of assuming directly that prices are bounded - which is not all that unappealing - there are two known ways of going about it. The first of these is to consider the classic case in which the price adjustment functions, $F^i(\cdot)$, which appear on the right-hand side of (2.2.1), are linear through the origin. Whether we work in terms of absolute prices or in terms of prices relative to that of the numéraire (utility-yielding money in the Hahn Process model), it is not hard to show that (provided the numéraire would be in excess demand if it were priced at zero - an innocuous assumption) there is an ellipsoid in the space of the prices, outside of which prices cannot go. If the units in which quantities are measured are appropriately chosen, this amounts to showing that the sum of squares of the prices is bounded above. The same result can be extended to the case in which the price adjustment functions, $F^i(\cdot)$, are not necessarily linear themselves, but are bounded above by rays through the origin.

This is a strong result, basically depending on limiting speeds of adjustment in a particular way. Boundedness of relative prices can also be accomplished without such a limitation if one is willing to restrict demands. Thus, it is possible to show boundedness if one is willing to assume that whenever any subset of prices becomes high enough relative to all others, then the highest priced good is in excess supply. Such an assumption attempts to capture the notion that it is possible to price oneself out of the market.[27]

Boundedness of individual commodity or commitment holdings is a potentially more delicate matter than that of prices, although it is relatively simple in the contexts we have so far considered. Under pure exchange there is, of course, no problem, since total commodity stocks do not change. Once we introduce firms, however, there is at least the large potential difficulty that firms may wish to undertake unbounded

[27] The possibility of proving boundedness of prices in this way was first noticed in Fisher (1972b), but the first correct version is in Fisher (1974). As shown in Chapter 3, all of these problems can be avoided in overly simple cases where there is no natural numéraire and each price is divided by the sum of all the prices.

commitments, even though they cannot fulfill them. This would occur, for example, under constant returns since firms are not supposed to take resource limitations directly into account. As it happens, however, constant returns have already had to be ruled out of the models we have been discussing because of the necessity of having excess demands be continuous functions of the prices, and indeed, in the context of the Hahn Process model with firms but no production, it is in any case necessary to assume that each firm has a unique profit-maximizing position continuous in the prices. Since prices are to be bounded, such an assumption already implies boundedness of commitments and gets us out of the problem.

It would be very shortsighted to let it go at that, however. Constant returns is important; the introduction of consumption and production makes the problem more complex; and there is a natural way to go about it. That way uses what we know about the role of the price system in a world of limited resources. As resources become scarce, their prices ought to rise. Accordingly, it is possible to argue that unbounded commitments cannot be profitable since the unit costs of production would rise above the price at which output can be sold. Such an argument requires both the boundedness of prices and a fairly careful specification of the technology making limited or primary resources a nonnegligibly required input for every good, either directly or indirectly. It also turns out to require care in restricting speeds of adjustment.

Returning now to stability in the Hahn Process model with firms (but no production), the final step is a proof that, given the initial conditions, all limit points are the same. In the case of pure exchange, this was done by using the strict quasi-concavity of the utility function as described above. That proof can be extended to the present case. What is involved is the use of the fact that, at equilibrium prices, households are minimizing expenditure for given utilities while firms are maximizing profits, given their technologies. However, since target profits and target utilities decline out of equilibrium, and since every limit point is an equilibrium (quasi-stability), each household has the same target utility and each firm the same target profits at any one limit point equilibrium as at any other limit point equilibrium. At the prices of equilibrium A, therefore, the commitments of equilibrium B would be worth less to firms than the commitments of equilibrium A itself. On the other hand, those same equilibrium B commitments must cost households more than would those of equilibrium A. Since the net commitments of the production sector are made only to the household sector, and vice versa, this establishes a contradiction in a rather pretty way unless the equlibria are the same as regards commitments (ignoring free goods). One can then go on and complete the proof by a fairly straightforward assumption as to the uniqueness of relative prices.

2.7 Consumption and production out of equilibrium: Commodity dating, nonperformance, and the Present Action Postulate

We now come to the obviously important step of allowing real economic activities other than trading to go on before equilibrium is reached. Although, as I shall describe in a moment, one can produce a Hahn Process model in which disequilibrium consumption and production are allowed to take place with agents still unconscious of what is happening,[28] perhaps the most illuminating part of such analyses turns out to be not the resulting stability proof, but the way in which a number of underlying issues are pushed into the open when consumption and production are to be included. Perhaps surprisingly (and perhaps not) it turns out to be easier to deal with those difficulties by introducing what seems an additional complication - the crucial step of allowing agents to realize what is going on. That development, which generalizes the Hahn Process in a sense, is discussed in Part II.

Let me begin, however, by describing the way in which the relatively naive Hahn Process extension to production and consumption operates. It is convenient to work in continuous time. Every household has a utility functional, which is defined over its past and future consumption profiles of all commodities. At any given moment, however, the past is irreversible and the household can only attempt to optimize with respect to consumption yet to be undertaken. (In a sense, the utility functional of the household is allowed to change as a result of its past consumption.) It performs such optimization (in this naive model) assuming that current prices will last forever and subject to a budget constraint which involves its share of the target profits which it expects to receive from firms.

Firms are analogously situated. The technological opportunities open to a firm at any given time depend in part on the input and output actions it has taken in the past. Given its own past actions, the firm attempts to maximize profits with respect to its planned pattern of inputs and outputs, also assuming that prices will be constant.

The essential difference between this model and the preceding one with firms but no production is that firms and households take irreversible

[28] The models described in this section are Fisher (1976a) and (1977). There are some minor technical errors in these papers related to the handling of the hysteresis effect.

actions which change their optimizing actions later on. In the case of the household, such actions change the utility functional; in the case of the firms, they change the set of feasible production points; in both cases, they change the stock of commodities available for trade. We know, however, that if such actions were reversible, then target profits for firms and target utilities for individuals would decline out of equilibrium, given the other assumptions of the Hahn Process model, for we would then be back in the previous case. However, profits for firms or utilities for households can never be higher given the restrictions imposed by irreversible actions than they would be could those actions be undone at will. It is therefore not hard to show that target profits for firms and target utilities for households are still declining out of equilibrium; indeed, the declining utility and profit feature of the Hahn Process makes it particularly adaptable to the case of disequilibrium consumption and production.

Given this result, it is possible to go on to prove the global stability of the adjustment process along the lines of the previous model, although there are some technically rather tricky details. These are related to a property of equilibrium in this model which is of substantive interest. That property has already been mentioned in the preceding chapter. It appears both realistic and inevitable. Because the optimizing problems of firms and households change as a result of irreversible past actions, the set of competitive equilibria at any moment is not merely path-dependent in the sense that it depends on current endowments which adjust in the course of trade. Such path dependence is already present in all trading process models. When production and consumption take place out of equilibrium, path dependence is complicated by a further effect. The equilibrium set in such models depends on the past history of the system through its dependence on past production and consumption decisions – a hysteresis effect. Such effects do not disappear asymptotically. As discussed in the first chapter, this nondisappearing path dependence and, a fortiori, hysteresis makes comparative statics and computational algorithms largely, if not totally, irrelevant. In addition, it makes results on global stability quite tricky, because the nature of the space in which convergence must be proved is such as to make compactness a quite complex matter.[29]

As already stated, however, the interesting thing about the introduction of disequilibrium production and consumption may not be the global stability results but the problem which it pushes to the fore. I have

[29] As the problems arise in the same form in the full-blown model of Part II, I shall not discuss them here. They are not handled correctly in Fisher (1976a) and (1977).

already discussed some of these in the context of earlier work, but it is now appropriate to consider them again.

The first of these problems has to do with the dating of commodities. It is common and sensible to suppose that the same commodity at two different dates is to be treated as two different commodities. On this view, dates on commodities matter.

The question arises, however, of whether or not the dates on commodities are reached during the adjustment process. So long as we remain in the unreal world of tâtonnement and even so long as we permit trading but no other activity out of equilibrium, we can suppose that those dates are not reached, although this is a bit sticky in the latter case. As soon as we permit production and consumption to take place during the adjustment process, however, we are forced to assume that some commodity dates are reached before equilibrium. One cannot now consume tomorrow's toothpaste.

Note that this means that we are forced to leave the Arrow–Debreu world behind. In that world, commodity dates are but one more way of distinguishing commodities, no different from commodity colors in this respect. But a world in which all markets open and close before anything else happens is not a world in which disequilibrium consumption or production can be analyzed.

The reason that all this creates a difficulty lies in the fact that trading in *past* as opposed to *future* goods does not take place combined with the assumption that participants expect their trades to be consummated and fail to realize the disequilibrium nature of their circumstances. Hence, at the moment that a particular commodity date is passed, trading in that commodity is suspended and, out of equilibrium, there will be individuals who expect to trade further in that commodity and now suddenly realize that they cannot do so. Such individuals will now have to reoptimize subject to the suddenly imposed constraint that they are stuck with whatever they have of the dated commodity in question. Since, out of equilibrium, that constraint will be unexpected and will generally matter, its imposition can easily cause a discontinuity in the excess demand functions. This violates Lipschitz Conditions, the usual sufficient conditions for the existence of solutions to differential equations which are continuous in the initial conditions. I shall refer to this as "the dated commodities problem."

Now we know perfectly well why the dated commodities problem sounds somewhat contrived. It seems obviously unreasonable for people to care at midnight on December 31 that they cannot buy last year's toothpaste when they can obviously buy a perfect substitute, namely, this year's toothpaste. A little reflection, however, reveals that this is not an adequate way out of the difficulty. The reason that I am generally indifferent between buying last year's and buying this year's toothpaste as of the transitional moment is that I generally find that they are trading for the same price as of that moment. There are, of course, excellent reasons why that should be so, but they are mostly *equilibrium* reasons. There is certainly nothing in the price adjustment mechanisms of the models so far discussed that guarantees that prices will come together by the time the transition takes place. This is not merely a matter of permitting arbitrage but also of building a model in which arbitrage is sufficiently effective to erase such discrepancies by the crucial times. This cannot be done by assuming those discrepancies away.

We shall see in later chapters that this difficulty stems from the impersonal price adjustment process which we have been using. Where a single agent announces the price at which he will sell today's and tomorrow's toothpaste, that agent will take care to see that those prices come together as today blends into tomorrow, for it will be to his or her advantage to do so. While modeling individual price adjustment is not easy, it is plain that the dated commodities problem has its source in the refusal to undertake such modeling.

The dating of commodities also exacerbates another problem. Suppose we allow firms and households to deal in promises rather than only in actual deliveries. When commodities are dated, this means allowing agents to deal in futures contracts rather than in spot transactions only. Out of equilibrium, there may then be agents who find they cannot carry out their production or consumption plans because promised delivery of the goods they believe they own does not materialize. We must face the question of how to treat such cases of nonperformance, where short sellers of 1985 toothpaste, for example, are still short when 1985 rolls around. Such cases are very similar to those avoided by the Positive Cash assumption, which ensures that agents are not prevented from acting because money they assumed they would have is not paid to them. I consider these issues at length in Chapter 8; they are present whether or not commodities are dated but at least more visible in the presence of such dating.

If commodity dating makes these problems worse, one is tempted to ask, why not attempt to avoid them, at least initially, by avoiding commodity dating. This amounts to assuming that there are no futures markets for commodities and allowing only spot transactions.[30] Aside from questions of realism, such an approach has two difficulties. First, it

[30] This is the tack taken in Fisher (1976a). Fisher (1977) goes the other way and assumes complete dating but no discontinuities.

eliminates an important source of possible arbitrage by eliminating futures markets. Even though agents in the naive models under discussion do not see most arbitrage opportunities because they believe that prices will not change, the existence of different prices for the same commodity at different dates permits arbitrage through storage or the timing of production. To remove this seems a step backward, since we wish to ask whether the arbitraging actions of agents perceiving disequilibrium opportunities will in fact cause those opportunities to vanish and the system to be driven to equilibrium. Further, speculation may be a source of *in*stability. Still, there is little room for arbitrage in these models already.

The second problem which removal of futures markets and commodity dating exacerbates is at least as important as the lack of arbitrage. It is the problem of the Present Action Postulate. We have already seen that it is crucial in a model in which prices are driven by excess demands that such demands be expressed currently. Just as demands which are not backed up with purchasing power can have no effect on price, so too demands which remain merely gleams in the eye of the demander can have no effect. Yet all stability proofs assume that it is the excess demands derived from optimizing calculations that the demander attempts to exercise, at least to some degree. We must now examine this more closely.

Let us begin with households. In all the models we have considered, agents believe that current prices will rule forever, since they are not aware of disequilibrium. This means that a household believes that it can always trade toothpaste at the current price. Once we leave the essentially timeless Arrow–Debreu world, as we must, this leads to difficulty. If a household currently has a stock of toothpaste sufficient to satisfy its needs for some time to come but expects to need toothpaste sometime in the future, why should it *now* begin to acquire the extra toothpaste rather than wait until it is needed? (I abstract from questions of perishability and storage costs.) This seems particularly strange if we allow the household sufficient consciousness of what is going on that it becomes aware that it has a cash constraint. Indeed, since the household expects to be able to trade at the same price forever, its purchase plans are not determined even though its consumption pattern is, since it can buy more toothpaste than it needs and sell off the excess later or do the reverse, acquiring cash in the process.

This problem is present whether or not there are futures markets in the model but is exacerbated if such markets do not exist. It is bad enough to require that a household which expects to need toothpaste in 1990 should immediately enter the futures market for 1990 toothpaste and attempt to acquire it; it seems even more unreasonable to require that such a household should attempt to make such acquisitions in a world without dated commodities or futures markets by immediately entering the spot market for toothpaste. The best that can be said for this is that it forces the household to take a particular one of a set of equally optimal actions, given the assumptions under which it operates. Some vague notions as to transactions costs can be imported from outside those assumptions to justify this.

Unfortunately, not even such handwaving will do for firms, if commodities are not dated. For firms, the Present Action Postulate requires that they look into the future and consider whether they will end up being a net supplier or purchaser of any given commodity. If they find that over all future time it is best for them to sell a particular commodity, then they have to begin to offer it for sale right away. This is unreasonable both because their output of that commodity may not become positive for a long time to come and because it rules out technologies in which a given firm can find it optimal at given stationary prices first to buy a good for use as an input and then later to produce more of it as an output. Such problems are less disturbing when there are futures markets but, even then, the problems remain the same as for households.

Clearly, a principal source of such difficulties is the continuing assumption that participants fail to realize that they are in disequilibrium. Indeed, the most convincing argument that I know of in favor of the Present Action Postulate depends on allowing some such realization. In the presence of the Hahn Process, any participant hanging back from *full* present action (no matter how small) to satisfy each of his excess demands will quickly find that prices are changing perversely (from his point of view) and that he had better act before things get worse.

Nevertheless, such a way out of the problem requires us to step outside the model and allow consciousness of disequilibrium. This cannot be done adequately by attempting to impose a theory of the equilibrium behavior of agents on a disequilibrium process. Rather, we must allow agents fully to realize that they are in disequilibrium and to perceive and take advantage of arbitrage opportunities. When this is done – as in the model of Part II – the difficulties with the Present Action Postulate disappear. Agents expecting prices to change and acting on that expectation and agents realizing that it may not be possible to complete all possible transactions at any time will care about *when* they transact. A model which starts with the optimizing behavior of agents in such circumstances will not need a Present Action Postulate since excess demands will be defined in part by their timing.

2.8 Individual price adjustment

For the final topic in this chapter, I consider the question of dispensing with the fictional auctioneer, who lurks behind the price adjustment process (2.2.1), and allowing individuals to set prices. The importance of doing so has already been seen. How to do it is, however, a very deep matter, closely related to the problem of how to allow consciousness of disequilibrium to occur in the behavioral assumptions of stability models. For, as already remarked, in a world in which everyone assumes that prices are given, how do prices ever change? Indeed, it is a very serious question whether or not one can have individualistic price-setting models together with consciousness of disequilibrium and still end up at the competitive equilibrium. This is as much of a problem for analyses of single markets as it is for general equilibrium analysis, although we perhaps know more about it in the partial context.

One obvious thing to do, if one is going to have individual price adjustment, is to assume that participants on one side of each market set their own prices and then that participants on the other side search over prices to find the most advantageous one.[31] For convenience, I shall speak of the price setters as the sellers and of the searchers as the buyers, but there is not reason why it can't be the other way round in particular markets.

If one considers such a model in the general equilibrium context in which we have been working,[32] it becomes natural to deal with the wares of different sellers as different commodities, even if they are physically identical. This, of course, raises the issue of whether or not one can ensure that the prices of two such "seller-differing" commodities (i.e., the prices charged for the same commodity by two different sellers) will be the same in equilibrium. Not surprisingly, they will be if buyers are good at searching and they will not be if some sellers have persistent locational advantages in terms of buyer search, in which case the difference between the commodities is in some sense real even in equilibrium. The information possessed or gained by agents naturally affects the outcome of the process.

The interesting thing about distinguishing commodities in this way, however, is that, if one does so, the Hahn Process assumption becomes

[31] There is a burgeoning literature on such search models, most of which are not directly concerned with the question of whether one can end up in competitive equilibrium but with the no less interesting question of where one does in fact end up. For a good early critical survey, see Rothschild (1973).

[32] The ensuing discussion of the general equilibrium issues is drawn from Fisher (1972b). Kurz and Wilson (1974) discuss equilibrium with individual prices.

so natural as almost to be compelled. In such a context, that assumption amounts to saying that, at any one time, if a given seller (who is the only one on the supply side of the market for the commodity he sells) finds that he cannot sell as much as he would like to sell at the prices he sets, then there are not also buyers (with money) who know about him and would like to buy more from him at that price. Similarly, if there are such buyers, then the seller can sell all he wants. This is so clearly reasonable as to provide an independent very strong reason for interest in the Hahn Process.

There is another reason as well which stems from assuming individual price adjustment. Perhaps the most bothersome assumption in the Hahn Process model is that of Positive Cash - that participants do not run out of money before equilibrium is reached. Now, when prices are controlled anonymously, there are two ways that individuals can run out of money. First, they may have spent all their money and have for sale only things now valued at zero prices; second, they may have spent all their money and have for sale things which have positive prices but which are in oversupply. There is nothing about individual price adjustment which takes care of the case in which someone is offering a zero-priced good; but the other case, of goods with positive prices but in oversupply, can be handled. The reason for this is that such cases are essentially ones in which a seller is pricing himself out of the market. When prices are anonymously controlled, the seller can do nothing about this, but when he has control over his own price he can lower it and can lower it the more quickly the closer he is to bankruptcy. Hence the Positive Cash Assumption, while still strong, becomes more palatable when we allow individual price setting to take place.

Thus the Hahn Process, for two reasons, becomes an appealing one in an individualistic price adjustment context. Indeed, Fisher (1972b) shows that (with some complications involving the switching of buyers among sellers as search proceeds) the Arrow-Hahn version of the Hahn Process in pure exchange can be extended to allow individual price adjustment while still proving stability. The same can doubtless be done for the more complicated versions involving firms, consumption, and production, which I have already discussed.

There is one big catch to this, however, and that is the issue of just how individuals set prices in disequilibrium. The extension of the Hahn Process results to individual price adjustment just mentioned depends on sellers being rather foolish about what is happening. It requires each seller to set a price believing that there is a market equilibrium price and then to adjust that price up or down depending on whether he finds he can sell more or less than he wished at that price. In other words, the seller behaves like a little auctioneer and adjusts his own price according to the excess demand which occurs on his own personalized market. While one can rationalize such behavior in terms of a rule of thumb for finding an unknown equilibrium price, this really is not very plausible. As Rothschild (1973) has pointed out, not only is it unreasonable to make sellers act while setting such prices just as they would if they were certain that they had set equilibrium prices but also it is hard to suppose that sellers fail to notice that their demand curves are not flat and that the number of searching buyers who attempt to purchase from them depends on the prices they set.

These difficulties, of course, are but part of the general one that all these models make the participants base their behavior on the obviously erroneous belief that equilibrium has been reached and their transactions will be consummated. Nevertheless, the problem seems particularly acute as regards price adjustment behavior perhaps just because we do have some notion as to how price setters ought to behave in such a situation. Putting aside the uncertainty issue (which is very difficult) it appears evident that sellers facing a declining demand curve, as these do, ought to behave as monopolies.

What happens if they do? Is it nevertheless possible to get convergence to competitive equilibrium or does some residual monopolistic element remain in any search model?[33] So far as general equilibrium is concerned, this is an important but so far wholly open question. The problem, however, arises also in the context of a single market and here one seems able to make a little progress.[34]

Let me thus restate the problem in the context of a single market so as to emphasize how fundamental it is. Just about the first thing new students of economics encounter is a demonstration that competitive markets end up where supply equals demand. They are told that if price is such that supply exceeds demand, then there will be unsold goods and sellers will offer lower prices to get rid of them; similarly, if demand exceeds supply, unsatisfied buyers will bid up the price. This basic idea lies behind the price-adjustment process (2.2.1) which we have been discussing. Like that process, however, it presupposes a model of how price gets changed out of equilibrium and it is hard to come to grips with this in a context in which everyone takes price as given. Even at this level, we lack a satisfactory, fully rigorous disequilibrium model of price adjustment.

Suppose then that we try to build such a model by allowing sellers to set prices and buyers to search for low prices. If sellers behave in the not

[33] As suggested by Arrow (1958).

[34] Indeed, practically all the search literature is about single markets. The ensuing discussion is based on Fisher (1970) and especially (1973).

very sensible way indicated above for general equilibrium, setting prices, behaving as though their demand curves were flat, and adjusting prices according to whether or not they sell out all their supplies, then it is not hard to show, given reasonable restrictions on the search behavior of buyers, that the process can be made to converge to competitive equilibrium.[35]

Suppose, however, that we allow sellers to realize what is happening and to know the declining demand curves they face. Can we nevertheless get to competitive equilibrium allowing sellers to use that information in a profit-maximizing way? It turns out to be possible to tell such a story with a competitive ending, but the only such story that has been successfully told, as far as I know, turns out to be very complex and perhaps something of a fairy tale. It depends first, on demand curves flattening out at low enough relative prices as buyers find firms with usually low enough prices and second, on buyers gradually learning where the minimum price they can find can be expected to be if it persists long enough.[36] Whether even such unsatisfactory results can be carried over into the analysis of general equilibrium stability is an open question.

As we shall see in Part II, the questions raised by allowing individual price adjustment are largely unsolved. While we shall prove that - under wide circumstances - such price adjustment is compatible with stability, whether or not the system converges to a *competitive* equilibrium depends heavily on the specifics of the price-adjustment process. More specifically, it depends on how agents perceive the demand and supply curves they face. This is not an easy question and it arises, as we shall see, not only in the context of search, but, more generally where agents perceive themselves as constrained in the amount of their transactions.

The circumstances under which perceived monopoly or monopsony power disappears in the limit is an important but largely unsolved question. Nevertheless, it must be faced if we are to escape from the question-begging straightjacket of the auctioneer price-adjustment process, (2.2.1).

[35] See Fisher (1970).
[36] See Fisher (1973).

CHAPTER 3*

Hahn Process models: Formal treatment

3.1 Introduction

In this chapter, I return to the Hahn Process models discussed in Chapter 2 and treat them more precisely than was done there. This enables the introduction of the notation used later in the book. More important, it facilitates understanding of some issues which arise again in the context of more complex and satisfactory models. For the most part, these issues were discussed in the previous chapter and nontechnical readers may proceed directly to Chapter 4 with little loss of continuity.[1]

Two models are discussed in the present chapter. First, I treat the case of pure exchange without the introduction of money. As explained in the previous chapter, this model embodies the basic feature of the Hahn Process. It is very easy to see what is going on in a context that lacks the increasingly complex apparatus of later versions.

The second model treated below adds the complications of firms and of money. However, actual production and consumption out of equilibrium are not permitted. The analysis of this model permits an understanding of the role of firms and introduces a number of the problems which later appear. Production and consumption out of equilibrium will not be separately treated. As explained in the preceding chapter, they are easiest to introduce in the context of a relatively rich disequilibrium model where agents understand what is happening and care about the timing of their actions. Hence, disequilibrium production and consumption are introduced only in the full model of Part II.

[1] Such readers will, however, have less understanding of the subject matter than will those who read this chapter. As the mathematics is not very difficult, readers are urged to read the present chapter if at all possible.

3.2 Pure exchange and no money: Notation and model

I adopt some notational conventions which will be followed wherever possible. Variables relating to individual agents are in lowercase; economy-wide variables, such as sums over agents, or variables common to all agents such as prices are denoted by capital letters. Agents are superscripted h for households and (later) f for firms. Subscripts are reserved for commodities. The numbers of households, H, firms, F, and commodities, n, are fixed. For convenience, agent superscripts are often omitted when the context makes clear what is involved. Similarly, the time argument, t, is often left implicit. Dots over variables denote differentiation with respect to time. Vectors are to be thought of as columns where it matters. Inner products, however, are written as though the vectors were scalars, $\mathbf{P}\mathbf{x}$ rather than $\mathbf{P}'\mathbf{x}$, for example, to avoid burdening the notation further. Vectors are printed in boldface.

I begin with pure exchange with no special role for money. Household h maximizes a utility function, $u^h(\cdot)$, defined over its demands, a vector $\mathbf{x}^h$. (Since consumption does not take place until equilibrium is reached we can think of the components of $\mathbf{x}^h$ as either stocks or flows.) $u^h(\mathbf{x}^h)$ is assumed weakly monotonic, locally nonsatiated, and strictly quasi-concave (save that strong monotonicity is not required). $u^h(\mathbf{x}^h)$ is also assumed bounded below, which (as pointed out in footnote 20 of Chapter 2) is innocuous in an ordinal context.

The household has a nonnegative vector of current endowments, $\bar{\mathbf{x}}^h$, which changes through time as trading progresses. It stupidly expects current prices, $\mathbf{P}$, to last forever and hence chooses $\mathbf{x}^h$ to maximize $u^h(\mathbf{x}^h)$ subject to:

$$\mathbf{P}(\mathbf{x}^h - \bar{\mathbf{x}}^h) = 0 \tag{3.2.1}$$

$\mathbf{x}^h$ so chosen is assumed continuous in prices and endowments. It will sometimes be convenient to give a separate notation to *excess* demand and define

$$\mathbf{z}^h \equiv \mathbf{x}^h - \bar{\mathbf{x}}^h \tag{3.2.2}$$

Denoting *total* excess demand by $\mathbf{Z} \equiv \sum \mathbf{z}^h$, it is elementary that (3.2.1) implies Walras' Law:

$$\mathbf{P}\mathbf{Z} \equiv 0 \tag{3.2.3}$$

Definition 3.2.1. A (Walrasian) equilibrium is a set of prices, $\mathbf{P}$, and endowments, $\bar{\mathbf{x}}^h$ $(h = 1, \ldots, H)$ at which $\mathbf{z}^h \leqq 0$ for all h.[2]

[2] I use the usual conventions for vector inequalities. $\mathbf{x} > \mathbf{y}$ means $x_i > y_i$ all i; $\mathbf{x} \geqq \mathbf{y}$ means $x_i \geqslant y_i$ all i; $\mathbf{x} \geqslant \mathbf{y}$ means $\mathbf{x} \geqq \mathbf{y}$ but $\mathbf{x} \neq \mathbf{y}$.

Note that the definition requires each agent to have nonpositive excess demands in equilibrium. The familiar practice of merely requiring that *aggregate* excess demands be nonpositive is not adequte. It leaves open the possibility that aggregate excess demands might sum to zero by accident even though there are individual agents with unsatisfied excess demands on both sides of a particular market. Of course, it is natural to rule this out by an assumption as to the orderly nature of markets. This is precisely what the Hahn Process assumption (Assumption 3.4 below) does. Thus this is not an issue in the present context. It is a possible problem in alternative models, however.

It is easy to see that Walras' Law (3.2.3) implies that goods which an agent has in excess supply are free in equilibrium.

Lemma 3.2.1. In equilibrium $P_i z_i^h = 0$ $(i=1,\ldots,n;\ h=1,\ldots,H)$ so that $P_i Z_i = 0$.

Proof. In equilibrium $\mathbf{z}^h \leqq 0$ and $\mathbf{Z} \leqq 0$. Since prices are nonnegative, the desired result follows immediately from (3.2.3).

I come now to the laws of motion for this economy. Despite the fact that agents never expect prices to change, prices do move all the same as in (2.2.1) of the previous chapter. That is:

Assumption 3.2.1. (Price Adjustment).

$$\dot{P}_i = \begin{cases} F^i(Z_i) & \text{unless } P_i = 0 \text{ and } Z_i < 0 \\ 0 & \text{if } P_i = 0 \text{ and } Z_i < 0 \end{cases} \tag{3.2.4}$$

where the $F^i(\cdot)$ obey a Lipschitz Condition (and are therefore continuous), are sign-preserving, and are bounded away from zero except as $Z_i > 0$.

The rest points of (3.2.4) are obviously the economic equilibria of the model.

Note that this price-adjustment process does not involve a numéraire. Treatment of a similar model with a numéraire involved is given below when money is introduced; there is no point in duplicating that development here. Of course the time path of prices (and hence of other variables) depends on whether the adjustment in (3.2.4) is in terms of relative or absolute prices, but the stability theorems are essentially unaffected by this potentially important issue.

The other basic variables which adjust in this model are the endowments, $\bar{\mathbf{x}}^h$, which change because of trade. Trading rules are not specified precisely but are subject to four general restrictions.

First, write the trading rules as:

$$\dot{\bar{x}}_i^h = G_i^h(\bar{\mathbf{x}}^1,\ldots,\bar{\mathbf{x}}^H;\mathbf{P}) \quad (h=1,\ldots,H; i=1,\ldots,n) \tag{3.2.5}$$

These equations, together with (3.2.4), form the differential equations of the system and we assume that trade takes place sufficiently smoothly that the system of differential equations has a solution continuous in the initial conditions, as discussed in the Appendix.[3]

Second, the fact that we are dealing with pure exchange means that the total amount of any commodity is fixed. We thus assume:

Assumption 3.2.2 (Pure Exchange).

$$\sum_h \bar{\mathbf{x}}^h \equiv \bar{\mathbf{X}} \tag{3.2.6}$$

where $\bar{\mathbf{X}}$ is a fixed vector.

This assumption will, of course, be discarded when firms are introduced and replaced with more complex versions reflecting the closed nature of the economy being studied. The following assumption will also take on more complex forms, but starts out quite simply. Trading takes place by differential movements as agents exchange goods at what they all believe are fixed prices. Hence no agent will ever give up something unless what he gets for it is of equal value. We express this as:

Assumption 3.2.3 (No Swindling)[4]*:*

$$\mathbf{P}\dot{\bar{\mathbf{x}}}^h \equiv 0 \quad (h=1,\ldots,H) \tag{3.2.7}$$

The final assumption on trade is the crucial one of the Hahn Process. Trade is assumed to take place instantaneously or outside of time so that we are always looking at endowments *post*-trade, given the prices. It is assumed that markets are *orderly,* that is, *after* trade there are not both unsatisfied suppliers *and* unsatisfied demanders for any given good.[5]

[3] This would be guaranteed if the functions $G_i^h(\cdot,\ldots,\cdot;\ \cdot)$ satisfied Lipschitz Conditions, but Fernando Saldanha has pointed out to me that such satisfaction is unlikely. Consider a particular commodity, i, which is in excess supply and an agent, h, for whom $x_i^h < \bar{x}_i^h$. As the price of i drops, h may switch from attempting to sell to attempting to buy. By the Hahn Process Assumption (Assumption 3.2.4, below), such an attempt must succeed if i remains in net excess supply. This means that $\dot{\bar{x}}_i^h = \dot{x}_i^h$ after h switches, while it is not at all plain that this is reasonable so long as h is trying to sell; indeed, $\dot{\bar{x}}_i^h = 0$ and $\dot{x}_i^h \neq 0$ may very well hold before the switchover.

[4] Negishi (1962) calls this the "Condition of Barter" but "No Swindling" seems a more expressive name and one that will continue to be applicable when money is introduced.

[5] Note that such an assumption makes sense only post-trade. Before trade takes place, there will come a moment as prices change when suppliers and demanders look at each other with a wild surmise. Of course, continuous time is an abstraction here. One must think of such pretrade moments as outside of time.

Assumption 3.2.4 (Hahn Process).

$$z_i^h Z_i > 0 \text{ unless } z_i^h = 0 \quad (h=1,\ldots,H; i=1,\ldots,n) \tag{3.2.8}$$

There are no further restrictions on the trading process. Note in particular that agents foolishly expect to be able to complete their transactions at fixed prices.

3.3 The behavior of target utilities

As indicated in the previous chapter, the way the Hahn Process works is that target utilities, the $u^h(\mathbf{x}^h)$, which are the utilities which households expect to get when their transactions are completed, decline until plans become mutually compatible and equilibrium is reached. It will be convenient to define:

> *Definition 3.3.1.* An agent is in *personal equilibrium* if he can complete all of his transactions with the possible exception of his ability to dispose of free goods.

Note that an equilibrium for the system is a point at which all agents are in personal equilibrium. (See Definition 3.2.1 and Lemma 3.2.1.)

> *Theorem 3.3.1.* For every $h=1,\ldots,H$, $\dot{u}^h \leqslant 0$ and $\dot{u}^h < 0$ unless h is in personal equilibrium.

Proof. The Lagrangian for h's optimization problem is:

$$L^h \equiv u^h(\mathbf{x}^h) - \lambda^h \mathbf{P}(\mathbf{x}^h - \bar{\mathbf{x}}^h) \tag{3.3.1}$$

When the problem is solved, the optimized value of u^h in fact depends only on the variables which are outside of h's control and which h takes as parameters. These are prices, $\mathbf{P}$, and the current state of h's endowments, $\bar{\mathbf{x}}^h$. Thus, we can use the Envelope Theorem for constrained optimization to evaluate the derivatives of target utility with respect to these parameters and write

$$\dot{u}^h = \sum_{i=1}^{n} \frac{\partial u^h}{\partial P_i} \dot{P}_i + \sum_{i=1}^{n} \frac{\partial u^h}{\partial \bar{x}_i^h} \dot{\bar{x}}_i^h = \sum_{i=1}^{n} \frac{\partial L^h}{\partial P_i} \dot{P}_i + \sum_{i=1}^{n} \frac{\partial L^h}{\partial \bar{x}_i^h} \dot{\bar{x}}_i^h$$

$$= -\lambda^h(\dot{\mathbf{P}}\mathbf{z}^h - \mathbf{P}\dot{\bar{\mathbf{x}}}^h) = -\lambda^h \dot{\mathbf{P}}\mathbf{z}^h \equiv -\lambda^h \sum_{i=1}^{n} \dot{P}_i z_i^h \tag{3.3.2}$$

where the last substantive step follows from the No Swindling assumption (Assumption 3.2.3).

We know, however, that $\lambda^h > 0$. Further, by the Hahn Process assumption (Assumption 3.2.4), total excess demand for commodity i, Z_i, has the same sign as individual excess demand, z_i^h, wherever the latter is non-zero. Finally, by the Price Adjustment assumption (Assumption 3.2.1), $\dot{P}_i$ and Z_i have the same sign wherever $Z_i \neq 0$ except where $Z_i < 0$ and $P_i = 0$ so that unsatisfied excess demand involves disposal of a free good. The theorem now follows from (3.3.2).

With this result in hand, the first of our stability results is immediate. It is:

> *Corollary 3.3.1.* The dynamic process given in (3.2.4) and (3.2.5) is quasi-stable.

Proof. Choose $V \equiv \Sigma_h u^h(\mathbf{x}^h)$.[6] Since we have assumed $u^h(\mathbf{x}^h)$ to be continuous and bounded below, so is V. Theorem 3.3.1 shows that V is declining out of equilibrium (i.e., except at rest points). Hence V is a Lyapounov function, and the corollary is proved.

3.4 Compactness

As discussed in the previous chapter, the next step in a stability analysis after a proof of quasi-stability is a discussion of compactness. Since we are working in a Euclidean space in the present model, this means we must show that the time paths of the state variables (endowments and prices) remain in a closed and bounded set. Closure is obviously trivial here; what matters is boundedness.

As it happens, even boundedness is trivial in the context of the present greatly oversimple model. As we move to more complex and satisfactory models, boundedness and, more generally, compactness become matters of increasing depth. Some of the issues which will then arise can be introduced by studying the matter in the present case.

The first state variables for which boundedness must be established are the individual endowments, $\bar{\mathbf{x}}^h$. Here boundedness is trivial because of the fact that we are dealing with pure exchange. Assumption 3.2.2 guarantees that the total stock of each commodity in the economy does not change. Since $\bar{\mathbf{x}}^h \geqq 0$, by assumption, this must mean that each of the $\bar{\mathbf{x}}^h$ remains bounded.

Note, however, that this easy result not only rests on pure exchange but also on the assumption that the holdings of households must be non-negative. If we were to allow short sales, this would no longer be the case. Of course, boundedness would still be guaranteed (under pure exchange) if such short sales were bounded below for legal or other

[6] No special significance attaches to the unweighted sum – any Bergson social welfare function continuous and strictly monotonic in individual utilities would do as well.

reasons, but we would then need to consider the reasons for such bounds. This is not unrelated to issues raised by constant returns in production. In both cases boundedness requires that agents be kept from promising delivery of unbounded amounts of goods which in fact cannot be produced.

The boundedness of prices is also a simple matter in the present context, precisely because that context is not really very satisfactory. To see this, observe the following. It is evident that the homogeneity of degree zero in the prices of the excess demand function which stems from the homogeneity of the budget constraints (3.2.1) means that we cannot hope to prove convergence of absolute prices. Indeed, there is nothing in this model to tie down the units of those prices, and it will be completely satisfactory to prove convergence of relative prices. We can thus take as the price variables of interest,

$$\tilde{P}_i \equiv \frac{P_i}{\sum_{j=1}^{n} P_j} \quad (i=1,\ldots,n) \tag{3.4.1}$$

which obviously lie in a compact set, the unit simplex.[7]

Of course, we can get away with this precisely because we have not introduced any good with a special role as numéraire. Once we introduce money in all transactions below, it will not suffice to show that relative prices constructed as in (3.4.1) remain bounded, rather we must show that prices *in terms of money* do so. This will require some analysis of the special features of money as a numéraire good. In fact, as we shall see, we cannot wholly escape such considerations even in the present model. When we prove global stability below, we will need to assume that any pair of equilibria has at least one good with a positive price at both.

Despite the fact that there is no formal need to consider the boundedness of absolute prices in this model, we nevertheless digress to do so as this introduces a method to be extended below. Boundedness of the absolute prices can be accomplished if we are willing to bound the price adjustment functions $F^i(\cdot)$ of (3.2.4). In essence this means bounding the speeds with which prices respond to excess demands.

Lemma 3.4.1. Suppose there exist n positive scalars, k_i ($i=1,\ldots,n$), such that

$$F^i(Z_i) \leqslant k_i Z_i \quad (i=1,\ldots,n) \tag{3.4.2}$$

Then absolute prices remain bounded.

[7] Note that Walras' Law and the Price Adjustment assumption will keep the sum of the prices from being zero at any finite time. This is all that is required for compactness here.

Proof. Define

$$Q \equiv \frac{1}{2} \sum_{i=1}^{n} \frac{P_i^2}{k_i} \tag{3.4.3}$$

Differentiating Q with respect to time and using (3.2.4), we obtain

$$\dot{Q} = \sum_{i=1}^{n} \frac{P_i \dot{P}_i}{k_i} = \sum_{i=1}^{n} \frac{P_i F^i(Z_i)}{k_i} \leqslant \sum_{i=1}^{n} P_i Z_i = 0 \tag{3.4.4}$$

where the last statement follows from Walras' Law (3.2.3). (Note that the cases in which price changes are not given by $F^i(Z_i)$ do not matter here.) Thus Q is never increasing and prices must be bounded since they remain on or within a finite ellipsoid determined by the initial value of Q.

3.5 Global stability

We are now nearly ready to show that the process (3.2.4) and (3.2.5) is globally stable. Before doing so, however, two matters must be considered. The first is the question of just what it is that we can hope to prove; the second concerns two more necessary (and not particularly objectionable) assumptions.

Part of the question of what it is we can hope to prove has already been mentioned. In this model, only relative prices can possibly be expected to converge. In a sense, that is true of all later models as well in that prices relative to the price of money are shown to converge. It is in this sense that "relative prices" should be interpreted in Definition 3.5.1 below.

The other part of the nature of convergence that must be mentioned concerns quantities. A little thought will reveal that there is nothing in the model that will determine the ultimate holdings of the goods which turn out to be free at the asymptotic equilibrium. Who gets caught holding the bag when the music stops is not determined; in fact, there is nothing to keep agents from passing free goods back and forth after equilibrium has been reached. Plainly, however, it is not sensible to count either this phenomenon or the fact that relative, rather than absolute, prices converge as a failure of stability. Accordingly, we define:

> *Definition 3.5.1.* A process such as (3.2.4) and (3.2.5) will be called *essentially* globally stable if, starting from any initial condition (a) relative prices converge to some limit and (b) all other state variables converge to some limit with the possible exception of the holdings of goods which are free at the limiting prices.

In fact, the proof of convergence in the present (and later) models proceeds by first showing convergence of holdings of nonfree goods. To show that this implies convergence of prices requires an additional assumption. I shall first give such an assumption and then discuss it. For any price vector, **P**, define:

$$S(\mathbf{P}) \equiv \{i \mid P_i > 0\} \tag{3.5.1}$$

so that $S(\mathbf{P})$ is the set of commodities with positive prices.

Assumption 3.5.1 (Indecomposability of Equilibrium). Let $(\mathbf{P}^*, \bar{\mathbf{x}}^{*1}, \ldots, \bar{\mathbf{x}}^{*H})$ be any equilibrium. Let R be any nonempty proper subset of $S(\mathbf{P}^*)$. Then there exists an $i \in R$, a j in $(S(\mathbf{P}^*) - R)$, and an h, $1 \leqslant h \leqslant H$, such that $\bar{x}_i^{*h} > 0$ and $\bar{x}_j^{*h} > 0$.[8]

This assumption ensures that the economy does not split at equilibrium into two (or more) sets of agents and commodities with the first group of agents holding the first set of commodities and the second group of agents holding the second set of commodities, each group having corner-solutions with respect to the commodities it does not hold. If such a split were to occur, the relative prices of the commodities within each set would be determined, but there would be nothing to pin down the relative prices of two commodities drawn from different sets.

Assumption 3.5.1 is obviously quite acceptable. It guarantees that there will be a unique set of relative prices supporting any particular equilibrium. In later applications, when the model becomes more complex, I shall simply assume this directly rather than write down the more complicated - but not more informative - versions of Assumption 3.5.1 which will guarantee it.

In the context of the present model, even Assumption 3.5.1 will not quite guarantee convergence of relative prices, although the parallel assumption will do once money is introduced. We have now reached the point at which we can no longer wholly do without a numéraire. We add the following reasonably innocuous assumption.

Assumption 3.5.2 (Pairwise Numéraire). Let $\mathbf{P}^*$ and $\mathbf{P}^{**}$ be prices correponding to two equilibria. Then $S(\mathbf{P}^*) \cap S(\mathbf{P}^{**}) \neq \varnothing$.

That is, for any pair of equilibria there is at least one good whose price is positive at both.

We can now proceed to the principal result for this simplest of Hahn Process models.

[8] In fact what is wanted is that the first-order conditions for an optimum of $u^h(\mathbf{x}^h)$ should hold as equalities for i and j. This could happen even if one or both of $\bar{x}_i^h$ and $\bar{x}_j^h$ were zero. There seems no point in complicating the text to include such a generally measure-zero case, however.

Theorem 3.5.1. The process given in (3.2.4) and (3.2.5) is essentially globally stable.

Proof. Since we know that the relevant variables remain in a compact set, we need only show that the limit points of the time path of the system which correspond to a given initial condition are all the same. (See Theorem A.2.2.) We do this by using the fact that, by quasi-stability, such limit points are rest points and that rest points are Walrasian equilibria. Consider any two such equilibria. Denote values of variables in the first one by $*$ and in the second by $**$.

Begin by considering the target utility of any household, h. By Theorem 3.3.1, u^h is nonincreasing and we have assumed it bounded below, hence it must approach a limit, say, $\bar{u}^h$. This limit must be the same for *any* infinite sequence of times, so $u^h = \bar{u}^h$ both at $*$ *and* at $**$, that is,

$$u^h(\mathbf{x}^{*h}) = u^h(\mathbf{x}^{**h}) = \bar{u}^h \tag{3.5.2}$$

Now, $u^h(\cdot)$ is strictly quasi-concave, so that the fact that $\mathbf{x}^{*h}$ and $\mathbf{x}^{**h}$ lie on the same indifference curve must mean that $\mathbf{x}^{**h}$ costs more than $\mathbf{x}^{*h}$ in the prices ($\mathbf{P}^*$) at which $\mathbf{x}^{*h}$ is chosen, unless $\mathbf{x}^{*h}$ and $\mathbf{x}^{**h}$ differ only in goods which are free at those prices. Formally,

$$\mathbf{P}^*\mathbf{x}^{*h} \leqslant \mathbf{P}^*\mathbf{x}^{**h}$$

and (3.5.3)

$$\mathbf{P}^*\mathbf{x}^{*h} < \mathbf{P}^*\mathbf{x}^{**h} \quad \text{unless } x_i^{*h} = x_i^{**h}$$

for all $i \in S(\mathbf{P}^*)$.

Since $**$ is an equilibrium, the excess demands of every agent are nonpositive at $**$, so that $\mathbf{x}^{**h} \leqq \bar{\mathbf{x}}^{**h}$. Using this fact and the budget constraint (3.2.1) at $*$, together with (3.5.3), we obtain:

$$\mathbf{P}^*\bar{\mathbf{x}}^{*h} = \mathbf{P}^*\mathbf{x}^{*h} \leqslant \mathbf{P}^*\mathbf{x}^{**h} \leqslant \mathbf{P}^*\bar{\mathbf{x}}^{**h} \tag{3.5.4}$$

so that

$$\mathbf{P}^*\bar{\mathbf{x}}^{*h} \leqslant \mathbf{P}^*\bar{\mathbf{x}}^{**h} \tag{3.5.5}$$

and the strict inequality holds if it holds in (3.5.3).

Now sum (3.5.5) over households, obtaining

$$\mathbf{P}^*\bar{\mathbf{X}}^* \leqslant \mathbf{P}^*\bar{\mathbf{X}}^{**} \tag{3.5.6}$$

with the strict inequality holding if it holds in (3.5.5) for *any* $h = 1, \ldots, H$. It is obvious, however, that (3.5.6) *must* be an equality since we are in pure exchange (Assumption 3.2.2) so that $\bar{\mathbf{X}}^* = \bar{\mathbf{X}}^{**}$. This establishes that

(3.5.5) (and (3.5.3)) must hold as equalities for every household; in other words, equilibrium holdings (and demands) of any commodity with a positive price at * must be the same in both equilibria. It is only a matter of notation to reverse the roles of * and ** in this proof. Hence equilibrium holdings (and demands) of any good with a positive price at *either* equilibrium must coincide.

A little reflection will show that it now only remains to prove convergence of the relative prices defined in (3.4.1) by showing that $\tilde{\mathbf{P}}^* = \tilde{\mathbf{P}}^{**}$. This is done by using Assumptions 3.5.1 and 3.5.2 together with the convergence of the holdings of nonfree goods. By Assumption 3.5.2 (Pairwise Numéraire), there exists some good which has a positive price at both * and **. Without loss of generality, suppose that this good is the first. If this is the only good with a positive price at either equilibrium, there is nothing more to prove. Hence we may suppose that at one of the equilibria, say, *, there is at least one other good with a positive price. Partition $S(\mathbf{P}^*)$ into $R \equiv \{1\}$ and $(S(\mathbf{P}^*) - R)$. Then Assumption 3.5.1 (Indecomposability of Equilibrium) shows that there exists some household, h, and some good with a positive price other than the first, such that h holds positive amounts of both the first good and this other good at *. Without loss of generality, we may take the other good in question to be the second. Then the fact that * is an equilibrium must mean:

$$\frac{u_2^h(\bar{\mathbf{x}}^{*h})}{u_1^h(\bar{\mathbf{x}}^{*h})} = \frac{P_2^*}{P_1^*} \tag{3.5.7}$$

Since $\bar{\mathbf{x}}^{*h}$ and $\bar{\mathbf{x}}^{**h}$ coincide in all nonfree components, it must then be the case that[9]

$$\frac{u_2^h(\bar{\mathbf{x}}^{*h})}{u_1^h(\bar{\mathbf{x}}^{*h})} = \frac{u_2^h(\bar{\mathbf{x}}^{**h})}{u_1^h(\bar{\mathbf{x}}^{**h})} = \frac{P_2^{**}}{P_1^{**}} \tag{3.5.8}$$

Putting this together with (3.5.7), we see that the ratio of the first two prices must be the same in both equilibria.

If these are the only two goods with a positive price at either equilibrium we are finished. If not, suppose that there is another such good at *. Repartition $S(\mathbf{P}^*)$ into $R' \equiv \{1, 2\}$ and $(S(\mathbf{P}^*) - R')$. Assumption 3.5.1 (Indecomposability of Equilibrium) assures us that there is some good with a positive price other than the first two and some household, h, such that, at *, h holds positive amounts of both the good in question

[9] The fact that holdings of free goods need not coincide does not matter. For indeterminacy in such holdings to occur, the marginal utility of such goods must be zero for all $\mathbf{x}^h$ that are convex combinations of $\mathbf{x}^{*h}$ and $\mathbf{x}^{**h}$. Thus the amounts of such goods cannot affect marginal rates of substitution which involve at least one nonfree good.

and at least one of the first two goods. Letting this good in question be good 3, it is evident that an argument substantively identical with that leading to (3.5.7) and (3.5.8) (together with those equations themselves) will show that

$$\frac{P_3^*}{P_1^*} = \frac{P_3^{**}}{P_1^{**}} \tag{3.5.9}$$

Proceeding in this way, we can reach any commodity with a positive price at either * or ** and the theorem is proved.

Note the special role played by commodity 1 in the proof of convergence of prices. In the more satisfactory models which follow, that role will be played by money and Assumption 3.5.2 will be replaced by the assumption that money has a positive price at all equilibria. (Such an assumption has its own difficulties, however; I take these up below.)

3.6 Firms (but no production)[10]

I now extend the model in two ways. The first of these is the introduction of firms; the second is that of money as the sole medium of exchange and the unit of account. As previously discussed, the introduction of money in some such role is practically compelled if we are to have a sensible disequilibrium model that includes firms. Accordingly, all prices are now to be considered in terms of money which is given a separate notation and is *not* one of the n commodities.

I begin by considering firms. In this version of the model, production, like consumption, does not take place until equilibrium is reached. Households in pure exchange can be thought of as trading in titles to commodities - pieces of paper carrying ownership of commodities. Firms are now to be thought of as also trading in such titles; however, firms, which have access to production technologies, do not merely trade titles of goods which they already possess. Rather they sell commitments to deliver outputs. In order to meet those commitments, firms must acquire the necessary inputs; hence firms purchase commitments to supply such inputs - these may be the output commitments of other firms or the factor supplies of households. If firms are unsuccessful at purchasing the inputs which will enable them to meet their output commitments, they must keep on trying or else repurchase the unfillable output commitments. Trade thus does not cease until all firms are in a feasible position. In all of this, money changes hands as commitments are traded, even though inputs and outputs do not physically change hands until equilibrium is reached.

[10] The remainder of this chapter is based on Fisher (1974). See also Arrow and Hahn (1971, chapter 13).

Note that in this process, the question of what happens when someone fails to deliver as promised never materializes. There are no fixed delivery dates and trade simply does not stop until all promised commitments can be met. Where production (or consumption) takes place out of equilibrium such nondelivery problems cannot be swept aside so easily.

I use a notation for firms which, so far as possible, parallels that used for households. The mnemonic convenience of doing this seems to me to overcome the slight technical ambiguities which result; these ambiguities are never of any substantive importance.

Thus, the firm's desired holdings of commodities (commitments) will be denoted by $\mathbf{x}^f$ and its actual holdings by $\bar{\mathbf{x}}^f$, with $\mathbf{z}^f \equiv \mathbf{x}^f - \bar{\mathbf{x}}^f$ its excess demand vector. *Note that this requires that we depart from the usual convention of having firm outputs measured positively and inputs measured negatively.* Here it is the other way round. Goods which the firm produces are *negative*; goods used as inputs are *positive*. This allows us to write excess *demands* as positive and excess *supplies* as negative, matching the notation for households and avoiding a confusing welter of minus signs.

The fth firm has a convex production technology with a differentiable efficient frontier:

$$\phi^f(\mathbf{x}^f) = 0 \quad (f = 1, \ldots, F) \tag{3.6.1}$$

Its target profits, π^f, which it expects to achieve when its transactions at current prices are complete (like households, firms stupidly believe prices will not change) are given by:

$$\pi^f = -\mathbf{P}\mathbf{z}^f + \bar{\pi}^f \quad (f = 1, \ldots, F) \tag{3.6.2}$$

where $\bar{\pi}^f$, to be defined explicitly in a moment, denotes the cash profits it has already received.

The way to think about (3.6.2) is as follows. The firm as of time t - the time as of which (3.6.2) is written - has a current position in commodity commitments, $\bar{\mathbf{x}}^f$. It plans to trade to achieve a new, optimal position, $\mathbf{x}^f$. When it does so (it believes), it will achieve a (positive or negative) increment to profits given by $-\mathbf{P}(\mathbf{x}^f - \bar{\mathbf{x}}^f) = -\mathbf{P}\mathbf{z}^f$, where the minus sign comes about because *outputs* are measured negatively. This will be added to the cash already received through past trades, $\bar{\pi}^f$, to obtain total target profits, π^f. Note that profits, like prices, are measured in terms of money.

Actual profits, $\bar{\pi}^f$, are given by

$$\bar{\pi}^f(t) \equiv -\int_0^t \mathbf{P}(\tau)\dot{\bar{\mathbf{x}}}^f(\tau)\, d\tau + \bar{\pi}^f(0) \quad (f = 1, \ldots, F) \tag{3.6.3}$$

Here, the dependence on time has been made explicit. Starting with an arbitrary initial date, time 0, at each moment in time up to the present (time t), the firm has adjusted its then current position, $\bar{\mathbf{x}}^f(\tau)$, by trading at the then current prices, $\mathbf{P}(\tau)$. Actual profits as of t consist of the profits achieved through such sales plus actual profits as of the starting date (which may be zero). Again the minus sign appears because of the notational convention as to the respective signs of inputs and outputs. Note that $\bar{\pi}^f$ measures actual profits on a cash, rather than an accrual, basis; future costs of meeting obligations already undertaken are not included.

The firm at each moment in time chooses $\mathbf{x}^f$ to maximize profits (3.6.2) subject to (3.6.1). (In so doing, it (stupidly) expects current prices to continue forever and expects to complete its transactions.) Unfortunately, it is necessary (or at least desirable) in this version to assume that this results in a unique optimizing choice for $\mathbf{x}^f$ which is continuous in the prices. This is unfortunate because it rules out constant returns. It is necessary if excess demands are to be continuous functions of prices and the equations of motion given by differential equations with rates of change given as functions of the state variables rather than as relations. If we were to permit constant returns, many of the same results would go through,[11] but the mathematics would become more complex and, quite naturally, while total output would converge, the distribution of output over individual firms would fail to be determined. In general, it is simpler to avoid such complexities. (In Part II, I permit constant returns where there are transaction costs which make optimal policies unique.)

The firm may (indeed must) retain some of its actual earnings to finance transactions, as discussed below, but it eventually pays out its earnings to its stockholders. It is unnecessary to be very explicit about dividend policy. It suffices to assume:

(1) The firm decides on its dividend policy after solving its profit maximizing problem; it does not alter its profit-maximizing plans because of dividends.

(2) The firm's dividend policies are continuous (and obey Lipschitz Conditions) in the state variables so that existence and continuity of solutions to the differential equations of the model are unaffected.

(3) Denote by g^f the *total* dividends paid out by the firm up through t (the integral, *not* the flow paid at t). Then

$$\bar{\pi}^f \geqslant g^f \quad (f=1,\ldots,F) \tag{3.6.4}$$

so that the firm never pays out more than it has earned in cash. This is a convenient assumption rather than a necessary one.

[11] See Henry (1973a,b) and Champsaur, Drèze, and Henry (1977) for existence and continuity of solutions in such cases.

(4) It is natural to assume that the firm *ultimately* plans to pay out all its profits, since it exists for the benefit of its owners. However, this is not necessary. It follows from the results below that in fact all profits do get paid out.

Beyond this assumption, the dividend policy of the firm is a matter of negotiation between ownership and management. The kinds of considerations involved will appear below.

Note that money appears in this model only as the medium of exchange and the unit of account; it is possible to give it a separate role in the productive process; it turns out to be somewhat inconvenient to do this, however, and accordingly I assume that money is neither produced nor used as an input.

3.7 Households, money, and firm ownership

The appearance of firms and of money alters the analysis of the household somewhat. We must take account of the fact that firms are owned by households; this is straightforward, and I shall get to it in a moment.

As explained in the previous chapter, the naivete of agents and the nature of equilibrium in this model make the transactions demand for money disappear at equilibrium. Since this is the only reason for holding money as such, we cannot use money as a numéraire unless we give agents an additional reason to hold money even in equilibrium. As already stated, it is not particularly convenient to do this by allowing money a separate role in production;[12] I adopt the traditional dodge used when faced with this problem in general equilibrium theory and assume that money enters the utility functions of households. It is not necessary to go deeply into the way in which households derive utility from money; the simplest thing is to think of money as another commodity with a utility-producing use such as gold jewelry. When we get to more reasonable models, this rather awkward treatment will not be necessary.

Accordingly, I denote by m^h the hth household's desired money holdings and by $\bar{m}^h$ its actual money holdings. The price of money, of course, is fixed at unity.

The household now maximizes a strictly quasi-concave, weakly monotonic, utility function $u^h(\mathbf{x}^h, m^h)$ which I assume bounded below. It does so subject to a budget constraint – but we must now take account of the fact that firms are owned by households.

In the present model everyone has the same (incorrect) expectations so there is no disagreement about the profits of firms. Hence there appears

[12] This was done (in addition to putting it into utility functions) in Fisher (1974) on which the present development is based.

to be no reason for trading in shares. The other reason for such trading, involving the intertemporal liquidity needs of households and firms, also does not appear. Liquidity problems, as described below, only arise as an afterthought in this model and consumption and production take place after equilibrium is reached. So I shall postpone such matters until Part II, simplify for the present, and assume that ownership of firms is fixed. Let k_f^h denote the fraction of the fth firm which is owned by household h. Then

$$k_f^h \geqslant 0; \quad \sum_{h=1}^{H} k_f^h = 1 \quad (f=1,\ldots,F) \tag{3.7.1}$$

Now, as of time t, the household regards itself as entitled to and about to receive a share in the profits of the firms it owns. Define:

$$s^h \equiv \sum_{f=1}^{F} k_f^h \pi^f; \quad d^h \equiv \sum_{f=1}^{F} k_f^h g^f \quad (h=1,\ldots,H) \tag{3.7.2}$$

Then s^h is the household's share of *total* target profits, and d^h is its share of *already distributed* profits which it has received in the form of dividends. As of t, such distributed profits are held by the household as part of its money stock, $\bar{m}^h$, or have already been used to make purchases of other commodities, $\bar{\mathbf{x}}^h$. What the household regards its ownership of firms as adding to its wealth in addition to the value of its current holdings of money and commodities is thus $(s^h - d^h)$, its share of *undistributed* target profits.

We can thus write the budget constraint for the household as:

$$\mathbf{P}\mathbf{x}^h + m^h = \mathbf{P}\bar{\mathbf{x}}^h + \bar{m}^h + s^h - d^h \quad (h=1,\ldots,H) \tag{3.7.3}$$

3.8 Walras' Law and equilibrium

We can now combine the analyses of the firm and the household and discuss the relations which obtain for the economy as a whole. Sum the budget constraints (3.7.3) over households, obtaining:

$$\mathbf{P}\left(\sum_{h=1}^{H} \mathbf{z}^h\right) + (M - \bar{M}) = \sum_{h=1}^{H} (s^h - d^h) \tag{3.8.1}$$

where M and $\bar{M}$ are the sums of m^h and $\bar{m}^h$, respectively. From (3.7.2) and (3.7.1) we see that

$$\sum_{h=1}^{H} (s^h - d^h) = \sum_{h=1}^{H} \sum_{f=1}^{F} k_f^h (\pi^f - g^f)$$

$$= \sum_{h=1}^{H} k_f^h \sum_{f=1}^{F} (\pi^f - g^f) = \Pi - G \tag{3.8.2}$$

where $(\Pi - G)$ are the total undistributed profits of firms. Going back to the definition of profits, (3.6.2), and summing over firms, we obtain:

$$\Pi - G = -\mathbf{P}\left(\sum_{f=1}^{F} \mathbf{z}^f\right) + (\bar{\Pi} - G) \tag{3.8.3}$$

Substituting (3.8.3) into (3.8.2) and (3.8.2) into (3.8.1), we arrive at:

Proposition 3.8.1 (Walras' Law).

$$\mathbf{PZ} + M - (\bar{M} + (\bar{\Pi} - G)) \equiv 0 \tag{3.8.4}$$

where **Z** is the sum of firms' *and* households' excess demands for ordinary commodities.

It is easy to see that this is indeed Walras' Law for the present economy by realizing that only households have been given any reason to demand money, given that all agents believe that equilibrium is imminent. Hence, M is the economy's *target* demand for money, while $\bar{M}$ is the money stock held by households and $(\bar{\Pi} - G)$ the money stock held by firms.

We can now proceed to define equilibrium for this economy.

Definition 3.8.1. A (Walrasian) equlibrium is a set of prices, **P**, and commitment levels for households and firms, $(\bar{\mathbf{x}}^1, \ldots, \bar{\mathbf{x}}^H)$, $(\bar{\mathbf{x}}^1, \ldots, \bar{\mathbf{x}}^F)$, at which

(a) $\mathbf{z}^h \leqq 0 \quad h = 1, \ldots, H$

(b) $\mathbf{z}^f \leqq 0 \quad f = 1, \ldots, F$

(c) $m^h \leqq \bar{m}^h \quad h = 1, \ldots, H$

The comments made after Definition 3.2.1 apply here also. In (c) of this definition I have allowed money to be in excess supply in equilibrium, but this is illusory as shown in the following theorem.

Theorem 3.8.1. In equilibrium:

(a) $P_i z_i^h = 0$; $P_i z_i^f = 0 \quad (i = 1, \ldots, n), (h = 1, \ldots, H), (f = 1, \ldots, F)$ and hence $P_i Z_i = 0$ so that any agent only has excess supplies of free goods.[13]

(b) $m^h = \bar{m}^h \quad (h = 1, \ldots, H)$ so excess demand for money is zero.

(c) $\pi^f = \bar{\pi}^f = g^f \quad (f = 1, \ldots, F)$ so target and actual profits coincide and are totally paid out to stockholders.

Proof. Rewrite Walras' Law (3.8.4) as

$$(\mathbf{PZ}) + (M - \bar{M}) - (\bar{\Pi} - G) = 0 \tag{3.8.5}$$

Total retained earnings $(\bar{\Pi} - G)$ are nonnegative, since they have been assumed nonnegative for each firm in (3.6.4). In equilibrium, **Z** and

[13] Note that the fact that this is true for every agent and not simply for aggregates has nothing to do with the Hahn Process. It is a property of equilibrium.

$(M-\bar{M})$ are both nonpositive, while $\mathbf{P}$ is of course nonnegative. Hence (3.8.5) can only hold in equilibrium if each of the three terms in parentheses is zero. This, together with the fact that individual excess demands are all nonpositive in equilibrium, establishes (a) and (b). Given (3.6.4), $(\bar{\Pi}-G)$ is zero if and only if $\bar{\pi}^f = g^f$ for every firm, so this proves the second equality in (c). The first equality – that realized and target profits coincide in equilibrium – is very natural. It follows from (a) and the definition of profits (3.6.2), since the firm with unsatisfied excess demands can only be attempting the disposal of free goods.

3.9 The dynamics of the model: Money and trade

I come now to a description of the laws of change in this model, of how endowments and prices change over time. To do this, I must be somewhat more explicit about the role of money than has hitherto been necessary.

As stated, I assume that all trade takes place for money. Since agents realize this, they must take it into account when making their offers to buy. In the present model, however, such liquidity considerations enter only as an afterthought in the following manner.

Agents first formulate "target" excess demands, $\mathbf{z}^h$ or $\mathbf{z}^f$. These are the demands that they believe they can fulfill at current prices. Offers to supply do not require money to back them up, so negative components of target excess demands require no adjustment. Positive excess demands, however, must be backed up with money to become effective or "active" demands so agents ration their current money stocks over their positive target excess demands so as to take account of what they regard as a temporary financial inconvenience.

Formally, let $\mathbf{a}^h$ ($\mathbf{a}^f$) denote the household's (firm's) active excess demand vector. Let $\mathbf{z}^{+h}$ ($\mathbf{z}^{+f}$) be the subvector of $\mathbf{z}^h$ ($\mathbf{z}^f$), which is positive and $\mathbf{P}^{+h}$ ($\mathbf{P}^{+f}$) the corresponding subvector of prices.

Assumption 3.9.1 (Formation of Active Excess Demands).

1. Households. For every $h=1,\ldots,H$ and $i=1,\ldots,n$,
   (a) $z_i^h \leqslant 0$ implies $a_i^h = z_i^h$.
   (b) If $\bar{m}^h > 0$, then $z_i^h > 0$ implies $0 < a_i^h \leqslant z_i^h$ and $\mathbf{P}^{+h}\mathbf{a}^{+h} \leqslant \bar{m}^h$.
   (c) If $\bar{m}^h = 0$, then $z_i^h > 0$ implies $a_i^h = 0$.
2. Firms. For every $f=1,\ldots,F$ and $i=1,\ldots,n$,
   (a) $z_i^f \leqslant 0$ implies $a_i^f = z_i^f$.
   (b) If $(\bar{\pi}^f - g^f) > 0$, then $z_i^f > 0$ implies $0 < a_i^f \leqslant z_i^f$ and $\mathbf{P}^{+f}\mathbf{a}^{+f} \leqslant (\bar{\pi}^f - g^f)$.
   (c) If $(\bar{\pi}^f - g^f) = 0$, then $z_i^f > 0$ implies $a_i^f = 0$.

It does not matter beyond this how money is rationed over positive demands, provided that the rules used are sufficiently smooth to guarantee the existence and continuity of solutions to the differential equations below. I assume this without further comment.

Note the strict inequality in (b). It is sensible that agents faced with temporary liquidity problems should not demand more than their target amounts, but it is not innocuous to assume that they make a positive offer for *every* good for which they have a positive excess demand. As discussed in the preceding chapter, this is a version of the Present Action Postulate.

Given active demands, we can now discuss price adjustment. Prices react to active rather than target demands, so defining $\mathbf{A} \equiv \Sigma_h \mathbf{a}^h + \Sigma_f \mathbf{a}^f$, we replace Assumption 3.2.1 with:

Assumption 3.9.2 (Price Adjustment).

$$\dot{P}_i = \begin{cases} F^i(A_i) & \text{unless } P_i = 0 \text{ and } A_i < 0 \\ 0 & \text{if } P_i = 0 \text{ and } A_i < 0 \end{cases} \tag{3.9.1}$$

where the $F^i(\cdot)$ obey a Lipschitz Condition, are sign preserving, and are bounded away from zero except as $A_i \to 0$.

The Hahn Process Assumption (Assumption 3.2.4) must also be altered to reflect the fact that it is active demands that count.

Assumption 3.9.3 (Hahn Process). For every $h = 1, \ldots, H$, $f = 1, \ldots, F$, and $i = 1, \ldots, n$

$$a_i^h A_i > 0 \quad \text{unless } a_i^h = 0, \tag{3.9.2}$$

$$a_i^f A_i > 0 \quad \text{unless } a_i^f = 0. \tag{3.9.3}$$

The remaining assumptions on the dynamics of the previous model, Pure Exchange and No Swindling – Assumptions 3.2.2 and 3.2.3, respectively – must also be altered, but the alteration here is caused by the introduction of firms rather than of money.

The first such alteration is in Assumption 3.2.2 (Pure Exchange) which we replace by:

Assumption 3.9.4 (Closed Economy).

$$\sum_{h=1}^{H} \dot{\mathbf{x}}^h + \sum_{f=1}^{F} \dot{\mathbf{x}}^f \equiv 0, \tag{3.9.4}$$

$$\bar{M} + (\bar{\Pi} - G) \text{ is a fixed constant.} \tag{3.9.5}$$

The second part of this assumption, (3.9.5), merely repeats the fact that (for convenience) money is neither produced nor destroyed so the total money stock of the economy is a constant. The first part, (3.9.4), can also be read as stating that the total stock of commitments in commodities is constant, but it is somewhat misleading to so interpret it. In the case of pure exchange (Assumption 3.2.2) or in the case of money stocks, what is involved is the statement that a fixed stock of something is merely redistributed among agents each of whom holds a nonnegative amount. The assumption embodied in (3.9.4) is somewhat different. It states that changes in the net total commitments of the production sector must be matched by changes of the opposite sign in the net total position of the household sector. This reflects the fact that the economy is closed so that commitments made by one agent are received by another. The crucial difference between this and pure exchange is that the commitments made by firms do *not* have to be nonnegative. Indeed, commitments to produce outputs are (by definition) negative ones. We will thus not be able to use Assumption 3.9.4 to establish boundedness of positions in any trivial way.

The change that must be made in Assumption 3.2.3 (No Swindling) preserves the assumption that trading at constant prices must involve the exchange of items of equal value. In the present model, this means exchange of commodities for money. For firms, there is no need to assume this directly; we have built it into their accounting in the definition of actual profits (3.6.3). For households, however, we still need to assume it.[14]

Assumption 3.9.5 (No Swindling).

$$\mathbf{P}\dot{\mathbf{x}}^h + \dot{m}^h = \dot{d}^h \quad (h=1,\ldots,H) \tag{3.9.6}$$

Thus the value of a household's holdings of commodities (commitments) and money can change. It can change, of course, through capital gains or losses; however, with prices constant, that value can only change through the receipt of dividends; it cannot change through trade.

3.10 Target profits, target utilities, and quasi-stability

We can now proceed to show that target profits decline when the firm is not in personal equilibrium (able to complete all of its transactions save possibly the discarding of free goods). In doing so it is simplest to assume that firms remain in operation, never finding it optimal to go out of business and distribute their remaining cash and other assets to their stockholders. (Bankruptcy discontinuities are discussed in the context of the richer model of Part II.)

[14] Note in the proofs of Theorem 3.10.1 and 3.10.2 the parallel roles played by (3.63) and the No Swindling assumption.

Theorem 3.10.1. For every $f=1,\ldots,F$, provided that $(\bar{\pi}^f - g^f) > 0$, $\dot{\pi}^f \leqslant 0$ and $\dot{\pi}^f < 0$ unless f is in personal equilibrium.

Proof. Write the Lagrangian for the firm's maximization problem (3.6.2) and (3.6.1) as

$$L^f = -\mathbf{P}\mathbf{z}^f + \bar{\pi}^f + \delta^f \phi^f(\mathbf{x}^f) \tag{3.10.1}$$

where δ^f is a Lagrange multiplier. By the Envelope theorem for constrained maximization, we can evaluate $\dot{\pi}^f$ by differentiation of (3.10.1) with respect to those variables which the firm takes as parameters, $\mathbf{P}$, $\bar{\mathbf{x}}^f$, and $\bar{\pi}^f$, multiplying the respective derivatives by the corresponding derivatives of $\mathbf{P}$, $\bar{\mathbf{x}}^f$, and $\bar{\pi}^f$ with respect to time. This yields:

$$\dot{\pi}^f = -\dot{\mathbf{P}}\mathbf{z}^f + (\mathbf{P}\dot{\bar{\mathbf{x}}}^f + \dot{\bar{\pi}}^f) \tag{3.10.2}$$

Examining the definition of $\bar{\pi}^f$, (3.6.3), we see that

$$\dot{\bar{\pi}}^f = -\mathbf{P}\dot{\bar{\mathbf{x}}}^f \tag{3.10.3}$$

reflecting the fact that achieved cash profits change through trade. Hence the term in parentheses in (3.10.2) is zero, and

$$\dot{\pi}^f = -\sum_{i=1}^{n} \dot{P}_i z_i^f \tag{3.10.4}$$

Now, since $(\bar{\pi}^f - g^f) > 0$, Assumption 3.9.1 (Formation of Active Excess Demands) shows that every nonzero target excess demand, z_i^f, corresponds to a nonzero active excess demand, a_i^f, of the same sign. Assumption 3.9.3 (Hahn Process), however, shows that nonzero active excess demands for the firm correspond to total active excess demands of the same sign. Finally, Assumption 3.9.2 (Price Adjustment) states that price moves in the direction of total active excess demand save for the case of free good disposal. Putting this all together, it is plain that (for $i=1,\ldots,n$) $\dot{P}_i z_i^f \geqslant 0$ and $\dot{P}_i z_i^f > 0$ unless either $z_i^f = 0$ or $z_i^f < 0$ with $P_i = 0$. This proves the theorem in view of (3.10.4).

With this in hand, it is possible to go on to generalize Theorem 3.3.1 to show that household utilities decline unless the household *and* the firms in which it owns shares are all able to complete their non-free-good-disposal transactions.

Theorem 3.10.2. For every $h=1,\ldots,H$, provided that $\bar{m}^h > 0$, *and* $\bar{\pi}^f - g^f > 0$ for all f for which $k_f^h > 0$, it is the case that $\dot{u}^h \leqslant 0$ and $\dot{u}^h < 0$ unless both h *and* every f for which $k_f^h > 0$ are in personal equilibria.

Proof. Write the Lagrangian for the household's optimization problem as

$$L^h = u^h(\mathbf{x}^h, m^h) - \lambda^h\{\mathbf{P}(\mathbf{x}^h - \bar{\mathbf{x}}^h) + (m^h - \bar{m}^h) - s^h + d^h\} \quad (3.10.6)$$

where λ^h is a Lagrange multiplier (see (3.7.3)).

Applying the Envelope Theorem technique to the evaluation of $\dot{u}^h$, we obtain:

$$\dot{u}^h = -\lambda^h\{\dot{\mathbf{P}}\mathbf{z}^h - (\mathbf{P}\dot{\bar{\mathbf{x}}}^h + \dot{\bar{m}}^h - \dot{d}^h) - \dot{s}^h\} \quad (3.10.7)$$

Using Assumption 3.9.5 (No Swindling), we see that this reduces to

$$\dot{u}^h = -\lambda^h\dot{\mathbf{P}}\mathbf{z}^h + \lambda^h\dot{s}^h \quad (3.10.8)$$

Now, λ^h is the marginal utility of wealth and is readily seen to be positive. By Theorem 3.10.1, $\dot{s}^h$, which is the household's share of the target profits of the firms it owns is nonpositive and is strictly negative unless all those firms are in personal equilibria. Finally, an argument from Assumptions 3.9.1 through 3.9.3 identical with that made for firms (in the proof of Theorem 3.10.1) shows that $\dot{\mathbf{P}}\mathbf{z}^h \geqslant 0$ and $\dot{\mathbf{P}}\mathbf{z}^h > 0$ unless h is in personal equilibrium. This proves the theorem.

We can now generalize the quasi-stability result of Corollary 3.3.1 to the present case. To do so, however, will obviously require us to assume:

Assumption 3.10.1 (Positive Cash). For all finite times sufficiently large, $\bar{m}^h > 0$ $(h = 1,\ldots,H)$ and $(\bar{\pi}^f - g^f) > 0$ $(f = 1,\ldots,F)$.

Thus no one runs out of money. As already discussed in the previous chapter, this is awkward. Until we allow agents to realize that liquidity may be a problem, it is hard to do anything about this. (Note that we have also assumed that firms do not voluntarily go out of production.)

Corollary 3.10.1. The dynamic process under study is quasi-stable.

Proof. Once again define

$$V \equiv \sum_h u^h(\mathbf{x}^h, m^h)$$

Then V is continuous, bounded below, and, by Theorem 3.10.2, it is decreasing except at rest points (= equilibria). Hence V is a Lyapounov function.

Note that the fact that firms are owned by households makes it possible to continue using the sum of household target utilities as a Lyapounov function. It would not be possible to stop with Theorem 3.10.1 and merely use the sum of target profits because of the possibility that firms might be in personal equilibria while households still want to trade. The ownership position of households means that they are still revising their target utilities downward if the firms they own are unable to complete their non-free-good-disposal transactions.

It would be possible - although perhaps less elegant - to use the sum of all target utilities and profits together as a Lyapounov function. No less meaning attaches to the sum of profits and utilities than to the sum of utilities over different individuals. (In a later chapter, I shall make use of such a construction.) Target profits have already been assumed bounded below by the assumption that firms always find it optimal to remain in business.

3.11 Compactness again

We are now once more at the stage where we must prove or assume that the state variables (prices, actual commitments, money stocks, actual profits, and paid-out dividends) remain in a compact set. As before this means showing that they remain bounded.

Now such boundedness remains trivial for money stocks. We have assumed all agents' money stocks nonnegative and in Assumption 3.9.4 (Closed Economy) have assumed the total stock of money fixed. Further, it is not hard to see that actual profits and actual dividends will remain bounded provided that prices and commitments do so. Hence we may concentrate on the behavior of prices and commitments.

Neither the boundedness of prices nor that of commitments is any longer the trivial matter which it was in Section 3.4 above, however. In the case of commitments this is because we have allowed negative holdings on the part of firms. The fact that firms and households trade with each other does not then permit the Closed Economy assumption (Assumption 3.9.4) to play the same role as did the Pure Exchange assumption (Assumption 3.2.2) in assuring boundedness for commodities other than money.

Somewhat more subtly, the fact that we are using money as a numéraire means we are no longer free simply to define relative prices to be in the unit simplex as in (3.4.1). Rather we must show that prices relative to that of money rather than relative to an arbitrarily weighted price index remain bounded.[15]

I begin with prices. There are two ways known to me to proceed. The first, along the lines of Theorem 3.4.1, restricts the price-adjustment process somewhat, but does not restrict the behavior of agents save to assure that money can always serve as a numéraire.[16] The second avoids restricting the process but does place some mild restrictions on the excess demands of agents.

The first route is as follows. Money will not be suitable as a numéraire if its price relative to that of other goods can drop to zero. Hence it is

[15] cf. Assumption 3.5.2 (Pairwise Numéraire).
[16] This is based on Arrow and Hahn (1971, Chap. 13).

natural to prevent this by assuming that if the relative price of money were low enough, there would be an excess demand for it. In the present model, this amounts to assuming that money not only enters the utility functions of households, but also that it does so in a nondisappearing way, that is, that there always exists at least one household for whom the marginal utility of money never approaches zero. Since all demands are homogeneous of degree zero in prices, this amounts to assuming:

Assumption 3.11.1 (Money a Suitable Numéraire). If $\mathbf{P}$ is sufficiently far from the origin, then

$$M \geqslant \bar{M} + (\bar{\Pi} - G).$$

In the present finite-dimensional context, the distance measure used here is unimportant.

Given this, we can extend Lemma 3.4.1.

Lemma 3.11.1. Suppose there exist n positive scalars, k_i $(i=1,\ldots,n)$ such that

$$F^i(A_i) \leqslant k_i A_i \quad (i=1,\ldots,n) \tag{3.11.1}$$

Then Assumption 3.11.1 implies the boundedness of prices.[17]

Proof. Define

$$Q \equiv \frac{1}{2} \sum_{i=1}^{n} \frac{P_i^2}{k_i} \tag{3.11.2}$$

Differentiating Q with respect to time and using (3.11.1) and the Price Adjustment Assumption (Assumption 3.9.2), we obtain:

$$\dot{Q} = \sum_{i=1}^{n} \frac{P_i \dot{P}_i}{k_i} = \sum_{i=1}^{n} \frac{P_i F^i(A_i)}{k_i} \leqslant \sum_{i=1}^{n} P_i A_i \tag{3.11.3}$$

(Note that free goods in excess supply do not affect this result.) Further, by Assumption 3.9.1 (Formation of Active Excess Demands), the active excess demand of any agent cannot exceed that agent's target excess demand. Thus

$$\sum_{i=1}^{n} P_i A_i \leqslant \sum_{i=1}^{n} P_i Z_i \equiv \mathbf{PZ} = \bar{M} + (\bar{\Pi} - G) - M \tag{3.11.4}$$

where the last equality follows from Walras' Law (3.8.4).

[17] I mention Assumption 3.11.1 explicitly in the statement of the theorem although other assumptions are used as well because, unlike those other assumptions, Assumption 3.11.1 is replaced by alternative versions in the present section.

Now suppose that **P** were to become very large. Then, by Assumption 3.11.1, the right-hand side of (3.11.4) would become negative. It would then follow from (3.11.4) and (3.11.3) that $\dot{Q} \leqslant 0$. Hence prices must stay bounded because if they got big enough to create excess demand for money as in Assumption 3.11.1, the ellipsoid (defined by a given value of Q) on which they lie would be shrinking.

This method of proceeding uses the fact that at unbounded prices all goods taken together, so to speak, must be in excess supply. It requires that the price adjustment mechanism be such as to allow the use of an appropriately weighted sum of excess demands as in (3.11.3). The alternate way to proceed is to assume directly that goods whose relative prices are very high are not in excess demand. Since it is relative prices which are involved, this does not seem too objectionable. Such an assumption can be made formally as:

> *Assumption 3.11.2 (Excess Supply of High-Priced Goods).* There exists a finite scalar, $N > 1$, such that for every set of commodities, J (not including money), whenever both (i) $P_j > NP_i$ for all $j \in J$, $i \notin J$ and (ii) $P_j > N$ for all $j \in J$, then $Z_{j^*} \leqslant 0$, where $P_{j^*} \equiv \max_{j \in J} P_j$.

In other words, whenever any set of commodities have prices sufficiently high relative to all others, including money, the highest priced commodity in the set is not in excess demand.

> *Lemma 3.11.2.* Under Assumption 3.11.2, prices are bounded.

Proof. Suppose not. Then there is a set of commodities, J, whose prices become unbounded. I shall show that this is impossible by establishing that the highest price of any commodity in J cannot increase beyond an upper bound given by the greater of its initial value and $N^k \alpha$, where k is the number of commodities in J and α is an upper bound to the prices of commodities not in J (including money). To do this, it suffices to show that the highest such price, P_{j^*}, is not increasing above $N^k \alpha$.

Thus, suppose that $P_{j^*} > N^k \alpha$. If all commodities in J have prices above $N\alpha$, then, by Assumption 3.11.2, target excess demand for j^* is nonpositive and, since (by Assumption 3.9.1) active excess demand cannot exceed target excess demand, P_{j^*} must not be increasing.

Suppose, therefore, that there is some commodity in J, whose price is not greater than $N\alpha$. Let J' denote the subset of J formed by deleting all such commodities. Suppose that all commodities in J' have prices higher than $N^2\alpha$. Then Assumption 3.11.2 applies to J' and P_{j^*} is nonincreasing as before.

Suppose, therefore, that there is some commodity in J' with a price no

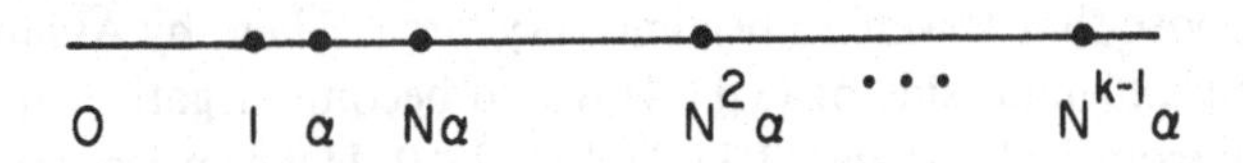

Figure 3.11.1.

greater than $N^2\alpha$. Let J'' denote the subset of J' formed by deleting all such commodities. If all commodities in J' have prices greater than $N^3\alpha$, then Assumption 3.11.2 applies to J'' and P_{j^*} is nonincreasing.

Proceeding in this way, either we find that P_{j^*} is nonincreasing or we find that all prices other than that of j^* are below $N^{k-1}\alpha$. In the latter case, Assumption 3.11.2 applies to the subset of commodities consisting of j^* only and P_{j^*} is nonincreasing. This proves the lemma.

A schematic idea of the proof can be obtained from Figure 3.11.1 above. The only way to avoid Assumption 3.11.2 as we delete more commodities from J is to have one price between α and $N\alpha$, one between $N\alpha$ and $N^2\alpha$, and so forth. But in this case we run out of commodities in J by the time we reach $N^{k-1}\alpha$. Note that this depends crucially on there being a finite number of commodities. In the development in Part II, such finiteness will not apply.

Lemmas 3.11.1 and 3.11.2 provide alternate reasons for supposing that prices are bounded and we shall henceforth assume that they are so bounded. The other boundedness issue with which we must deal is that of commitment positions (in commodities other than money), the $\bar{\mathbf{x}}^h$ and $\bar{\mathbf{x}}^f$. In the context of the present model, this turns out to be easy - indeed, embarassingly easy - to do.

The reason that it might be possible for commitment positions to become unbounded is that we have allowed firms, in promising to deliver output, to hold negative positions in commodities. While it is innocuous to assume that firms do not promise more than they believe they can deliver if they can get the required inputs (so that actual positions only become unbounded if desired ones do),[18] this is not enough. Firms, it is true, will not offer unbounded amounts of outputs unless they believe they can acquire unbounded amounts of inputs, but there is nothing so far in the model to prevent them from believing this. Indeed, to the extent that the input holdings of one firm are the output promises of other firms, there is so far nothing to prevent firms from making ever-growing output commitments believing that they have *already* acquired adequate inputs to produce the promised outputs.

As it happens, in the present model this is not a problem. We have

[18] Note that this puts an entirely reasonable, but so far unstated, restriction on trade. Agents may not be able to acquire (or sell) all they want, but they do not acquire (or sell) *more* than they want.

already assumed that the firm's optimum problem results in a unique choice for desired commitments, $\mathbf{x}^f$, which is continuous in the prices. In so doing, we ruled out constant returns. However, we have now assumed (or proved) that prices are bounded and hence lie in a compact set. It follows that every element of $\mathbf{x}^f$ has a finite maximum and a finite minimum as prices vary over that compact set, so $\mathbf{x}^f$ must be bounded. It is then totally innocuous to assume that actual commitments, $\bar{\mathbf{x}}^f$, are bounded as well. The boundedness of household commodity holdings, $\bar{\mathbf{x}}^h$, now presents no difficulty since these are nonnegative and the economy is closed (Assumption 3.9.4).

This line of attack will suffice for the present model, but it is obviously not wholly satisfactory as a general matter. One would like to be able to handle such boundedness problems in models which do permit constant returns, where the problem has not already been assumed away. It is plain that this is possible and, indeed, the tack to take is quite a natural one. I add a few words on it.

The possibility, described above, of firms expanding forever by taking in each other's washing, so to speak, lacks an obvious element of realism. What is missing is the notion that production somewhere requires primary factors and not just the outputs of firms as inputs. It is the fact that the Earth is finite that ultimately keeps production with constant-returns technologies bounded. More specifically, suppose we assume that the overall production set of the producing sector has the property that no output can be produced without an amount of some primary factor,[19] which is bounded above zero per unit of output. Then outputs can only become unbounded by generating an unbounded demand for primary factors.

This is not enough directly to prevent firms from making unbounded commitments under constant returns. After all, each competitive firm (believing that it is in equilibrium) believes it can buy all it wants of factors at the going price so that it believes that the overall limit on factor supply will not limit its own purchases. However, an unbounded demand for a primary factor which is limited in supply will lead to an unbounded excess demand for that factor. Provided one is careful about the mechanics of price adjustment for such factors, it is evident that the price system will do what it is supposed to do. The prices of primary factors will rise, signalling firms that they are limited in supply and making production of outputs which use them either directly or indirectly unprofitable since output prices are bounded.[20] This keeps firms from working to make

[19] Outputs which are known to be limited in supply would also serve.

[20] It is also true that factor prices are bounded so unbounded increases in factor prices cannot themselves occur. The reason that one must be careful about the mechanics of price adjustment is as follows: Suppose that desired output

greater output commitments and thus keeps actual commitments bounded in an economically more interesting (and aesthetic) way than simply ruling out constant returns by brute force.

There is no need to formalize this development here, however, and I shall simply assume henceforward that the state variables remain in a compact set.

3.12 Global stability again

We are almost ready for the principal result for this model, the proof that the dynamic process under study is globally stable. Before giving that proof, there are two matters that require attention.

The first of these concerns free goods. As in Theorem 3.5.1 above for the case of pure exchange, it will not be possible to guarantee convergence of the holdings of goods which are free in the asymptotic equilibrium price system. As in that case, what is proved here is essential global stability as defined in Definition 3.5.1 above.

Second, we must make an assumption such as Assumption 3.5.1 (Indecomposability of Equilibrium) to ensure convergence of prices.[21] This can be done by adapting Assumption 3.5.1 to include money in the set of goods that have positive prices at equilibrium and to allow for firms as well as households.[22] However, these changes present no difficulty and essentially no new material and I shall cut through further discussion by assuming directly:

Assumption 3.12.1 (Uniqueness of Support Prices). Let $(\mathbf{P}^*, \bar{\mathbf{x}}^{*1}, \ldots, \bar{\mathbf{x}}^{*H}, \bar{m}^{*1}, \ldots, \bar{m}^{*H}, \bar{\mathbf{x}}^{*1}, \ldots, \bar{\mathbf{x}}^{*F})$ and $(\mathbf{P}^{**}, \bar{\mathbf{x}}^{**1}, \ldots, \bar{\mathbf{x}}^{**H}, \bar{m}^{**1}, \ldots, \bar{m}^{**H}, \bar{\mathbf{x}}^{**1}, \ldots, \bar{\mathbf{x}}^{**F})$ be two equilibria. If (a) $\bar{m}^{*h} = \bar{m}^{**h}$ $(h = 1, \ldots, H)$; (b) for all $i \in \{S(\mathbf{P}^*) \cup S(\mathbf{P}^{**})\}$, $\bar{x}_i^{*h} = \bar{x}_i^{**h}$ $(h = 1, \ldots, H)$ and $\bar{x}_i^{*f} = \bar{x}_i^{**f}$ $(f = 1, \ldots, F)$, then $\mathbf{P}^* = \mathbf{P}^{**}$.

commitments do not become unbounded monotonically but cycle with ever-increasing peaks. Then excess demand for primary factors will also cycle. One must be sure that the price adjustment mechanism does not operate by having the prices of primary factors grow relatively slowly in periods of great excess demand, recovering all increases by decreasing rapidly in slack periods. Since excess demand for primary factors becomes unbounded and excess supply does not, it is reasonable to rule out such behavior and assume that the prices in question would become unbounded.

[21] Note that we need not again assume Assumption 3.5.2 (Pairwise Numéraire). We have already assumed that there is a good, namely money, whose price is positive in every equilibrium.

[22] Formally, we can do this by allowing money to be indexed as good 0 with price $P_0 = 1$, so that $0 \in S(\mathbf{P})$ in (3.5.1). The final statement of Assumption 3.5.1 must then allow there *either* to be an h such that $\bar{x}_i^{*h} > 0$ and $\bar{x}_j^{*h} > 0$ *or* an f such that $\bar{x}_i^{*f} > 0$ and $\bar{x}_j^{*f} > 0$. Further details are left to the reader.

In other words, if holdings at two equilibria coincide except for goods free at both equilibria, then the prices supporting these holdings are the same.

Cutting through the indecomposability issue with Assumption 3.12.1 allows us to concentrate on the places where the proof of global stability with firms (and money) is different from (although an extension of) the similar proof for pure exchange. Where the proofs are essentially the same, I do not give extended discussion.

Theorem 3.12.1. The dynamic process under study is essentially globally stable.

Proof. As in Theorem 3.5.1, we need only show that the limit point equilibria of the process (corresponding to a given initial condition) are all the same. As in the proof of Theorem 3.5.1, denote one such equilibrium by * and the other by **.

The same reasoning as in the proof of Theorem 3.5.1 shows that the target utility of any household converges so that

$$u^h(\mathbf{x}^{*h}, m^{*h}) = u^h(\mathbf{x}^{**h}, m^{**h}) \tag{3.12.1}$$

By strict quasi-concavity, this means

$$\mathbf{P}^*\mathbf{x}^{*h} + m^{*h} \leqslant \mathbf{P}^*\mathbf{x}^{**h} + m^{**h} \tag{3.12.2}$$

with the strict inequality holding unless $m^{*h} = m^{**h}$ and $x_i^{*h} = x_i^{**h}$ for all i for which $P_i^* \neq 0$. Since ** is an equilibrium, $\mathbf{x}^{**h} \leqq \bar{\mathbf{x}}^{**h}$ and $m^{**h} = \bar{m}^{**h}$. Hence

$$\mathbf{P}^*\mathbf{x}^{**h} + m^{**h} \leqslant \mathbf{P}^*\bar{\mathbf{x}}^{**h} + \bar{m}^{**h} \tag{3.12.3}$$

So far, this development has been substantively identical to that in the proof of Theorem 3.5.1.

Now consider the household's budget constraint (3.7.3). It implies:

$$\mathbf{P}^*\bar{\mathbf{x}}^{*h} + \bar{m}^{*h} = \mathbf{P}^*\mathbf{x}^{*h} + m^{*h} - (s^{*h} - d^{*h}) \tag{3.12.4}$$

However, * is an equilibrium and hence, by Theorem 3.8.1, all target profits have been achieved and paid out to shareholders so

$$s^{*h} - d^{*h} = 0 \tag{3.12.5}$$

Putting (3.12.2)–(3.12.5) together, and summing over households, we obtain:

$$\mathbf{P}^* \sum_{h=1}^{H} \bar{\mathbf{x}}^{*h} + \bar{M}^* \leqslant \mathbf{P}^* \sum_{h=1}^{H} \bar{\mathbf{x}}^{**h} + \bar{M}^{**} \tag{3.12.6}$$

with the strict inequality holding if it holds in (3.12.2) for any h.

We now turn to firms.[23] Since $\mathbf{x}^{*f}$ is the unique profit-maximizing commitment vector at prices $\mathbf{P}^*$, we have:

$$-\mathbf{P}^*\mathbf{x}^{*f} \geqslant -\mathbf{P}^*\mathbf{x}^{**f} \tag{3.12.7}$$

with the strict inequality holding unless $x_i^{*f} = x_i^{**f}$ for all i for which $P_i^* \neq 0$. Since ** is an equilibrium, $\mathbf{x}^{**f} \leqq \bar{\mathbf{x}}^{**f}$, so that

$$-\mathbf{P}^*\mathbf{x}^{**f} \geqslant -\mathbf{P}^*\bar{\mathbf{x}}^{**f} \tag{3.12.8}$$

Since * is an equilibrium, target and realized profits coincide at * (Theorem 3.8.1), so that, from the definition of profits (3.6.2),

$$-\mathbf{P}^*\bar{\mathbf{x}}^{*f} = -\mathbf{P}^*\mathbf{x}^{*f} - (\pi^{*f} - \bar{\pi}^{*f}) = -\mathbf{P}^*\mathbf{x}^{*f} \tag{3.12.9}$$

Putting (3.12.7) through (3.12.9) together and summing over firms, we obtain

$$\mathbf{P}^* \sum_{f=1}^{F} \bar{\mathbf{x}}^{*f} \leqslant \mathbf{P}^* \sum_{f=1}^{F} \bar{\mathbf{x}}^{**f} \tag{3.12.10}$$

with the strict inequality holding if it holds in (3.12.7) for any f.

Now, combine (3.12.6) and (3.12.10), obtaining:

$$\mathbf{P}^*\left(\sum_{h=1}^{H} \bar{\mathbf{x}}^{*h} + \sum_{h=1}^{H} \bar{\mathbf{x}}^{*f} \right) + \bar{M}^* \leqslant \mathbf{P}^*\left(\sum_{h=1}^{H} \bar{\mathbf{x}}^{**h} + \sum_{f=1}^{F} \bar{\mathbf{x}}^{**f} \right) + \bar{M}^{**} \tag{3.12.11}$$

with the strict inequality holding if it holds either for some h in (3.12.2) or for some f in (3.12.7). It is plain, however, that the strict inequality cannot hold in (3.12.11). This is so because the economy is closed (Assumption 3.9.4) so that the sum of household and firm commitments in ordinary commodities is fixed, while all profits are paid out in equilibrium (Theorem 3.8.1) so that (3.9.5) implies $\bar{M}^* = \bar{M}^{**}$. Hence (3.12.2) and (3.12.7) must hold as equalities for all h and f, respectively.

Essentially, what is going on in the proof is the following. Compare the economy at * and ** using the prices of *. From the point of view of consumers, their holdings at ** must cost at least as much as their holdings at * since they are on the same indifference curves. From the point of view of firms, however, their holdings at ** must be worth no more than their holdings at * since the latter maximize profits at the prices being used. Since all profits are distributed, these things cannot both be true unless they hold as equalities since any change in firm holdings from * to ** would be exactly matched by a change in household holdings.

[23] Since π^f is nonincreasing (Theorem 3.10.1) and bounded below (by assumption) it approaches a limit which must be the same in every equilibrium. This parallel to the case of utility, however, does not have to be used directly.

We now know that $\bar{m}^{*h} = \bar{m}^{**h}$ for all h. Further, $\bar{x}_i^{*h} = \bar{x}_i^{**h}$ and $\bar{x}_i^{*f} = \bar{x}_i^{**f}$ for all h, f, and those i for which $P_i^* \neq 0$. It is only a matter of interchanging the roles of * and ** to establish the latter statement for those i for which $P_i^{**} \neq 0$. Hence holdings of money coincide as do commitments of goods which are not free at both equilibria. The theorem now follows from Assumption 3.12.1.

PART II

A model of disequilibrium with arbitraging agents

CHAPTER 4

Allowing disequilibrium awareness

4.1 Toward a more sensible model

It is now time to consider developing the models so far considered in the direction of our final goal. We must allow production and consumption to take place out of equilibrium. More important, we must allow agents to realize that they are not in equilibrium and to act on arbitrage opportunities as they occur. This fundamentally requires that agents be permitted to do two things. First, they must recognize that prices may change. Second, they must recognize that they may not be able to complete their desired transactions. In forming their consumption and production plans, agents must take these things into account.

The fact that agents may not be able to complete their transactions is not unrelated to the fact that prices can change. Agents who believe that they face transaction constraints are also likely to believe that prices in markets with such constraints will change. This is particularly likely in a Hahn Process world of orderly markets in which agents can take their own inability to purchase as reflecting a general short supply. Moreover, agents facing such constraints may themselves make price offers to get around them.

Handling all of this is a tall order and is best done in pieces. In the present chapter, I consider in general how the analysis so far developed can be adapted to deal with these matters. The details - which are often very interesting indeed - are explored later on.

The first problem, that of permitting production and consumption out of equilibrium, is particularly suited for handling in terms of the Hahn Process. As already pointed out in Chapter 2, carrying out production and consumption decisions involves taking actions which are likely to be irreversible. If those actions are taken under expectations about prices and trading opportunities which turn out to be false, it will often be the case that the actions are regretted. Such actions lead to lower profits or utilities than would have been achieved had prices and trading opportunities been correctly anticipated. The Lyapounov function of the Hahn Process, however, depends on target profits and utilities declining out of equilibrium. The making of irreversible and regretted decisions can only aid in such decline. Hence it should be possible to incorporate disequilibrium production and consumption into a Hahn Process model without a great deal of change.

What does require change is the deeper matter of allowing agents to realize that they are not in equilibrium and to take advantage of arbitrage opportunities. Here one must step back and ask what stability propositions we can reasonably suppose might be true. I do so assuming that agents have point expectations, commenting on the more general case later.

In the first place, if agents perceive themselves as bound by transaction constraints, there can be no assurance (without further assumptions) that the rest point to which the economy converges (supposing that it does converge) is a Walrasian equilibrium. After all, if everyone always believes that he cannot transact at all, the dynamic system involved will be at a rest point and globally stable, but only because no one ever tries to do anything. Less trivially, where quantity constraints are involved, we cannot be sure that equilibria do not involve some such constraints as binding. Hence, at least without assumptions that ensure that such constraints will be tested, one cannot guarantee that the system, if it converges, does so to a Walrasian equilibrium.

This is not without its own interest, of course. The possibility of convergence to a non-Walrasian equilibrium with persistent underemployment is the problem treated by Keynes in the *General Theory of Employment, Interest and Money*. Further, the existence of such quantity-constrained equilibria has been the subject of much recent attention in the literature.[1] It would be surprising if – without further assumptions or analysis – such a situation could be ruled out in advance.

4.2 The appearance of new opportunities: No Favorable Surprise

Put aside the question of what sort of rest point a full-dress model is likely to approach, however, and consider the logically prior question of the circumstances under which such a model can be expected to converge at all. Can one expect to prove that an economy with rational agents

[1] See Drazen (1980) for a survey.

conscious of disequilibrium and taking advantage of arbitrage opportunities is driven (asymptotically) to *any* equilibrium, Walrasian or constrained? A little thought reveals that such convergence cannot hold as a uniformly true proposition, nor should one expect it to do so.

Imagine the following scenario. Equilibrium is about to be attained. Church bells are ready to ring announcing the great moment. Just as celebrations begin to break out, however, a nonnegligible number of agents sit up and say: "Wait a minute. The price of gold-plated chocolate bars will go up tomorrow." Believing this to be true, such agents perceive a new arbitrage opportunity; they rush out and buy gold-plated chocolate bars. Plainly, such actions delay convergence to equilibrium. If this sort of thing keeps being repeated in a nonnegligible way, convergence may never occur.

The point of this is as follows. It may well be true that an economy of rational agents who understand that there is disequilibrium and act on arbitrage opportunities is driven toward equilibrium, but not if these agents continually perceive new previously unanticipated opportunities for further arbitrage. The appearance of such new and unexpected opportunities will generally disturb the system until they are absorbed.

Such opportunities can be of different kinds. The most obvious sort is the appearance of unforeseen technological developments – the unanticipated development of new products or processes. There are other sorts of new opportunities as well. An unanticipated change in tastes or the development of new uses for old products is one; the discovery of new sources of raw materials is another. Further, efficiency improvements in firms are not restricted to technological developments. The discovery of a more efficient mode of internal organization or of a better way of marketing can also present a new opportunity. So long as such opportunities keep on arising, we cannot expect an economy with sensible agents to converge. The appearance of such opportunities, where they are unanticipated, are shocks which keep the economy moving.

To students of the history of economic thought, this discussion should have a familiar ring, even though it may not seem familiar to those narrowly focused on modern mathematical theories of general equilibrium and stability. It was the basic insight of Joseph Schumpeter, first enunciated in 1911 in his *Theory of Economic Development* (Schumpeter, 1951) and then developed in various ways in later works (Schumpeter, 1939, 1962) that it is the actions of the innovating entrepreneur, seizing on new opportunities that produce economic growth and change. For Schumpeter, indeed, it is the innovator who disturbs what he called the "circular flow" and what we would now call a position of general equilibrium and who, using credit markets, bids away the resources needed to follow his vision of a new opportunity. In Schumpeter's theory, the original innovator, if successful, is followed by imitators whose actions eventually cause the profits of the innovative activity to disappear, and, with the innovation now fully absorbed, equilibrium is restored unless and until the process repeats.

Schumpeter was right, even though his model was not a rigorous one by today's standards. So long as Schumpeterian innovators keep appearing, they provide the shocks which keep the economy moving. We cannot hope to prove that rational agents acting on arbitrage opportunities will drive the economy to converge to equilibrium unless we assume that new opportunities do not keep on appearing. Moreover, in a sense this is the most we should *want* to prove. This is that part of Schumpeter's model that describes the return to equilibrium as an innovation becomes absorbed through the actions of arbitraging agents - the imitators. To prove that there is stability in the presence of a continual stream of new innovations which do not die away would be to prove too much. It would show that competitive economies *never* move - whether disturbed or not.

What we can hope to prove, therefore, is that in a world with no unforeseen opportunities, stability will occur and equilibrium will be asymptotically achieved. To put it another way, we can hope to show that the continued *presence* of new unforeseen opportunities is a necessary condition for instability - for continued change.

The matter is more subtle than has so far appeared, however. The Schumpeterian list of opportunities given above does not exhaust the possibilities. This is because agents will act on opportunities if constraints which previously kept them from doing so are loosened and because agents may be mistaken in their perceptions of opportunities.

Consider the constraint question first. Where agents face constraints on their ability to raise capital, they may be kept from exploiting opportunities which they see. An unexpected increase in the availability of funds can therefore lead to an attempt to exploit such opportunities. But it is not the mere realization that a new opportunity exists that provides the Schumpeterian shock to the system; it is the actions that result from such a realization. In Schumpeter's own story, the entrepreneur uses the resources of the credit markets (together with his own) to bid resources away from their existing uses in order to take advantage of his innovative vision. More generally, agents require money to act on opportunities. An unexpected increase in their ability to raise such money will enable them so to act.

It is important to realize that an unexpected increase in an agent's ability to raise funds need not come about because of innovations in credit institutions or even because the agent's bank manager calls him up and offers a larger overdraft. Agents also finance their activities through the earnings they make from selling their endowments or from successful arbitrage or investment. If we are to assume - as we must - that new opportunities do not forever disturb the economy we are studying, we must therefore assume that agents who have been kept from exploiting potentially profitable opportunities for lack of funds do not experience nonnegligible windfall gains. This is not to say that agents can never have capital gains or engage in profitable arbitrage. It is to say that the profits so realized must not be *unexpectedly* high if the agents who receive them have been faced with a binding liquidity constraint.

Other constraints as well must not become unexpectedly looser where their stringency has kept agents from action. For example, agents may be kept from acting because they realize that the economy is in disequilibrium and believe that they will not be able to complete all the transactions which they would otherwise attempt. If such constraints become looser either because some improvement in the technology of transactions makes it easier to find trading partners or simply because agents change their views and become more optimistic as to the possibility of transacting, the behavior pattern of agents will change and progress toward equilibrium will be disrupted in the same way as if any other new opportunity had arisen.

This example brings me to the next point. What matters is not whether new opportunities are really there but whether agents believe that they are. Opportunity is in the eye of the beholder and it is the perceptions of agents which lead them to act - even though such perceptions may be wrong. The man who believes he can build a better mousetrap and is willing to spend resources to do so will initially act in the same way regardless of whether his invention is technologically sound. The man who believes that the world will beat a path to his door to buy his mousetrap will act as though the mousetrap will be profitable even if in fact he is mistaken. If we are to establish that a competitive economy tends to equilibrium in the absence of a stream of new opportunities, it must be in the absence of a stream of *perceived* new opportunities, real or imagined.

The fact that it is perceptions that count has further, perhaps more subtle implications for our analysis of loosening constraints. Perceptions of new opportunities need not be perceptions of current events in order to disturb the system. An agent who suddenly believes for the first time that the wheat harvest a year hence will be low will believe that wheat prices at that time will be higher than he had previously thought. Even if he also believes that the futures price of the wheat involved will not begin to rise for six months, he may begin to buy such futures immediately or, more generally, he may begin to rearrange his optimal program of investment so as best to take advantage of the new opportunity.

Similarly, consider an agent who expects to face a liquidity constraint some time hence. If such an agent changes his expectations and now believes that he will experience a previously unexpected capital gain, he will generally change his behavior so as to take optimal advantage of the new opportunity which his newly expected increase in later liquidity is expected to afford him.

The lesson is clear. Following Schumpeter, we cannot suppose it to be true that an economy in which new opportunities constantly arise will converge to equilibrium. Such "new opportunities" are to be broadly interpreted; apart from the traditional forms of Schumpeterian innovation - technology, new raw materials, new markets, new forms of organization, and so on - they include the weakening of previously binding constraints. A leading example here is that of the effect of windfall gains on constraints on borrowing. Further, it is agents' perceptions of new opportunities that matter rather than (directly) their reality. Finally, since agents plan over time, what must be ruled out is sudden optimistic revisions in agents' expectations. *There must be no favorable surprise.*[2]

It is important to understand what is being claimed. I do not pretend that an assumption of No Favorable Surprise is a realistic one. New opportunities do arise all the time (or are perceived to do so). That fact makes for economic growth and change. What I do claim is that convergence to equilibrium cannot be expected to hold unless such shocks become negligible. To put it a little differently, the position examined in the first chapter - that economies are best studied by studying their equilibria - makes sense if adjustment processes are stable and convergence swift. In such a case, the effects of shocks will quickly be absorbed. Even in such a case, however, shocks will generally displace equilibria; even when this does not happen, a rapid enough succession of shocks will keep the economy away from equilibrium. If we are to prove anything to justify looking only at equilibria, it follows that we must first show that individual shocks can be absorbed - that an economy once displaced has a tendency to converge to equilibrium if not displaced again. We cannot possibly show that an economy continually displaced converges - nor should we wish to do so. What we can hope to prove is that economies which are *not* disturbed again do converge (and converge quickly, although a proof of the latter proposition is beyond the scope of this book and possibly the state of the art). A basic, necessary first step in this

[2] In Fisher (1981), this was called "no optimistic surprise," but surprises, unlike agents, cannot be optimistic.

direction is to show that, under very general circumstances, economies with rational, arbitraging agents will converge to equilibrium given an assumption of No Favorable Surprise.

Unfortunately, such a proof is only the first step. Imagine an exogenous favorable shock to the economy - say, an unanticipated invention. We wish to show that the effects of such a shock will be (quickly) arbitraged away. To do so, it is natural to examine those effects while assuming that further exogenous shocks do not occur. No Favorable Surprise, however, does more than this; it rules out favorable surprises which arise in the course of absorption of the original shock - endogenous shocks, as it were - as well as simply optimistic (possibly incorrect) changes in expectations. Yet the really interesting stability question may lie in just how such "endogenous" shocks disappear.

There are deep issues here. In an ongoing economy, what constitutes an "exogenous" shock? How is such an original shock to be distinguished from the "endogenous" shock brought about by adjustment to the original shock? No Favorable Surprise may not be precisely what is wanted as an assumption in this area, but it is quite difficult to see exactly how to refine it.

A proof of stability under No Favorable Surprise, then, seems quite desirable for a number of related reasons. First, it is the strongest version of an assumption of No Favorable *Exogenous* Surprise (whatever that may mean precisely); hence, if stability does not hold under No Favorable Surprise it cannot be expected to hold under the more interesting weaker assumption. Study of the stronger case may shed light on the more interesting one.

Second, it is obvious (with point expectations) that stability requires the asymptotic disappearance of surprises of any kind, favorable or unfavorable, if those surprises lead to action.[3] Thus an assumption that favorable surprises cease after a long enough time is close to an assumption of something we know to be necessary for stability; a proof that such an assumption also suffices for stability comes close to providing a necessary and sufficient stability condition. Moreover, that condition is not at all trivial; it is not obvious, for example, that ruling out favorable surprises implies that *un*favorable surprises will cease asymptotically as a result of arbitrage, yet such is in fact the case if No Favorable Surprise implies stability.

Finally, in view of this, a proof that No Favorable Surprise implies stability can refocus the analysis of the stability question, for a central issue, given such a proof, becomes that of what adjustment processes,

[3] These are changes in what are called "relevant parameters" in Chapter 7.

what assumptions in expectation formation, are consistent with No Favorable Surprise. I shall give some examples of such assumptions in this book, but they are special and the general answer to this question appears to require more attention to the analysis of just how trade takes place in a disequilibrium setting than economists have so far given it. Such attention is badly needed if equilibrium economics is to be solidly based (and even more badly needed if it turns out not to be solidly based).

This is not to say that the examples of No Favorable Surprise which are easy to generate are without their own interest. Indeed, one such example is that of perfect foresight which, in a model with only point expectations, means rational expectations. Under perfect foresight, there are no surprises at all, and thus no unfavorable ones.[4]

This raises an important matter. The discussion has so far proceeded on the assumption that agents have point expectations - that they have no subjective uncertainty. This will also be true of the model and proofs to follow in later chapters. I do not apologize for this; it is necessary to learn to walk before one can run, and the model which follows is already quite complex, particularly when compared to most of the stability literature surveyed in Part I. Some discussion of the more general case is warranted, however.

Once subjective uncertainty is admitted, certain changes must be made. Thus, for example, equilibrium must be redefined, for, unless subjective uncertainty disappears, we can only hope for convergence to some stochastic equilibrium in which distributions are constant and the expected values of excess demands for nonfree goods are zero.[5] Further, No Favorable Surprise would have to be redefined as well. I now consider how this might be done.

With subjective uncertainty, there certainly will be surprises in the sense that when improbable events occur, some of those events will be favorable. Hence we cannot rule out favorable surprises in this sense. Moreover, it will not suffice to rule out new opportunities in the sense of ruling out favorable additions to the support of the agent's subjective probability distribution; even with an unchanging support, a shift in probability mass which makes a previously unattractive (but still available) program look better than the previously chosen one can upset convergence. However, the perception that this has occurred is itself, in

[4] Although we shall later see that perfect foresight is not a very interesting case in a disequilibrium model, this is for reasons unconnected with No Favorable Surprise; those reasons may not apply to more general forms of rational expectations.

[5] The persistence of such an equilibrium might itself cause subjective uncertainty to disappear, but this is beside the point.

some sense, the perception of a new opportunity, and ruling it out is quite in the spirit of No Favorable Surprise. Note that such an assumption includes the case of rational expectations.

There is a related point that requires discussion. As the time to the realization of an uncertain event gets shorter, it is reasonable to suppose that the uncertainty surrounding that event will diminish. This effect need not be ruled out by a stochastic version of No Favorable Surprise, because, although such reduction in uncertainty is favorable if agents are risk-averse, it is not a surprise. Such a natural reduction in uncertainty is likely to be expected by agents. Only an *un*expected reduction need be ruled out.

This is a special case of a general property of No Favorable Surprise which is quite important to understand. Returning to the case of point expectations, No Favorable Surprise does *not* require that things never get better, but only that they do not do so unexpectedly. No Favorable Surprise is quite consistent, for example, with expanding consumption opportunities brought about by technical advance; what is required is that agents not underestimate the extent of that expansion, that *changes* in expectations be in a pessimistic direction, not that expectations themselves be pessimistic.

Further, note that we need only require No Favorable Surprise to hold after some finite time (taken as already past in later chapters). Thus, speculative bubbles are permitted in a sense. Agents can initially become more and more optimistic about the future, so long as this process stops. Unending and expanding speculative bubbles are ruled out, but their bursting need not mean that agents become pessimistic, only that they become less optimistic than before.

Is there reason to believe that an attempt to prove stability in economies with arbitrage and No Favorable Surprise will prove successful? Indeed there is, and this brings us to another example of a process with No Favorable Surprise. Under such an assumption, new, previously unexpected favorable opportunities are never perceived to arise. Changes in expectations (if they occur) are in an unfavorable direction. Agents whose perceptions change come to perceive that old opportunities are not working out as well as they had hoped. If agents act on arbitrage opportunities, this is just what we should expect, since old opportunities will be arbitraged away. Hence, incidentally, the perceptions of agents will be generally correct in this regard. At best they will perceive themselves as no better off than before; more generally, they will feel themselves to be worse off as they see old opportunities disappearing.

Such a situation has a familiar sound to it, however; it is highly reminiscent of the results of the Hahn Process, which we studied at length in previous chapters. Indeed, it is fair to say that the Hahn Process rests on two logically separate insights. The first of these is that markets are *orderly* so that there is not, post-trade, both unsatisfied demand and unsatisfied supply. When this is so, every agent can take his own experience as a mirror of the overall situation. When all agents naively believe that the economy is in equilibrium, the assumption that markets are orderly leads to a situation in which agents perceive themselves as constantly becoming worse off in terms of target utilities or profits. This occurs because the things an agent wishes to buy and cannot buy are going up in price, while those things he wishes to sell and cannot sell are going down in price. In effect, the orderly market assumption plus the naive expectations of agents leads to a situation in which the opportunities which agents perceive disappear as they are acted on - even though the "arbitrage" involved is not deliberate.

The insight that old opportunities disappear when acted on so that agents will perceive themselves progressively worse off in terms of target utilities or profits is logicaly independent of the orderly market assumption, however. Once we drop the assumption that agents foolishly believe the system to be in constant equilibrium, the two insights of the Hahn Process fail to coincide. The view that old opportunities are perceived to disappear through arbitrage while new ones do not arise is precisely the kind of phenomenon we have been discussing in this chapter, however; it is a description of No Favorable Surprise. This suggests quite strongly the possibility that the Hahn Process models can be generalized to allow a proof of what I have argued is the basic step in the direction of a fully satisfactory stability theorem - that No Favorable Surprise implies stability - and this turns out to be the case.

4.3 The timing of optimal programs

Since we are going to allow production and consumption out of equilibrium, we must now distinguish commodities by date. Further, we must suppose that the dates on some commodities are passed before equilibrium is reached. This is because one can only consume, use as inputs, or actually produce as outputs currently dated commodities. Future pie is pie in the sky; one can plan to consume it but cannot actually do so until it is future no longer.

Since agents can only plan to consume commodities of dates which are current as of the time of use, they must plan to acquire such commodities no later than those dates. Moreover, since we are now to allow agents to realize that they are not in equilibrium, they will generally not be indifferent about when (before such dates) they acquire those commodities. Thus, agents who expect prices to change will wish to acquire or sell commodities at the most advantageous prices; agents who realize that their transactions at any one time may be limited will wish to take such limitations into account in planning when to transact. Hence optimal plans for agents will involve not only the optimal timing of consumption and production but also the optimal timing of transactions. Further, the necessity of planning the timing of transactions will be reinforced by the desire to take advantage of the arbitrage opportunities that are perceived because of the expectation of price change.

The fact that transactions and not just consumption and production are to be optimally timed naturally introduces some complexity into the model. The gains from that complexity are very substantial, however. Aside from the insights into speculative behavior that emerge in the results, the introduction of such timing totally resolves the difficulties connected with what was termed in Chapter 2 the "Present Action Postulate."

Only actions, not mere desires, can influence actual markets; hence agents' plans can influence current prices only through current actions. In models in which agents are indifferent about the timing of their transactions, this leads to a certain amount of awkwardness. One must assume, for example, that agents foreseeing an eventual need for a particular commodity begin to act immediately to acquire that commodity even though they may already have stocks of that commodity on hand and also be faced with cash problems in attempting to acquire other commodities for which their needs are more immediate. Where commodities are dated, the problem is alleviated but not eliminated. The postulate required is that agents must currently act on the futures market for any later dated commodity for which they have a nonzero excess demand. The problems connected with this sort of thing have not seemed pressing so far in this book, only because the models so far examined in detail have not allowed any consumption or production to take place out of equilibrium. Hence the necessity of acquiring goods before they are used has not appeared and we could generally remain within an Arrow–Debreu world in which commodities that differed only by dates bore no special relation to one another. In such a world it seems largely innocuous to assume that agents attempt immediately to act on the market for any good for which they have a nonzero excess demand.[6] When consumption

[6] That assumption is reflected specifically in Chapter 3 in Assumption 3.9.1, where positive target excess demands backed up by money result in strictly positive (and not simply nonnegative) active excess demands.

and production are allowed to take place out of equilibrium, however, the awkwardness of such a Present Action Postulate becomes more pressing.[7]

Fortunately, this difficulty is readily resolved by the introduction of what seems an additional complexity – the realization by agents that they are not in equilibrium so that the timing of transactions really can matter. Where planned demands are distinguished not only by commodities and commodity dates but also by the dates at which they are to be exercised, there is no longer any need artificially to force agents to act on future demands currently.

As this suggests, it will be necessary to have time in the model indexed in three ways. We must distinguish among the time at which planning takes place (the "present"); the time at which actions are to be taken; and the dates on commodities. To give an example, I can plan in 1983 to purchase 1995 wheat in 1990.[8] Since it will also be true that I have in 1983 expectations concerning the price of 1995 wheat which will obtain on the futures market for that wheat in 1990, it is evident that price expectations will also involve these three types of dating.

It is convenient to work in continuous time in dealing with optimal plans. This means that we date commodities continuously and that (in principle, at least) there is always a futures market for every commodity at every later date. The exploration of what happens with a system of incomplete markets is not undertaken.

The possibility of trading in commodities of every *future* date does not of course imply the possibility of trading in commodities whose dates have elapsed. Such "past" markets do not exist. This obvious fact has a number of consequences. First, as we have already observed, agents planning to use or consume commodities of a given date must plan to acquire those commodities by the time that date is reached. Second, we must include in a description of the technology available to households and firms the fact that perishable items such as dated labor disappear if not used, while nonperishable items are definitionally changed into different goods simply through the passage of time. To put it differently, 1983 labor can only be used in 1983. If it is not used then it disappears. A 1983 table, however, if left alone automatically becomes an input to a process which produces a 1984 (one-year-older) table the next year.

[7] See Fisher (1976a) and (1977) for papers in which such a postulate appears explicitly.

[8] Real plans are not made in such detail far in advance, but this is because of uncertainty and computational costs from which I abstract.

4.4 The Dated Commodities problem and individual price adjustment

More important than such essentially housekeeping phenomena, however, is the problem referred to in Chapter 2 as the "Dated Commodities problem." I briefly review what is involved.

Since there is no trading in commodities whose dates are past, agents, when a commodity's date is reached, must make do with their holdings of that commodity. This is a potential problem because agents may be mistaken concerning their ability to complete transactions. Hence, it may come as a surprise to them that they cannot in fact acquire or sell all they wish by the time trade terminates. Such surprise may lead to discontinuities in behavior.

Now, this problem may at first appear artificial. One supposes that a given commodity at a particular date will be a close substitute for the same commodity at a nearby date. Thus (ignoring continuous dating for ease of exposition), at midnight on December 31, 1983 agents will be indifferent between 1983 and 1984 commodities. The problem with this view is that it implicitly supposes that 1983 and 1984 commodities will trade at the same prices at that moment - but this is an equilibrium property which is not otherwise guaranteed.

The point may perhaps be made clearer by considering the role of arbitrage in such situations. Plainly it will generally be the case that divergence between the price of a commodity dated 1983 and the price of the same commodity dated 1984 will provide an opportunity for arbitrage as 1983 draws to a close. Hence we should expect that divergence to diminish and the prices to come together. We cannot simply assume that this happens, however, for it is the task of disequilibrium analysis and especially of a stability proof to *prove* that such disequilibrium phenomena are transitory. The problem exists not because arbitrage is absent from the model - arbitrage is present - but because we cannot be sure that arbitrage operates sufficiently quickly to bring prices into line before the crucial date is passed.

At first sight, these do not seem to be easy problems. As the discussion just given indicates, they are unlikely to be resolved satisfactorily within the context of an analysis that is capable of proving stability but is silent on questions of speed of convergence. Since the state of the art or, perhaps, our ability to specify dynamic adjustment processes in specific functional forms is insufficient to permit adequate treatment of convergence speeds, it seems unlikely that we will get much further here than the rather unsatisfactory assumption that such problems are unimportant.

Is such an assumption really unsatisfactory, however? Interestingly enough, the answer appears to be in the negative. There is a real sense in which the difficulties in which we find ourselves are of our own making. They arise because of the mechanical attitude toward price adjustment which has characterized stability analysis since the days of tâtonnement.

In most real markets prices are not simply set by an auctioneer. Rather, sellers and (less often) buyers make price offers, and transactions take place when a meeting of minds occurs. Now consider an agent - for convenience a seller - who is offering a particular commodity for sale. Aside from the fact that the same seller often sells the same commodity at different dates, the seller of a nonperishable commodity must realize that if he holds it, it will turn into the same (if older) commodity with a later date. Such a seller will quite naturally not be willing to set (or accept) a price for the 1983-dated commodity on December 31 which is much different from the price he sets (or accepts) for the 1984 commodity to be available on the next day. For him to do so is to invite arbitrage at his own expense. At the least he cannot expect positive sales to take place at both prices if storage is really costless so that the commodities are perfect substitutes.

Similarly, if buyers of perishable commodities such as labor are indifferent on December 31 between 1983 and 1984 versions at the same price, then they will not make different price offers. Moreover, sellers, realizing this, will not make different price offers either.

The point is that to the extent that commodities that differ only in date become perfect substitutes as their dates come together, it will be in the self-interest of agents who trade in them to have their prices also come together. Thus those agents will only set (or accept) prices which are continuous functions of the commodity dates. Further, given such continuity agents planning their demands will be able to contemplate smooth substitution of slightly later-dated commodities for earlier ones. The apparent discontinuities engendered by the dated commodities problem occur only because of a lack of attention to the way in which prices are in fact set. I discuss price adjustment more explicitly later on.

4.5 Nonperformance and bankruptcy

Now, although the discontinuities just discussed may be apparent rather than real, there are other discontinuities that may be real ones. These are induced primarily by the allowing of production and consumption out of equilibrium - but the dating of commodities sharpens the problem.

In general, we must suppose that agents trade not merely in actual commodities but in promises. This is obvious if we consider futures trading but, as seen in the examination of Hahn Process models with firms, it is in any case natural in the case of firms. Given this, we must be prepared to have agents hold short positions in certain commodities – positions which they plan to cover either through repurchase or through later production. If such short positions were impossible, no trading in futures could ever occur. The possibility of such short positions, however, raises the possibility that they will not *in fact* be covered because, out of equilibrium, agents find their plans are not realized. The consequences of such nonperformance on the agent who fails to perform must be considered, of course, but we must also be concerned with the consequences on other agents.

Consider, for example, agents who have bought December wheat and plan to use it either for consumption or for production. If, when December comes around, they find that they are merely holding empty promises which cannot be kept, their consumption or production plans will have to change. Worse still, if they did not foresee this event, those plans may have to change discontinuously.

To some extent, such discontinuities can be avoided by observing that the use of newly delivered commodities for consumption or production is often (or even usually) the use of a flow. Hence, since we work in continuous time, actual (as opposed to planned) consumption and production cannot be affected by nondelivery if every agent planning to receive that delivery already has a stock of (what will become when updated) the commodity in question on hand. Still, it is artificial to assume that this always happens. Since agents can plan to consume or create inputs out of newly delivered flows, we must pay at least some attention to the possibility that these flows fail to materialize so that actual and planned activities diverge in a discontinuous way.

In Chapter 8 I shall discuss some ways in which one can deal with this problem. For the present, I make three points. First, it is plainly easier to avoid these complications in a world in which agents understand that they are in disequilibrium than in a world in which they do not. Agents who realize that their own transactions may not be completed will at least plan to cover short positions taking that possibility into account. Agents who realize that the transactions of others may not be completed will when planning take into account the possibility that promised deliveries will not in fact take place. This will tend to smooth out discontinuities.

Second, the central position in the Hahn Process models of the previous chapter occupied by the assumption that agents never run out of cash now recedes. That assumption involved the problem of agents who planned to spend out of the proceeds of current sales. We now see that this is much the same problem as that of agents who plan to consume out of future purchases or deliveries. As with the delivery problem, the difficulties associated with the positive money stock assumption are at least greatly alleviated if we permit agents to optimize taking the cash constraint into account rather than having that constraint enter only as an afterthought.

Third, agents who fail to deliver on promises will be penalized. This will make them unhappy. Moreover, agents who fail to receive expected deliveries will also be unhappy; they will be worse off than they expected to be. But it is a fundamental feature of Hahn Process models that agents *do* find themselves to be worse off than previously expected. Further, as we have seen, that feature is precisely the one that must carry over into the stability models that it is natural to investigate - those characterized by No Favorable Surprise. This suggests that, provided we can deal with discontinuities, we can accommodate nondelivery quite naturally into such models.

4.6 The nature of equilibrium and the role of money

The fact that agents optimize the timing of their transactions has further consequences as well. One of these has to do with the nature of equilibrium. Up to this point all stability models have had in common the fairly undesirable equilibrium characteristic of the Arrow-Debreu model: Equilibrium has meant an exhaustion of trading opportunities, a situation in which all trades that are ever to be made are completed and the economy (unless further disturbed) lapses into autarky. This is not particularly reasonable.

Where agents care about and plan the timing of their transactions and form expectations about future prices, this rather artificial property of equilibrium does not appear. Rather than involving an exhaustion of trading opportunities, equilibrium will involve the carrying out of previously planned trades at correctly foreseen prices - a much more natural state of affairs. Such equilibria are rational expectations equilibria.

Further, the fact that equilibrium does not involve the cessation of trade provides at least a partial natural answer to another awkward problem, the question of the role of money in equilibrium. In the Hahn Process model with money (treated extensively in Chapter 3), it was necessary to assume that money entered the utility functions of households.[9] Without some such assumption, money could not have served as a numéraire since, in equilibrium, no one would wish to hold it, even though it was required for transactions purposes out of equilibrium.

[9] An alternative would have been to assume that money was needed as input for firms.

Where equilibrium involves continued transactions, however, the transactions demand for money does not disappear[10] (even though other reasons for holding money may do so). Hence it is not necessary to give agents an artificial reason for holding money in equilibrium, provided that it is not inferior as a store of value to other assets. Thus, while it turns out to be necessary to make money an interest-bearing asset in order to get agents to hold it in equilibrium, it is not necessary to go further to explain why money is held rather than other assets (including commodities) with the same equilibrium interest rate as money. This seems a definite gain.

[10] There is one exception to this. Where agents expect to encounter transaction constraints it is at least conceivable that equilibrium involves a point at which no agent believes he will *ever* be able to transact anything. At such a trivial equilibrium there will be no transactions demand for money, so nobody will wish to go on holding it. On the other hand, at such a point nobody will believe that he can dispose of money either, save by throwing it away, as the economy ceases to function and the question of whether money can serve as a numéraire becomes irrelevant. There is little point in treating such cases at length.

CHAPTER 5

The theory of the individual agent

5.1 Introduction

The matters discussed in the previous chapter are all quite complex, and it is best to deal with them one at a time where possible. In the present chapter, I explore the behavior of individual agents where disequilibrium consciousness is allowed and production and consumption take place out of equilibrium. To do so, I first ignore the (welcome) complications which arise from the realization by agents that they may not be able to complete their transactions. Further, I postpone consideration of how prices (and price expectations) are set. These and other matters are introduced later on.

I thus begin with the general setup of the model and the analysis of the optimizing behavior of agents who believe that prices will change. The analysis is complicated, but the results are appealing, being both interesting in themselves and required for what follows. The complexity seems inescapable if we are to deal with models in which time is essential and arbitrage over time takes place. No suitable, complete treatment of these matters seems available in the literature.

Because it seems desirable to continue to make the discussion accessible to relatively nontechnical readers without at the same time sacrificing continuity for those interested in a more rigorous treatment, this and succeeding chapters are organized a bit differently from the earlier ones. Each subject is discussed in one or more nontechnical sections. Those sections are followed by one or more technical ones, which are indicated by asterisks. The nontechnical reader may skip the sections

Much of the model of Part II is based on that in my Econometric Society Presidential Address (Fisher, 1981). See also Fisher and Saldanha (1982).

marked by asterisks, but the technical reader must read the sections not marked, since not all material is repeated.

5.2 Money, bonds, and relative prices

As explained in Chapter 4, agents in this model will care about the timing of their transactions. Thus, although all transactions will be assumed to take place for money, it is necessary to distinguish money at different dates. Further, it turns out to be convenient to treat prices and price expectations first by taking all prices which are expected to rule at a given date, v, relative to money at v and then transforming such current money prices for different v by taking them relative to the price of money at a common date, generally, but not always, date 0. It is natural to refer to this step as "discounting" and to the adjusted price as "discounted price," but all that is involved is a particular choice of numéraire (money at time 0).[1] The ways in which agents evaluate future opportunities emerge in the results of later sections.

Agents in this model come equipped with point expectations concerning prices; there is no subjective uncertainty. Prices are for n commodities (not including money), but each commodity is also dated so that for each physical commodity there is at any one time an entire function of commodity dates (a "profile") giving the prices of future dated versions. Thus, in 1983, there is a price for 1984 wheat, 1985 wheat, and so on. The price expectations of agents are expectations of what these price profiles will be in the future. Leisure is one of the dated commodities (more than one if labor of different skill types is distinguished).

Now among the commodities with such price profiles is one called "bonds." A θ-dated bond is a binding promise by the government to pay one dollar at date θ. (Private promises are also permitted but are called "notes.") Naturally, such promises of future money ordinarily sell at a discount so that the current dollar price of a θ-dated bond will typically be less than unity. The money supply at θ is simply the supply of maturing θ-dated bonds; it is best to think of the government as always ready to buy or sell bonds of extremely short maturity at the going price. In effect, this makes money an interest-bearing asset, since it consists of bonds of limitingly short maturity.

Relative prices are constructed as follows. The agents' expectations about bond prices imply at each future moment an expected instantaneous interest rate, the rate at which the price of bonds that are just about to mature will then be changing. Similarly, actual bond prices at

[1] The discussion of discounting in Fisher (1981) is misleading on this point.

past dates imply actual instantaneous interest rates for such dates. Because the government redeems bonds of very short maturities, such instantaneous interest rates are also the instantaneous rates of growth of the money supply.

We first express all prices which the agent encountered or expects to encounter at any date, v, in terms of the price of money encountered or expected at v, then we discount those prices back to time 0, using such instantaneous interest rates. This makes money at time 0 the numéraire in a consistent way.

Insight into this procedure may be gained by considering it as the continuous time limit of the following. Suppose that time were measured in discrete units, say, years, so that one year were the shortest maturity of any bond. For each year v, multiply the price occurring (or expected) at v by the price of a v-dated bond occurring (or expected) at $v-1$. This converts v-dated prices which are in terms of v-dated money to units of $(v-1)$-dated money. A sequence of such operations converts all prices to 0-dated money for use as the numéraire.

Note that, while there are other (less natural) ways of accomplishing such a conversion, two ways which might be thought appropriate will not work at all. First, simply dividing all later prices by the price of 0-dated money is not an available option; 0-dated money is not traded at the same time as v-dated prices hold, and its closing price is unity (by definition). Second (and more interesting), if the term structure of actual and expected interest rates is such as to permit arbitrage, which is quite possible out of equilibrium, the procedure described is not equivalent to using the interest rates implied by the price of v-dated bonds *at time 0* to convert v-dated prices to 0-dated money. Such a use would be inappropriate, however, since (except in long-run equilibrium on the bond market) it leads to *relative* prices (and hence the behavior of agents) being affected by the choice of a time origin and hence of a numéraire. The use of instantaneous interest rates in the way described does not present such a problem and, as we shall see, leads to obviously correct results with regard to arbitrage.

Now it is important to assure that the instantaneous interest rates expected by any agent are always bounded above zero so that there is always a discount factor bounded below one applied to later money flows.[2] There are two reasons for this.

The first such reason has to do with the way in which distances and convergence are measured. To see this, consider the fact that we must

[2] Note that this involves a very mild assumption as to time preference and capital productivity. It is enough if every agent believes correctly that all other agents have nonnegligible reasons for discounting the future.

require agents' optimizing problems to have the property that for any planning date, t, the value of all planned expenditures in t-dated money is finite. Since we certainly do not wish to assume that prices are expected to approach zero far in the future, this makes it natural to require that the t-dated money value of any future consumption or production stream *at unitary prices* be finite. If we do this, it then becomes natural to measure the distances between such consumption or production streams by the discounted value of the (absolute) differences between them. It turns out that this makes the natural measure of distance for any stream of *discounted* prices the supremum of the *undiscounted* prices, with the discount rate which it is convenient to use being the lower bound (infimum) of the instantaneous discount rates used by agents. Details are given in Section 5.3.

It is no mere technicality, however, that it becomes important to assume such a lower bound to be strictly greater than zero. While many of our results will hold without such an assumption, our full stability result appears to require it. This reflects the fact that, in a model with point expectations, even the transactions demand for money will not give agents a reason to hold money in equilibrium if money is not an interest-bearing asset. If the interest rate on money is allowed to fall to zero, money (which then has the same price at all dates) becomes unsuitable as a numéraire in equilibrium in the presence of other interest-bearing investments. It is thus no accident that proofs of convergence which use prices relative to money break down in such circumstances.

5.3* Instantaneous discount rates and topology

There are n ordinary commodities in addition to money. Each of these is distinguished by date and there is a futures market for every commodity for every future date. As of time t, the vector of prices of θ-dated commodities is given by $\hat{\mathbf{P}}(\theta, t)$. Here (and, generally later) θ is in $[0, \infty)$ with $\hat{\mathbf{P}}(\theta, t)$ for $\theta \leqslant t$ being fixed at the closing prices which obtained at θ; in other words, $\hat{\mathbf{P}}(\theta, t) = \hat{\mathbf{P}}(\theta, \theta)$ for all $t \geqslant \theta$. 0 is an arbitrary initial date. $\hat{\mathbf{P}}(\theta, t)$ is assumed continuous in θ (for reasons discussed in the previous chapter) and differentiable in t. Derivatives of any function with respect to t will be denoted by dots.

Agents have expectations about prices. We let $\hat{\mathbf{p}}^a(\theta, v, t)$ denote the vector of prices of θ-dated commodities which, at time t, agent a expects to encounter at time v. $\hat{\mathbf{p}}^a(\theta, v, t)$ is assumed continuous in θ and differentiable in v and t. Furthermore, $\hat{\mathbf{p}}^a(\theta, v, t) = \hat{\mathbf{p}}^a(\theta, \theta, t)$ for all $v \geqslant \theta$. We further assume that the agent knows correctly all present and past prices so that $\hat{\mathbf{p}}^a(\theta, v, t) = \hat{\mathbf{P}}(\theta, v)$ for all $t \geqslant v$. Individual actual prices are introduced later.

We can now formally derive the instantaneous discount rate discussed in the preceding section. Let $\hat{\sigma}^a(\theta, v, t)$ (one of the elements of $\hat{\mathbf{p}}^a(\theta, v, t)$) be the price which, as of t, agent a expects to encounter at v for θ-dated bonds. Suppose for a moment that bonds are only available in maturities of discretely differing dates with maturity dates differing by a small time interval, Δv. Divide the interval from t to θ into k equal parts of length Δv, so that $\theta = t + k\Delta v$. If money is transferred from θ to t by a series of k purchases of bonds of length Δv, then the implied discount factor $\hat{\rho}^a(\theta, t; \Delta v)$ is given by

$$\begin{aligned}\log \hat{\rho}^a(\theta, t; \Delta v) &= \sum_{j=1}^{k} \log \hat{\sigma}^a(t + j\Delta v, t + (j-1)\Delta v, t) \\ &= \sum_{j=1}^{k} (1/\Delta v)[\log \hat{\sigma}^a(t + j\Delta v, t + (j-1)\Delta v, t) \\ &\qquad - \log \hat{\sigma}^a(t + (j-1)\Delta v, t + (j-1)\Delta v, t)]\Delta v\end{aligned} \tag{5.3.1}$$

using the fact that $\hat{\sigma}^a(v, v, t) = 1$ for all v. Passing to the limit, assuming $\hat{\sigma}^a(\theta, v, t)$ to be continuously differentiable at $\theta = v$, and denoting the limiting discount factor by $\hat{\rho}^a(\theta, t)$,

$$\begin{aligned}\log \hat{\rho}^a(\theta, t) &\equiv \lim_{\Delta v \to 0} \log \hat{\rho}^a(\theta, t; \Delta v) \\ &= \int_t^\theta \left. \frac{\partial \log \hat{\sigma}^a(v', v, t)}{\partial v'} \right|_{v'=v} dv = \int_t^\theta \frac{\hat{\sigma}_1^a(v, v, t)}{\hat{\sigma}(v, v, t)}\, dv \\ &= \int_t^\theta \hat{\sigma}_1^a(v, v, t)\, dv\end{aligned} \tag{5.3.2}$$

where the subscript denotes differentiation in the obvious way, and I have used again the fact that $\hat{\sigma}^a(v, v, t) = 1$.

Now, in this definition, I have used the instantaneous interest rates which the agent expects to encounter after t; it turns out generally to be convenient to discount back to a fixed date, 0. In so doing, I merely use the actual bond prices prevailing at each date before t. Thus, letting $\bar{\sigma}(\theta, v)$ denote the actual price of θ-dated bonds which prevailed at v, the discount rate for all agents from t back to 0 for our purposes will be given by

$$\log \bar{\rho}(t, 0) = \int_0^t \bar{\sigma}_1(v, v)\, dv \tag{5.3.3}$$

and the discount factor for agent a from any later date, θ back to 0 by

$$\rho^a(\theta, 0) \equiv \bar{\rho}(t, 0)\hat{\rho}^a(\theta, t) \quad (5.3.4)$$

Notice that $\rho^a(\theta, 0)$ is a combination of actual and expected rates. We shall take $\rho^a(\theta, 0) = \bar{\rho}(\theta, 0)$ for $\theta \leqslant t$.

It turns out to be notationally convenient for most of the analysis to work with all prices (and later all revenue streams) discounted back to 0. Accordingly, define:

$$\mathbf{P}(\theta, t) \equiv \hat{\mathbf{P}}(\theta, t)\bar{\rho}(t, 0); \quad \mathbf{p}^a(\theta, v, t) \equiv \hat{\mathbf{p}}^a(\theta, v, t)\rho^a(v, 0) \quad (5.3.5)$$

Note that $\mathbf{p}^a(\theta, v, t)$ includes expectations as to discount rates.[3]

Now, it is natural to take consumption, production, and other quantity profiles as lying in a normed linear space with prices in the normed dual of that space. But what space? In the ensuing discussion, in a notation restricted to this section, I denote scalar quantity profiles generally by $Q(\cdot, t)$. In such a profile, for example, $Q(\theta, t)$ could be consumption of some commodity expected as of t to take place at θ and so forth.

It will usually be convenient to take $Q(\theta, t)$ to be defined for $\theta \in [0, \infty)$ with 0 an arbitrary starting date. For $\theta > t$, $Q(\theta, t)$ will be a planned quantity; for $\theta \leqslant t$ it will be an actual, historical magnitude. This domain for $Q(\cdot, t)$, however, is not a convenience when considering convergence. This is so because the mere passage of time will fix more and more of the early part of such profiles with only the part from t on remaining free. It would obviously be silly to adopt a norm in which that fact alone implied convergence. This consideration will be very restrictive, however, if we insist on counting the fixed part of such profiles, the part in $[0, t]$.

Clearly, the natural thing to do is to count only the free tail, the part in $[t, \infty)$. We can readily do this by a change of variables (used only in the present section) by measuring commodity dates from t rather than from 0. In this notation, all commodity profiles from t onward lie in $[0, \theta)$. I shall denote such profiles by $\tilde{Q}(\cdot)$, suppressing the t argument. Similarly, I shall denote the correspondingly redated tail of the corresponding scalar price profile, *discounted back to time t*, rather than to time 0, by $\tilde{p}(\cdot)$, omitting the agent's superscript.[4] The renormalized commodity dates will be denoted by $\tilde{\theta}$.

Now the model below will only make sense if the value of commodity profiles discounted back to t is finite. Since we do not wish this necessarily to imply that t-discounted prices approach zero, we must require

[3] I hope it is not misleading that the prices *without* the carets are the discounted ones; to reverse it would mean carrying the hat notation everywhere.

[4] There are actually many such profiles corresponding to the differing expectations of different agents; I ignore this in the present discussion. Note that $\tilde{p}(\theta)$ here refers to the price of a particular commodity at θ, *not* to the price of a θ-dated commodity.

that the integral of any commodity profile, $\tilde{Q}(\cdot)$, itself discounted back to its beginning (t) be bounded.

All of this suggests that the commodity profiles should be assumed to lie in a space in which such integrals are bounded. It is mildly inconvenient to do this directly, however, because the discount rates involved vary from agent to agent and from time period to time period (although I shall later show their convergence to a common profile for all agents).[5] Accordingly, I shall adopt a somewhat more restrictive version than is strictly necessary.

Thus, using the earlier analysis of discount rates, let

$$\rho \equiv -\underset{a}{\text{Max}} \underset{\{t,v\}}{\text{Sup}}(\hat{\sigma}_1^a(v,v,t)) \tag{5.3.6}$$

Then, from (5.3.2)

$$e^{-\rho\tilde{\theta}} \equiv e^{-\rho(\theta-t)} \geqslant \rho^a(\theta,t) \tag{5.3.7}$$

for all a, t, and θ, so that all agents always discount the future at a rate at least as great as the constant rate ρ. Thus convergence of the improper integral $\int_0^\infty |\tilde{Q}(\tilde{\theta})| e^{-\rho\tilde{\theta}}\, d\tilde{\theta}$ for some profile $\tilde{Q}(\cdot)$ implies convergence of the improper integral $\int_0^\infty |\tilde{Q}(\tilde{\theta})| \hat{\rho}^a(\tilde{\theta},t)\, d\tilde{\theta}$ for that same $\tilde{Q}(\cdot)$ and for all discount factor profiles used by agents. (Here the vertical lines denote absolute value.) Accordingly, the commodity profiles, $\tilde{Q}(\cdot)$, will be taken to lie in the space of functions defined on $[0,\infty)$ with norm $\int_0^\infty |\tilde{Q}(\tilde{\theta})| e^{-\rho\tilde{\theta}}\, d\tilde{\theta}$. That space will be denoted in this section by $\mathbf{Q}$.

As pointed out earlier, it is important to assume $\rho > 0$. This amounts to assuming that expected bond prices are always such as to bound instantaneous discount rates away from zero. (It also implies that $\mathbf{Q}$ is not L_1 – an uninteresting case, in any event.) It is also natural to assume $\rho < \infty$.

Now, denote the normed dual of $\mathbf{Q}$ by $\mathbf{Q}^*$. The t-discounted price profiles, $\tilde{p}(\cdot)$, will be taken to lie in $\mathbf{Q}^*$. This means that the norm of any such t-discounted price profile will be

$$\text{Norm}(\tilde{p}(\cdot)) = \underset{\substack{\tilde{Q}(\cdot)\in\mathbf{Q} \\ \tilde{Q}(\tilde{\theta})\neq 0}}{\text{Sup}} \frac{\left|\int_0^\infty \tilde{p}(\tilde{\theta})\tilde{Q}(\tilde{\theta})\, d\tilde{\theta}\right|}{\int_0^\infty |\tilde{Q}(\tilde{\theta})| e^{-\rho\tilde{\theta}}\, d\tilde{\theta}} = \underset{\tilde{\theta}}{\text{Sup}} |\tilde{p}(\tilde{\theta})| e^{\rho\tilde{\theta}} \tag{5.3.8}$$

The last step in (5.3.8) can perhaps be seen most conveniently by observing that since $(\tilde{Q}(\tilde{\theta})e^{-\rho\tilde{\theta}})$ forms a profile which lies in L_1, $(\tilde{p}(\tilde{\theta})e^{\rho\tilde{\theta}})$ must form a profile in L_∞ and thus have the sup norm.[6]

[5] But not to a constant value. There is no reason why equilibrium cannot occur with different (but correctly foreseen) instantaneous interest rates for different moments in time, depending on the (possibly changing but correctly foreseen) time preferences and technological opportunities of agents.

[6] Since prices are continuous in $\tilde{\theta}$, there is no need to distinguish between the supremum and the essential supremum. See Luenberger (1969).

The meaning of this result is that the appropriate norm for t-discounted prices is the supremum of the undiscounted prices which would correspond to them at the constant interest rate ρ. This is not quite the same as the supremum of the actual expected undiscounted prices (the difference occurring because of the inconvenience avoided by choosing a norm for $\mathbf{Q}$ which is independent of time period and agent). However, it is plain that, because of the definition of ρ, discounted prices in $\mathbf{Q}^*$ will be bounded if the supremum of the actual expected undiscounted prices over future dates is bounded for every agent as t goes to infinity.

We can now return to discounting prices back to time 0.

5.4 The arbitraging firm: Assumptions

I now consider the theory of the firm when prices are expected to change. Since the firm holds these expectations with certainty, and since we have postponed any consideration of transaction difficulties, we must expect to encounter discontinuous ("bang-bang") behavior as the firm rushes to take advantage of every perceived opportunity. This difficulty will disappear later on and the study of the speculative behavior of the firm under such circumstances is both instructive and useful for later purposes.

The firm, like all agents in this model, comes equipped with price expectations as described. This induces a discount rate profile. Given that profile, the firm is assumed to maximize the present value of its profit stream – that is, its profits expressed in terms of the numéraire.[7] In so doing, as of time t, the firm faces a number of constraints, some of them the legacy of its own past decisions.

The firm has access to a convex set of technological possibilities in which a stream of inputs generates later outputs. The firm operates by buying goods to be used as inputs and selling goods produced with these inputs; it may also buy and sell without production intervening if its price expectations lead it to think it profitable to do so. Naturally, only currently dated goods can actually be used as inputs or produced as outputs and the firm must take this into account. It will typically – but not always – plan to buy and sell such goods before their actual dates by trading on futures markets. In so doing, however, the firm must plan to produce in a technologically feasible manner so that it must either acquire the inputs

[7] This assumption is not trivial. In disequilibrium the firm and its owners may disagree as to future profits and dividend policy. I shall largely ignore such complexities and assume that there are a large number of shareholders for every firm and, as below, a market in shares, with the market perfect enough that dissatisfaction with the policies of management results in selling the shares of the firm. This becomes explicit in the theory of the household below when considering dividends.

it needs to produce the outputs it sells or else buy back its output commitments. I shall return to this.

At any moment of time, therefore, the firm has, as a result of its past actions, stocks of commodities (positive or negative) representing past commitments. In the case of currently dated commodities these may be physical goods (or services); in the case of future-dated commodities they are merely titles or promises to deliver. In the course of acquiring such stocks, the firm, by buying and selling, has already achieved some actual profits (on a cash basis); this too is a legacy from the past.

More important than this, however, is the fact that the firm will already have made certain decisions about production. With an eye to the production of future outputs, the firm will have put inputs into production. The furnaces may have been fired up; the production line begun; inventories of partly finished goods accumulated. Such activities, undertaken in the pursuit of what seemed at the time the optimal profit (present-value) maximizing program, may not now seem so desirable with the benefit of hindsight and revised expectations, but they cannot now be undone. As a result, the production opportunities the firm *now* faces are affected by its past production decisions; further, the decisions it now takes will affect its future opportunities. In effect, while (assuming no technical change) the firm's long-run feasible production set as of any fixed time remains constant, the part of that set which describes current opportunities is constantly changing since the firm cannot return to its birth and remake its past decisions. Rather it must optimize over the future in the light of those decisions.

Now it is important to understand what is incorporated in the technology of the firm in this model. Since goods are dated (and dated continuously), there is more involved than is usually meant by production possibilities. For example, as observed in Chapter 4, there is formally no such thing as allowing a currently dated commodity to sit unused. A new 1983 table automatically becomes a one-year-old 1984 table in 1984 if nothing else is done to it. Perishable commodities such as labor, on the other hand, also are involved in production even if not used to produce other goods. Thus, 1983 labor, if employed by the firm, is always an input into production, even if the workers spend their time sitting on their hands; such 1983 labor simply becomes an input without any corresponding output. (When we get to the household, the parallel case – that of outputs with no inputs – will become that of endowment flows, labor again being a prime example.)

The firm not only faces the constraints imposed by technology, it also faces economic constraints, some of which may be thought of as legally imposed. In selling its future outputs or in speculating or, indeed, in selling bonds or its own private notes (which are promises to deliver money), the firm may wish to take short positions and sell things that it does not already have. We must therefore impose restrictions that will ensure that short positions do not last beyond the dates of the commodities involved, but that the firm plans to deliver on its promises. We do this by placing a bound on the extent to which the firm can be short or plan to be short in any commodity with the bound approaching zero as the date on the commodity approaches. For commodities involved in the firm's production plans, the firm counts its planned net output (output less input) in calculating its short position; thus the firm must have a feasible production plan consistent with these constraints. For commodities not involved in production, these constraints simply require the firm to plan to clear its (bounded) short positions by repurchase. Note, in particular, that this requires the firm to plan to redeem its maturing notes and clear any short position in maturing bonds.

I shall refer to the constraints just described as "short constraints." They can be regarded either as internally imposed or (as I think preferable) as legal requirements which are imposed from outside the model.[8] They stem in part from the recognition that large transactions at the last moment may not be possible. More extensive discussion is given later.

Such short constraints do not exhaust the constraints which the firm faces, however. Purchases take place for money and the firm must take this into account in its planning. Naturally, the necessity of buying with cash would not be much of a constraint if we allowed the firm to hold negative money balances, paying directly with promises instead of cash, so I impose what I shall call the "money constraint" that the firm's planned money stock must always be nonnegative. Some further discussion is in order.

In the first place, note that the money constraint does *not* prevent the firm from going into debt. The firm can acquire money by issuing notes or selling bonds or future commodities. The limitations on its doing so – on its ultimate ability to raise cash – are provided by the short constraints. (For simplicity, I assume that the firm cannot issue new equity.)

Second, in calculating its money balances at future dates, the firm takes account of the availability of short-term bonds. Extra cash never lies around; rather (in the absence of more profitable opportunities) it is automatically rolled forward by investment in bonds of vanishingly short maturity, bringing in a return measured by the instantaneous interest rate. This means that the firm evaluates the cost of its future purchases not in the prices it will later have to pay but in the discounted value of

[8] Note that the enforcement of such requirements implies that the enforcement authorities know the firm's technology as well as having access to its books.

these purchases using money at a fixed time as a numéraire in the way described above.

Third, in all of this, I have not discussed the dividend policy of the firm and this is relevant here, for dividends reduce the firm's money balances. As in earlier chapters, it is not necessary to be explicit about dividend policies. It is enough to make the following fairly natural assumptions.

First, firms set dividend policies *after* making their optimal plans; they do not alter their profit-maximizing actions to achieve a particular dividend policy. As already mentioned, this may make some shareholders unhappy; such shareholders are free to sell their shares.

Second, suppose that the firm having embarked on an optimal policy and planned its dividend policy accordingly finds that it can complete its planned transactions and that its expectations about those prices and other variables which affect its optimal policy or its profits are fulfilled.[9] It is natural to assume that such a firm will not change its optimal policy and also that it will not alter its dividend plans.

Third, the firm commits itself only with regard to current dividend payments not future ones. It never pays out more cash than it has[10] and plans ultimately to pay out all its profits.

As long as it is consistent with these assumptions, dividend behavior is otherwise unrestricted save that dividend payments are smooth enough functions of the other variables of the system to permit the existence and continuity of solutions to the differential equations of motion of the system.

As in Chapter 3, I assume that the firm does not voluntarily go out of business. Relaxation of that assumption is discussed in Chapter 8.

5.5 The arbitraging firm: Optimal production and optimal arbitrage

When the firm maximizes the present discounted value of profits subject to all these constraints, certain results are obtained. Some of these relate to the firm's production plans and some to its arbitrage activities.

The principal result as to production plans is, of course, the expected one that where the firm plans actually to use an input at some future date, thereby securing additions to later outputs, it must be the case that marginal revenue product equals input price. What is interesting here is the question of the price system in which this familiar result is true.

[9] These are its *relevant* expectations as defined rigorously in Chapter 7.

[10] There are no capital levies on stockholders in this model and no new equity financing. Capital funds are raised by borrowing and through retained earnings.

There are several sets of prices that might be involved: prices that are expected to obtain as of the date the input is to be used; prices that are expected to hold as of the dates the resulting marginal additions to the stream of outputs occurs; futures prices holding as of the date at which plans are being made; or prices at other times at which the firm plans to buy or sell the goods involved. While it may at first seem natural that the planned input should be valued using the price expected as of the date of its use and resulting planned outputs similarly valued as of the dates of their production, this turns out not to be correct. Instead, the proposition that marginal revenue product equals factor price holds, using the prices on the futures market as of the date that plans are made.

The reason for this is instructive. Production plans enter the calculation of short positions. Thus, when the firm decides to use a unit of input at some future time, θ, it is taking a decision which affects its short position in that commodity not only at θ but at all times up to θ starting from time t, when its plans are made. The full opportunity cost of using that input, therefore, is not the cost of acquiring it at θ, the date at which it is to be used, or at any other time after t, but rather the cost of acquiring it immediately on the futures market at t for θ-dated goods. Note that this is so even if the optimal program calls for actually acquiring the input at some later time because its (discounted) price is expected to fall. In such a case, as shown below, the firm will find it desirable to sell the commodity short, clearing its position after the price has fallen. The decision to use the input at time θ affects the firm's short position starting at time t, the planning time. That decision keeps the firm from selling short at t to the same extent as if the input were not to be used, thus foregoing the receipts from such a short sale - an opportunity cost reflected in the price obtaining at t. The fact that the input is to be purchased at a later time does not matter - that purchase will be made at the same price regardless of whether the input is to be used at θ or sold short at t. At the margin, therefore, the firm must be indifferent between the two ways of using the commodity in question - selling it at t or using it as an input at θ.

Similarly, the marginal revenue product of the planned input must be evaluated not with the prices that were expected to rule when the outputs physically appear but with the prices which hold at the planning date, t, on the futures markets for those outputs. This is because the production of an additional unit of some commodity at a later date, θ', relieves the firm's short position in that commodity at all earlier times back to t. It is the equivalent of having another unit of the commodity purchased on the futures market at t and must be valued at the prices holding on that market. Note that this will be so even if prices are expected to rise so that the firm plans to wait to sell the output until some later time when price is at its peak. If price is expected to rise, the firm can also take advantage of that rise by buying the commodity in question at t and selling it at the same peak price. The revenue from the sale will be the same no matter how the commodity is acquired. Production of a unit of the commodity thus relieves the firm of the necessity of buying it on the futures market at t - at the margin the firm must be indifferent between the two alternatives of purchasing the commodity at t or producing it at θ'.

The other type of result as to the firm's optimal behavior concerns its decisions as to the timing of purchases and sales. Partly this is a matter of its decisions as to when to purchase inputs and when to sell outputs; partly it is a matter that need not be related to production but involves pure arbitrage on the opportunities it sees. As the explanation above shows, however, these decisions are not unrelated to the firm's optimal production plans.

The first set of results as to optimal arbitrage concerns arbitrage between two commodities. If the price of one commodity relative to another is expected to be falling at some future date, v, then, at v the short constraint for the commodity whose relative price is falling must be binding. This reflects the fact that it cannot pay to be holding such a commodity at v; the firm will wish to sell as much of such a commodity as it can in order to invest the sale proceeds in a more profitable opportunity. Such an opportunity certainly exists in the form of the other commodity whose price is involved in the comparison and the firm will either be putting its cash into that commodity or into something else.

A partial converse to this proposition also holds. If there are two commodities such that at some future date, v, the short constraint is binding for the first but not for the second, then the firm must expect the price of the first commodity to be falling relative to that of the second at v. Naturally, if this were not the case, the firm would have no reason to sell one commodity short but not the other.

Now these propositions relate to *relative* prices. They hold even if the (discounted) prices of both commodities are expected to rise, giving rise to the firm's choice between two profitable opportunities rather than between an unprofitable and a profitable one. Similarly, these propositions hold even if both (discounted) prices are expected to fall. The question of how the firm behaves when considering not relative but absolute price movements is the question of how it looks at arbitrage that involves not the holding of one commodity rather than another but the holding of commodities rather than money - more precisely, the investment of money in commodities rather than in instantaneous bonds.

The results in this area are quite similar to those already described. If the discounted price of some commodity is expected to fall at some future date v, then the short constraint for that commodity will surely be binding as of v, reflecting the fact that holding instantaneous bonds is a better investment than holding the commodity. It is possible, however, for the short constraint on a commodity to be binding as of some future date even though the discounted price of that commodity is not expected to be falling or is even expected to be rising at v; this is because it may be the case that some other discounted price is expected to be rising faster. If this is the case, then in line with the results on arbitrage between commodities, the firm will wish to sell the commodity with the slowly rising discounted price short to invest in one whose discounted price rises more quickly. In this case, however, the firm will certainly not wish to be holding cash or instantaneous bonds at v; hence it is natural to find that, if the short constraint for a particular commodity is binding as of some future date v, but the *money* constraint (which is, in effect, the short constraint for money) is not binding as of v, then the price of the commodity must be expected to be falling as the firm prefers holding instantaneous bonds to holding the commodity.

Similar results apply to the case in which the discounted price of a commodity is expected to rise. In such a case, it is the money constraint which must be binding as it cannot be optimal for the firm to hold cash balances (rolled forward at the instantaneous bond rate). On the other hand, the money constraint can perfectly well be binding at some future v without it being true that the discounted price of some particular commodity is expected to rise; this will be so if the discounted price of some *other* commodity is expected to rise. In this latter case, the firm will wish not only to invest its free cash in the second commodity but also (in accordance with the results described earlier) to sell the first commodity short. Accordingly, we find that if the money constraint is binding as of some future date v, but the short constraint for a particular commodity is *not* binding as of v, then the discounted price of that commodity *must* be expected to rise.

The only drawback to the very natural appeal of these results is the "bang-bang" property already referred to (which arises because of the absence of subjective uncertainty). The firm rushes from one opportunity to another and, indeed, from one corner solution to another in pursuit of even very small profits. This will be taken care of when we introduce transaction costs in Chapter 6.

One final result ties together, in a way, the theory of optimal production and the theory of optimal arbitrage. Because of the money constraint, the true price of money is neither unity nor totally reflected in the instantaneous interest rate. Rather it is the shadow price of money (the

Lagrange multiplier of the money constraint) which reflects the value of future opportunities to use it. Similarly, every planned purchase or sale of a commodity will be evaluated as to its effect on the availability of money – its shadow price in the same terms. In the case of optimal production, the proposition that marginal revenue product equals factor price for inputs which the firm plans actually to use is true in such shadow prices; since, as we have seen, the price system involved is the same for inputs and outputs, being that of the planning time, t, the shadow price of money at t drops out making the proposition true simply in ordinary prices. Where, however, the firm plans to purchase a commodity and hold it either for later sale or for use as an input, the shadow price of money comes into full play. At the margin it must be true that the marginal revenue *in terms of the shadow price of money* which the firm would receive from selling the commodity during or at the end of the holding period just balances the marginal cost of acquiring it evaluated in shadow prices *as of the time of acquisition.*

Note that this has the natural corollary that, if the discounted money price of an input is not expected to rise *and* if there is something profitable to invest in before the input is needed, the firm will plan to delay its acquisition of the input until the last possible moment (still continuing to abstract from transactions difficulties).

5.6* The arbitraging firm: Formal treatment

I now proceed to give the formal model of the arbitraging firm and to prove all the above results. Since this section involves only a single agent, the firm, I omit the superscript which would indicate that agent's identity. In later developments, when clarity requires it, firms will be denoted by f.

In what follows (and for the parallel case of the household) there is a triple notation for time as there was for prices. In general, t denotes the current period, the time at which plans are made and expectations formed; v denotes the time at which something is to happen; and θ denotes the date on a commodity. These are all defined, in general, on $[0, \infty)$, where 0 is an arbitrary starting date. Events that have occurred before t are fixed; the firm can only hope to influence later events.

The firm has a program of planned (or, in the case of dates already passed, actual) sales and purchases of ordinary commodities. As in Chapter 3, it is convenient to measure sales negatively and purchases positively so that excess demands will be positive and excess supplies negative. We denote by $\mathbf{z}(\theta, v, t)$ the n-vector of purchases of θ-dated commodities which the firm plans to make at v. Obviously it makes sense to define $\mathbf{z}(\theta, v, t) = 0$ for $v > \theta$. Actual purchases made at v will be denoted by $\bar{\mathbf{z}}(\theta, v)$ with a similar convention for $v > \theta$.

We can now write the discounted profits expected by the firm, $\pi(t)$, as

$$\pi(t) \equiv -\int_0^{\infty}\int_t^{\infty} \mathbf{p}(\theta, v, t)\mathbf{z}(\theta, v, t)\,dv\,d\theta + \bar{\pi}(t) \tag{5.6.1}$$

where the product in the integrand is to be taken as an inner product (and similarly throughout) and $\bar{\pi}(t)$ denotes profits (on a cash basis) already achieved at time t. Thus

$$\bar{\pi}(t) \equiv -\int_0^{\infty}\int_0^{t} \mathbf{P}(\theta, v)\bar{\mathbf{z}}(\theta, v)\,dv\,d\theta + \bar{\pi}(0) \tag{5.6.2}$$

I now turn to the technology of production. The firm's vector of inputs is denoted $\mathbf{y}(\cdot, t)$. Here, $\mathbf{y}(v, t)$ is a vector of actual inputs for $v \leqslant t$ and planned inputs for $v \geqslant t$. Note that only a dual notation for time is used here; this reflects the fact that only v-dated commodities can be used as inputs at v.

As a result of its past actual and planned future input activities, the firm at t expects to have at each time, $\theta \geqslant t$, a flow of outputs of θ-dated goods. That flow is given by a concave production *functional*, $\phi(\mathbf{y}(\cdot, t), \theta, t)$, which is assumed continuously Fréchet differentiable.[11] A few more words about this are in order.

In the first place, outputs at θ only depend on inputs up to θ - on $\mathbf{y}(v, t)$ for $v \leqslant \theta$. Moreover, apart from the case of joint production, it is sensible to suppose that the outputs of particular commodities depend on the inputs devoted to the production of those commodities and not just on total inputs as the notation would indicate. There is no point in burdening the notation with such matters, however. Instead, the argument, t, in part indicates that the way in which the inputs have been and are planned to be used depends on the history of actions taken up to t and the expectations of the firm at t. The suboptimization decisions of the firm are kept implicit.[12]

This is a different point from the erroneous one that there is something wrong because the same inputs keep on producing outputs regardless of what is taken out of the process in earlier periods. Only θ-dated goods can be outputs at time θ. As earlier discussed (and as we shall formally state in a moment), θ-dated goods which are not sold but remain on hand

[11] For those unfamiliar with Fréchet differentiation, it is the appropriate extension of ordinary differentiation to spaces such as that in which we are now working. See Luenberger (1969). Some heuristic comments are given in footnote 15 below.

[12] Expected technical change can also be placed in this notation.

at θ cannot remain θ-dated goods. This being so, we may as well think of them as automatically becoming inputs into the production process, even if that process becomes in part the trivial one of storing commodities so that their dates change. Hence later outputs do depend on earlier output decisions. They in effect depend on how much of earlier outputs remain as inputs. Perhaps the easiest way to think about this is to take $\phi(\mathbf{y}(\cdot,t),\theta,t)$ as denoting the availability of outputs of θ-dated goods at θ.

While the production process can only produce θ-dated goods at θ, the firm can acquire such goods at other times through purchase. Thus, for $t \leqslant v \leqslant \theta$, let $\mathbf{x}(\theta, v, t)$ be the stock of θ-dated goods which the firm, at t, expects to have acquired through purchase and have on hand at v. For $v \leqslant t$, the actual stock on hand will be denoted by $\bar{\mathbf{x}}(\theta, v)$. We shall think of trade as occurring instantaneously or outside of time, so that $\mathbf{x}(\theta, v, t)$ and $\bar{\mathbf{x}}(\theta, v)$ are to be evaluated after trade at v. Thus

$$\mathbf{x}(\theta, v, t) \equiv \bar{\mathbf{x}}(\theta, t) + \int_t^v \mathbf{z}(\theta, a, t)\, da \quad v \geqslant t \tag{5.6.3}$$

and

$$\bar{\mathbf{x}}(\theta, t) \equiv \bar{\mathbf{x}}(\theta, 0) + \int_0^t \bar{\mathbf{z}}(\theta, a)\, da \tag{5.6.4}$$

Now, as stated, θ-dated commodities on hand after trade at θ automatically become inputs. Formally

$$\mathbf{y}(\theta, t) = \phi(\mathbf{y}(\cdot, t), \theta, t) + \mathbf{x}(\theta, \theta, t) \tag{5.6.5}$$

I now turn to the statement of the short constraints. I assume that for every $(\theta, v, t), \theta \geqq v \geqq t$, there is imposed an n-component vector, $\epsilon(\theta, v, t) \geqq 0$, continuous in its three arguments, nonincreasing in v and with the property that $\epsilon(v, v, t) = 0$ such that[13]:

$$\mathbf{x}(\theta, v, t) + \phi(\mathbf{y}(\cdot, t), \theta, t) - \mathbf{y}(\theta, t) + \epsilon(\theta, v, t) \geqq 0 \quad \text{for all } 0 \geqslant v \geqslant t \tag{5.6.6}$$

Note that the firm is entitled to count at each v its anticipated net output of θ-dated goods, evaluating its position as though its purchases of such goods had to stop at v.

As of time t, the firm has paid out dividends and plans to pay dividends in the future. We denote by $g(v, t)$ the flow of dividend payments

[13] A special (and sensible) case would be to have $\epsilon(\theta, v, t)$ depend only on $(\theta - v)$ for given t. Note that I have assumed that the constraint for a given commodity is never looser at later planned transaction dates than at earlier ones.

which the firm, as of t, expects to make at v (actual for $v \leqslant t$), and by $\bar{G}(t)$ the total payments already made by the firm. Then

$$\bar{G}(t) \equiv \int_0^t g(v,t)\,dv + \bar{G}(0) \tag{5.6.7}$$

We assume

$$\bar{G}(t) \leqq \bar{\pi}(t) \tag{5.6.8}$$

so that the firm never pays more than it actually takes in in cash. The strict inequality may very well hold out of equilibrium as the firm retains earnings. It is also natural to assume

$$\bar{G}(t) + \int_0^\infty g(v,t)\,dv = \pi(t) \tag{5.6.9}$$

so that the firm plans ultimately to pay its profits to its stockholders. Other assumptions about dividend behavior were given in Section 5.4.

The constraint that the firm must plan to have a nonnegative money stock (its "money constraint") can now be written as

$$\bar{\pi}(t) - \bar{G}(t) - \int_0^\infty \int_t^v \mathbf{p}(\theta,a,t)\mathbf{z}(\theta,a,t)\,da\,d\theta \geqslant 0 \quad \text{for all } v \geqslant t \tag{5.6.10}$$

Note that this makes firms take into account the fact that purchases must be made with money. Note also that *future* dividend policy is not a constraint; it can be altered if profit maximization requires it.

As the final constraint, it is convenient to require explicitly that planned inputs, $\mathbf{y}(\theta,t)$, be nonnegative. This is implicit in (5.6.5) and (5.6.6), but the latter constraints are best thought of as assuring the nonnegativity of the stock of goods available for inputs rather than of inputs themselves.[14]

The firm chooses inputs, $\mathbf{y}(\cdot,t)$ and transactions $\mathbf{z}(\cdot,\cdot,t)$ so as to maximize discounted profits (5.6.1) subject to these various constraints (and the fact that past events are fixed). Substituting (5.6.3) into (5.6.5) and (5.6.6), the appropriate Lagrangian is given by

$$L(t) = \bar{\pi}(t) - \int_0^\infty \int_t^\infty \mathbf{p}(\theta,v,t)\mathbf{z}(\theta,v,t)\,dv\,d\theta$$

$$-\int_t^\infty \boldsymbol{\lambda}(\theta,t)\left\{\mathbf{y}(\theta,t) - \boldsymbol{\phi}(\mathbf{y}(\cdot,t),\theta,t) - \bar{\mathbf{x}}(\theta,t) - \int_t^\theta \mathbf{z}(\theta,v,t)\,dv\right\}d\theta +$$

[14] Without an explicit nonnegativity constraint on inputs one has to be careful about whether certain integrals of Lagrange multipliers are automatically zero when upper and lower limits of integration coincide. (Of course the Lagrange multipliers of these various constraints are related.)

$$+\int_t^\infty \int_t^\theta \boldsymbol{\mu}(\theta, v, t)\left\{\bar{\mathbf{x}}(\theta, t)+\int_t^v \mathbf{z}(\theta, a, t)\, da+\boldsymbol{\phi}(\mathbf{y}(\cdot, t), \theta, t)\right.$$

$$\left.-\mathbf{y}(\theta, t)+\boldsymbol{\epsilon}(\theta, v, t)\right\} dv\, d\theta$$

$$+\int_t^\infty \mu_0(v, t)\left\{\bar{\pi}(t)-\bar{G}(t)-\int_0^\infty \int_t^v \mathbf{p}(\theta, a, t)\mathbf{z}(\theta, a, t)\, da\, d\theta\right\} dv$$

$$+\int_t^\infty \boldsymbol{\gamma}(\theta, t)\mathbf{y}(\theta, t)\, d\theta \qquad (5.6.11)$$

Here, $\boldsymbol{\lambda}(\cdot, t)$, $\boldsymbol{\mu}(\cdot, \cdot, t)$, $\boldsymbol{\gamma}(\cdot, t)$, and $\mu_0(\cdot, t)$ are Lagrange multiplier functions, the first three being vectors.

Since the production functional is concave, we need only examine first-order conditions. These are (in addition to the constraints)

$$\boldsymbol{\lambda}(\theta, t)+\int_v^\theta \boldsymbol{\mu}(\theta, a, t)\, da=\mathbf{p}(\theta, v, t)\left\{1+\int_v^\infty \mu_0(a, t)\, da\right\} \quad \theta \geqslant v \geqslant t \qquad (5.6.12)$$

and

$$\boldsymbol{\lambda}(v, t)+\int_t^v \boldsymbol{\mu}(v, a, t)\, da-\boldsymbol{\gamma}(v, t)$$

$$=\int_t^\infty \left\{\boldsymbol{\lambda}(\theta, t)+\int_t^\theta \boldsymbol{\mu}(\theta, a, t)\, da\right\}\boldsymbol{\phi}_{\mathbf{y}(v,t)}(\mathbf{y}(\cdot, t), \theta, t)\, d\theta \quad \theta \geqslant v \geqslant t \qquad (5.6.13)$$

where the subscript denotes the value of the Fréchet derivative at v.[15] Here, (5.6.12) is obtained by differentiation with respect to $\mathbf{z}(\theta, v, t)$ and (5.6.13) by differentiation with respect to $\mathbf{y}(v, t)$, roughly speaking. Note that changing $\mathbf{y}(v, t)$ affects short positions *before* as well as after v.

Since certain of the integrals in (5.6.12) and (5.6.13) occur frequently in the following discussion, it will be convenient to adopt a notation for them. Accordingly, we define:

$$\mathbf{I}(\theta, v, t) \equiv \int_v^\theta \boldsymbol{\mu}(\theta, a, t)\, da \quad v \leqslant \theta \qquad (5.6.14)$$

[15] It is best to be precise about the notational convention used. The vector of Fréchet derivatives of $\boldsymbol{\phi}(\mathbf{y}(\cdot, t), \theta, t)$ would be denoted $\boldsymbol{\phi}_{\mathbf{y}}(\mathbf{y}(\cdot, t), \theta, t)$. It is a vector of entire functions defined over v (one component for each element of $\mathbf{y}$). It is convenient to have a notation for the values of those functions at a specific v; this is given by $\boldsymbol{\phi}_{\mathbf{y}(v,t)}(\mathbf{y}(\cdot, t), \theta, t)$. This notation, which will be abbreviated $\boldsymbol{\phi}_{\mathbf{y}(v,t)}$ wherever possible, is mnemonic because it reminds us of the fact that the value of each component is the limit of the derivative with respect to a constant added to a given element of $\mathbf{y}(\cdot, t)$ from $v-\epsilon$ to $v+\epsilon$ as ϵ goes to zero. A similar convention is used for utility and storage functionals below.

and

$$J(v,t) \equiv 1 + \int_v^\infty \mu_0(a,t)\, da \tag{5.6.15}$$

The separate components of $\mathbf{I}(\theta, v, t)$ will be denoted by subscripts.

I now proceed to prove the results discussed in the previous section. The result that marginal revenue product equals input price in the price system as of t is

Theorem 5.6.1.

$$\int_v^\infty \mathbf{p}(\theta,t,t)\phi_{\mathbf{y}(v,t)}\, d\theta \leqq \mathbf{p}(v,t,t) \tag{5.6.16}$$

with equality holding for those commodities which the firm actually plans to use as inputs at v.

Proof. Note that the first two terms on the left-hand side of (5.6.13) are the same as the right-hand side of (5.6.12) with θ and v replacing v and t, respectively. Evaluate the right-hand side of (5.6.13) by setting $v=t$ in (5.6.12). This yields

$$\mathbf{p}(v,t,t)J(t,t) - \gamma(v,t) = J(t,t)\int_v^\infty \mathbf{p}(\theta,t,t)\phi_{\mathbf{y}(v,t)}(\mathbf{y}(\cdot,t),\theta,t)\, d\theta \tag{5.6.17}$$

The desired result now follows on observing that $J(v,t)>0$ while $\gamma(v,t) \geqq 0$ with equality holding only in those components for which the nonnegativity constraint is not binding at v.[16]

I now prove the arbitrage results.

Theorem 5.6.2. Consider a pair of ordinary commodities, i and j, with respective dates θ_i and θ_j. Call these dated commodities (i,θ_i) and (j,θ_j), respectively. Consider a time v^*, $t \leqslant v^* < \min(\theta_i, \theta_j)$.

(A) Suppose that at v^* the expected price ratio $p_i(\theta_i, v^*, t) \div p_j(\theta_j, v^*, t)$ is decreasing in v. Then the short constraint for (i,θ_i) is binding at v^*.

(B) If at v^*, the short constraint for (i,θ_i) is binding but that for (j,θ_j) is not binding, then the expected price ratio must be decreasing in v at v^*.

[16] Throughout, I define a "binding" constraint as one for which the associated Lagrange multiplier is positive. Note the appearance of the full shadow price of money at t, $J(t,t)$, in (5.6.17) so that the theorem holds in shadow prices as well.

Proof. Differentiating the relevant parts of (5.6.12) with respect to v, we obtain:

$$\frac{\partial \log p_i(\theta_i, v, t)}{\partial v} - \frac{\partial \log p_j(\theta_j, v, t)}{\partial v}$$
$$= \frac{\mu_j(\theta_j, v, t)}{\lambda_j(\theta_j, t) + I_j(\theta_j, v, t)} - \frac{\mu_i(\theta_i, v, t)}{\lambda_i(\theta_i, t) + I_i(\theta_i, v, t)} \tag{5.6.18}$$

However, the Lagrange multipliers and their integrals are all nonnegative. Hence, if the left-hand side of (5.6.18) is negative at v^*, $\mu_i(\theta_i, v^*, t)$ must be strictly positive. Similarly, if $\mu_i(\theta_i, v^*, t) > 0$ but $\mu_j(\theta_j, v^*, t) = 0$, the left-hand side of (5.6.18) must be negative.

Corollary 5.6.1. If the firm plans to hold two commodities (i, θ_i) and (j, θ_j) over the entire interval $[v^*, v']$, $t \leqslant v^* < v' \leqslant \min(\theta_i, \theta_j)$, then $p_i(\theta_i, v^*, t)/p_j(\theta_j, v^*, t) = p_i(\theta_i, v', t)/p_j(\theta_j, v', t)$.

In particular,

Corollary 5.6.2. If at some time $v^* < \theta$, the firm plans to buy two θ-dated commodities, i and j, and to hold them until θ for use as inputs, then $p_i(\theta, v^*, t)/p_j(\theta, v^*, t) = p_i(\theta, \theta, t)/p_j(\theta, \theta, t)$.

Note that this does not imply that the price of each such input is expected to be the same at v^* as it is at θ, only that they are expected to change in the same proportion. The question of whether such prices are expected to change at all involves the money constraint. The theorem as to arbitrage between commodities and money is

Theorem 5.6.3. Consider a commodity, i, with date θ, and a time v^*, $t \leqslant v^* < \theta$.

(A) If, at v^*, $p_i(\theta, v, t)$ is decreasing in v, then the short constraint for the commodity is binding at v^*.

(B) If, at v^*, the money constraint is not binding but the short constraint for the commodity is binding, then $p_i(\theta, v, t)$ must be decreasing in v at v^*.

(C) If, at v^*, $p_i(\theta, v, t)$ is increasing in v, then the money constraint is binding at v^*.

(D) If, at v^*, the short constraint for the commodity is not binding, but the money constraint is binding, then $p_i(\theta, v, t)$ must be increasing in v at v^*.

(E) If, at v^*, neither the short constraint for the commodity nor the money constraint is binding, then $\partial p_i(\theta, v, t)/\partial v = 0$ at v^*.

Proof: Differentiate the ith component of (5.6.12) with respect to v and rearrange terms, obtaining

$$\frac{\partial p_i(\theta, v, t)}{\partial v} = \frac{p_i(\theta, v, t)\mu_0(v, t) - \mu_i(\theta, v, t)}{J(v, t)} \tag{5.6.19}$$

The desired results all follow immediately from the nonnegativity of the Lagrange multipliers.

The final result in this section has to do with equality of discounted expected shadow prices when commodities are held. It is

> *Theorem 5.6.4.* Suppose that the firm plans to buy or to hold at v a commodity i with date θ. Suppose that it plans to continue holding that commodity until at least v' $(t \leqslant v < v' \leqslant \theta)$. Then

$$p_i(\theta, v, t)J(v, t) = p_i(\theta, v', t)J(v', t) \tag{5.6.20}$$

Proof. This follows immediately from (5.6.12) and the fact that the short constraint for the commodity is not binding at any time in $[v, v')$.

As discussed in the previous section, this fact can be interpreted (as can (5.6.17) and hence Theorem 5.6.1) as marginal revenue product equals factor price taking account of the shadow prices of money at the appropriate dates. Note, moreover, that Theorem 5.6.4 applies to the purchase and holding of commodities which are later to be used as inputs.

5.7 The arbitraging household: Assumptions

I now turn to the theory of the household which in some respects parallels that of the firm and differs from it in others.

The household maximizes utility by deciding on a consumption plan. That plan is defined over past and future consumption, but, of course, past consumption is already fixed and, at the planning time t, the household can only alter future consumption. Since it is unduly restrictive to take the extremely special case where total utility is an integral of instantaneous utilities, this means, in effect, that one can think of the household's objective function (strictly, functional) as changing as a result of past consumption activities. It is preferable, however, to think of that objective function as fixed with the household's past consumption activities changing the constraints under which it operates by fixing more and more of the arguments of its utility functional, as it were.

Like the firm, the household has access to a convex technology, which we shall refer to as "storage," although it includes other phenomena. This technology gives outputs in terms of past input activities. Apart from the possibility of household production in other than a notational sense, this includes the redating of goods which the household keeps on hand. It also includes the endowment of the household; the flow of time which the household can dispose of as labor or leisure, for example, can simply be thought of as outputs which require no previous inputs. In general, all the discussion of the technology of the firm applies here as well.

As with the firm, the household can take short positions in commodities and those positions are constrained. In evaluating its short position in any commodity the household takes account of its planned net output of that commodity from storage just as the firm takes account of its planned net output from production.

There is one matter involving the short constraints for households that is not the same as for the firm, however. That is the question of whether or not the household subtracts its own planned consumption of future commodities when calculating its short positions in those commodities. The answer turns out to depend on what it is that the short constraints are thought to represent.

The view that the household should take account of its consumption in evaluating short positions is the view that the household is required to have a totally consistent plan which recognizes that the danger of being caught short and unable to carry out its plans if transactions do not materialize in a given dated commodity increases as the date on that commodity approaches. This is certainly a sensible way for the household to behave; however, if the household does so behave it is because of its own internal restrictions rather than because of outside legal constraints. Such outside constraints can force the household to plan to be able to deliver on its commitments to *others*; it is hard to see why society should care about the household's delivery to *itself*, as it were. To put it slightly differently, if, as the date on 1990 chocolate bars approaches, the household is not short in that commodity *except* for the amount required for its own planned consumption, one would suppose that legal requirements were satisfied. In such a case, all the risk of not being able to obtain further 1990 chocolate bars rests on the household itself. If it cannot do so, it will have to reduce its own consumption of 1990 chocolate, but it will still be able to meet its outside commitments.

Thus, if we view the short constraints on commodities as imposed from outside, it makes sense to exclude consumption considerations; if we take the view that the short constraints stem from a self-imposed recognition of the possibility that transactions may not be completed, then it makes sense to include consumption. While I favor the former view – the exclusion of consumption – there is something to be said on both sides. Accordingly, I perform the analysis both ways. It makes an interesting, but not wide-ranging difference, affecting, as we shall see, the question of the price system in which marginal utility of consumption equals price and the interpretation of that condition.

The household also differs from the firm in another important aspect: Households own firms, receive dividends, and participate in the market for shares.[17] As we shall see, the fact that there is a market for shares reflects not merely the possibility of disagreement about future prices and profits but also the fact that, with prices expected to change, the dividend policies of firms will be evaluated differently by different households with different intertemporal liquidity needs. This comes out very clearly in the results below. The point is closely related to that made in footnote 7 as to the ability of households to sell shares in firms whose managers adopt policies they do not like.

In any event, the fact that households can buy and sell shares means that they must be assumed to have expectations as to share prices and also expectations as to the future dividend policies of firms. Moreover, it means that we must impose constraints on the household's short positions in shares. In so doing, there is no need to require that such positions be cleared by any finite time, for shares, unlike commodities, are undated. We do require that such short positions be cleared eventually.

I now turn to monetary considerations. Defining profits for the firm in terms of money, we guaranteed that the firm would evaluate purchases and sales in terms of money. In the case of the household, one must impose this constraint separately as an accounting identity which specifies that the value of money which the household plans to receive through trade in commodities and shares just balances the value of its planned net sales at every future moment of time. It is not the case, however, that this constraint is (by itself) an instantaneous budget constraint; rather, it is a definition of money received through trade. The budget constraints arise when we also impose on the household money constraints similar to those imposed on the firm requiring nonnegative money stocks.

Such money constraints differ from those imposed on the firm in two respects. First, the money flow received by the household does not merely consist of money received in trade; it also includes dividends which the household can then spend. Secondly, although whether or not the money constraints on the household (or the firm) are binding as of any finite future time is an interesting question, there can be no question but that the household will not plan to hold a positive money stock

[17] Firms are not allowed to own other firms in the model; this is a matter of convenience. I have already assumed that firms cannot issue new shares.

forever, since money generates utility only by affording the wherewithal to attain consumption goods.[18] It is convenient explicitly to impose this constraint on households, something unnecessary in the case of firms which keep score as to profits in terms of money.[19] I shall refer to this long-run budget constraint as a "money constraint binding at infinity."

5.8 The arbitraging household: Results

When the household maximizes utility under these conditions, certain results emerge. These relate to its optimal consumption program, its optimal use of its storage technology, and its optimal arbitrage in commodities and shares as well as its holdings of the latter. Some of the results are identical to those obtained for firms and some are new.

I begin by considering the results with regard to consumption. Here, as we should expect, we obtain results in the familiar form that, for commodities that the household plans actually to consume, marginal utility is proportional to (discounted) price. However, the precise statement and interpretation of the results involve matters of some interest. The first issue is that of the price system in which such proportionality is to hold. This, not surprisingly, turns out to depend on which of the two interpretations of the short constraints discussed above one adopts.

Suppose first that one includes consumption in calculating short positions. In this case, the prices involved are not those that apply when the corresponding commodities are consumed, but rather the prices for those commodities on the futures markets as of the planning date, t. This is so for the same reason which led to a similar phenomenon for firms. The planned consumption of a given commodity at some future date, θ, affects the household's short position in that commodity at all times from t through θ, other things equal. Its effects on those positions can be offset precisely by the purchase of that commodity on the futures market as of t; this makes the price in that futures market the true opportunity cost of such consumption; hence it is that price that appears in the marginal conditions.

In fact, the full opportunity cost of such planned consumption in terms of utility has another component as well. If the commodity in

[18] This statement would still be true as a formal matter even if money entered the utility functional either as a stock or as consumption. In such a case money in trade can be thought of as one-for-one exchangeable with money in utility (gold coins for collections, for example) and it is the stock of money planned for use in trade that must go asymptotically to zero.

[19] The imposition of the requirement that firms plan ultimately to pay out all their profits in dividends is *not* the same thing since dividend policies do not *constrain* the firm in its profit-maximizing activities.

question is purchased on the futures market at t, it must be purchased with money. Because of the money constraint, such money has itself an opportunity cost. Not surprisingly, the factor of proportionality relating marginal utilities to prices is the marginal utility of money as of t. Note that this marginal utility is positive even though money does not itself directly enter the utility of the household; the marginal utility of money at t is the addition to utility which a little more money at t would permit attaining in an optimal program - the opportunity cost of such money in terms of utility. Measuring the cost of purchases in full shadow prices in terms of utility, marginal utilities equal utility shadow prices. (The opportunity cost of money does not drop out of that relationship as it did for the production plans of firms - and will for the storage plans of households - because the pay-off for the household is in terms of utility, rather than money.)

Turn now to the other alternative, that consumption is not involved in evaluating the short positions of the household. In this case, the result that marginal utility is proportional to price holds in the price system which the household expects to encounter when the consumption occurs - the prices on the spot market at θ rather than those on the futures market at t. This reflects the fact that the decision to consume at θ has no direct effect on matters at other times; what is foregone by such consumption is the opportunity to sell at θ regardless of when the good is purchased.

In this case, however, the full opportunity cost in terms of utility of consumption at θ involves the marginal utility (opportunity cost) of money at θ, rather than at t, and this is the factor of proportionality. Since, in general, that marginal utility will be higher at earlier times than at later ones, this means that marginal utilities of planned consumption at different future times will *not* in general be proportional to (discounted) *money* prices, although it will remain true that marginal utility is equal to the full shadow price of consumption in utility terms.

Note that this somewhat unexpected result is a consequence of the fact that the money constraint can be binding at finite times. Were this not so, these constraints would collapse into a single budget constraint over all future times. This may very well happen in equilibrium; it certainly happens in Walrasian equilibrium as discussed in Chapter 7 below. Out of equilibrium, however, it generally will not happen. As we have seen in considering the arbitrage results for the firm, it certainly will not happen if any discounted price is expected to rise. Hence we must expect that (if short constraints are legally rather than internally imposed), the standard result of marginal utility proportional to (discounted) money price will not generally hold in disequilibrium when comparing consumption in different time periods.

Turning to the optimal behavior of the household with regard to its storage technology, it is not surprising to find that the household manages the storage activity as if it were a profit-maximizing firm, setting marginal revenue product equal to input price for inputs actually stored with the prices involved being those on the futures markets as of the planning date, t. All the discussion of the firm's optimal production activities applies here and I shall not repeat it save to remind the reader that the appearance of prices as of t reflects the fact that storage inputs and outputs have effects on short constraints which can be exactly offset by purchase as of t. Since valuation of both inputs and outputs is as of the same date, the opportunity cost of money drops out of the marginal condition here.

Similarly, the household's optimal activities with regard to speculation in commodities are identical to those of the profit-maximizing firm. Further, where the household holds a commodity over some period, the full shadow price of that commodity in terms of utility must be constant over the period, any change in the discounted money price being just offset by an opposite change in the marginal utility of money. Since earlier money is no less valuable than later money, this requires the discounted money price of such a commodity to rise if there is any other profitable speculative use for money during the holding period.

Similar results hold regarding the household's speculation in and holding of shares. First consider speculation. Here the household behaves in terms of arbitrage between shares of different firms, between shares and commodities, and between shares and money essentially as it and firms do with regard to arbitrage between commodities or between commodities and money. The only difference is that, whereas for a commodity what matters is the price, for the shares of a firm what matters is the price *plus* the *dividend flow*. Hence, for example, a household may plan not to go short in a particular share even if the price of that share is expected to fall, since the expected dividend flow from holding the share may make it a worthwhile investment.

The role played by dividend expectations comes up again when we consider the circumstances under which a household will wish to hold the share of a firm over some time interval. Here, parallel to the result for holding commodities, we find that, in the optimal program, the marginal utility of the money represented by the (discounted) expected price of the share at the beginning of the holding period just balances the sum of the marginal utility of money represented by its (discounted) expected price at the end of that period *plus* the marginal utility of the money represented by the intervening (discounted) expected dividend stream. For shares that the household plans to hold forever, the marginal utility of the money represented by the (discounted) expected price of the share at any future time must be just matched by the marginal utility of the money represented by the (discounted) expected dividend stream from that time forward. If we interpret the marginal utility of money as the opportunity cost of money, these results can be given the form of marginal revenue product equaling input prices in terms of full shadow prices.

The fact that the money constraints make the household value money at different times differently and make it use those valuations in considering dividend streams provides the reason mentioned above for the existence of a securities market which is additional to that provided by differing expectations as to the profits of firms. The purchase or sale of the expected dividend stream which goes with the shares of a particular firm provides a way of transferring money among time periods that may not be available from transactions in bonds or other commodity futures. Out of equilibrium, households may very well find it to their advantage to engage in such transactions with each other even if there is uniform agreement as to the discounted future profits of the firms involved.[20]

5.9* The arbitraging household: Formal treatment

Households will later be superscripted h, but this superscript is omitted in the present section. Wherever possible, I deliberately adopt a notation identical to that used for firms.

The household maximizes a weakly monotonic, locally nonsatiated, strictly quasi-concave,[21] continuously Fréchet differentiable utility *functional* $U(\mathbf{c}(\cdot, t))$, where $\mathbf{c}(\theta, t)$ is the n-vector of consumption of ordinary commodities which the household expects at time t to consume at time θ. Obviously, this only makes sense for $\theta \geqslant t$. For $\theta \leqslant t$, $\mathbf{c}(\theta, t)$ denotes actual consumption.

As with firms, the household has expectations as to discounted prices,

[20] As previously stated, I assume that the liquidity considerations of the stockholders do not affect the profit-maximizing decisions of firms, although they may affect its dividend policies given those decisions. Note that firms never expect to pay dividends at times when their own money constraints are binding, in particular at times when they see profitable arbitrage opportunities for the money. Disgruntled stockholders will generally be those who see better uses still.

[21] For convenience, utility is defined over all goods including intermediate ones, like pig-iron. It is to be understood that strict quasi-concavity only applies when the Fréchet derivative is not identically zero over some range. Thus strong monotonicity is not implied and satiation in a particular commodity is possible. This permits continuity in prices when there are free goods.

denoted $\mathbf{p}(\theta, v, t)$, as before. It also has purchase plans for ordinary commodities, again denoted by $\mathbf{z}(\theta, v, t)$, with the same properties as for firms.

I denote by $\mathbf{k}(v, t)$ the vector of holdings of shares which, at time t, the household plans to have at time $v \geqslant t$; $\mathbf{k}(v, t)$ has one component for each firm. Actual holdings are denoted by $\bar{\mathbf{k}}(v)$. I normalize so as to make the total number of shares issued by any firm sum to unity and assume that all fractions between one and the permitted lower bound on short positions are possible.

It is convenient to have a separate notation for the household's purchases of shares; I denote the vector of such purchases which, at t, the household expects to make at $v \geqslant t$ by $\mathbf{q}(v, t)$. Purchases actually made are denoted by $\bar{\mathbf{q}}(v)$. I denote the corresponding vector of discounted share prices which the household expects to encounter at v by $\mathbf{w}(v, t)$. (Note that shares are not distinguished by date.)

The household's storage process is given the same notation as was the firm's production process. Inputs into storage, planned at t, to be made at v are denoted by $\mathbf{y}(v, t)$. The resulting planned availability of θ-dated goods is given by $\boldsymbol{\phi}(\mathbf{y}(\cdot, t), \theta, t)$, a concave Fréchet-differentiable functional. All of the remarks made in Sections 5.5 and 5.6 about the firm's production functional apply here.

Let $\mathbf{x}(\theta, v, t)$ denote the stock of θ-dated goods which the household, at t, expects to have acquired through trade after the close of trade at $v (t \leqslant v \leqslant \theta)$. For $v \leqslant t$, the actual stock on hand after trade at v will be denoted by $\bar{\mathbf{x}}(\theta, v)$. Then:

$$\mathbf{x}(\theta, v, t) \equiv \bar{\mathbf{x}}(\theta, t) + \int_t^v \mathbf{z}(\theta, a, t)\, da \quad v \geqslant t \tag{5.9.1}$$

and

$$\bar{\mathbf{x}}(\theta, t) \equiv \bar{\mathbf{x}}(\theta, 0) + \int_0^t \bar{\mathbf{z}}(\theta, a)\, da \tag{5.9.2}$$

where, as before, $\bar{\mathbf{z}}(\theta, a)$ denotes actual purchases made at a.

Now, θ-dated commodities on hand after trade at θ can come either from purchase or from storage. Such commodities are either consumed or automatically become inputs into storage, since their date must be changed. I write this as

$$\mathbf{x}(\theta, \theta, t) + \boldsymbol{\phi}(\mathbf{y}(\cdot, t), \theta, t) - \mathbf{c}(\theta, t) - \mathbf{y}(\theta, t) = 0 \tag{5.9.3}$$

I complete the description of technology by adding the explicit non-negativity constraints that $\mathbf{c}(\theta, t) \geqq 0$ and $\mathbf{y}(\theta, t) \geqq 0$.

The short constraints for commodities are written as in the case of firms, save for the decision as to the inclusion of planned consumption. Again I assume the imposition of a vector of continuous functions $\epsilon(\theta, v, t) \geqq 0$ defined for all $\theta \geqslant v \geqslant t$, with $\epsilon(v, v, t) = 0$. The short constraints for commodities are written as

$$\mathbf{x}(\theta, v, t) + \boldsymbol{\phi}(\mathbf{y}(\cdot, t), \theta, t) - \mathbf{y}(\theta, t) - b_c \mathbf{c}(\theta, t) + \boldsymbol{\epsilon}(\theta, v, t) \geqq 0 \tag{5.9.4}$$

where $b_c = 0$ if consumption is not to be counted and $b_c = 1$ if consumption is to be counted.

Short constraints for shares are simpler. I assume the imposition of a nonnegative vector of continuous functions, $\boldsymbol{\kappa}(v, t)$, nonincreasing in v and with $\lim_{v \to \infty} \boldsymbol{\kappa}(v, t) = 0$ such that

$$\mathbf{k}(v, t) + \boldsymbol{\kappa}(v, t) \geqq 0 \tag{5.9.5}$$

where

$$\mathbf{k}(v, t) = \bar{\mathbf{k}}(t) + \int_t^v \mathbf{q}(a, t)\, da; \quad \bar{\mathbf{k}}(t) = \bar{\mathbf{k}}(0) + \int_0^t \bar{\mathbf{q}}(a)\, da \tag{5.9.6}$$

Now, the household expects to earn dividends on the shares it owns. Let $\mathbf{d}(v, t)$ be a vector whose typical element is the total rate of dividend payments (discounted) that the household, at t, expects a particular firm to make at v (with actual payments denoted by $\bar{\mathbf{d}}(v)$). Then the total discounted dividend flow which the household expects at t to receive at v can be written as $\mathbf{d}(v, t)\mathbf{k}(v, t)$.

Note that a household with a short position in the shares of some firm is obligated for the dividend payments accompanying such shares; this is the case in practice.

Turning now to monetary matters, denote the discounted amount of money which the household, at t, expects to acquire at $v \geqslant t$ through trading by $z_0(v, t)$ and actual such acquisitions by $\bar{z}_0(v)$. We can now write the first of the financial constraints on the behavior of the household as

$$\int_0^\infty \mathbf{p}(\theta, v, t)\mathbf{z}(\theta, v, t)\, d\theta + \mathbf{w}(v, t)\mathbf{q}(v, t) + z_0(v, t) = 0 \quad \text{for all } v \geqslant t \tag{5.9.7}$$

This simply states that the household must plan to exchange money for things of equal value when trading. (Recall that $\mathbf{z}(\theta, v, t) = 0$ for $\theta < v$.)

Denote the household's actual stock of money at t by $\bar{m}(t)$, then:

$$\bar{m}(t) = \bar{m}(0) + \int_0^t \bar{z}_0(a)\, da + \int_0^t \bar{\mathbf{d}}(a)\bar{\mathbf{k}}(a)\, da \tag{5.9.8}$$

and the money constraints can be stated as

$$\bar{m}(t)+\int_t^v \{z_0(a,t)+\mathbf{d}(a,t)\mathbf{k}(a,t)\}\,da \geqslant 0 \quad \text{for all } v \geqslant t \tag{5.9.9}$$

$$\bar{m}(t)+\int_t^\infty \{z_0(a,t)+\mathbf{d}(a,t)\mathbf{k}(a,t)\}\,da = 0 \tag{5.9.10}$$

As with firms, note that households take into account the fact that purchases must be made with money. Equation (5.9.10) ensures that the household does not plan to hold a positive money stock forever - an obviously harmless restriction. Without such a separate statement, one can encounter a slightly inconvenient anomaly in cases in which the money constraints are not binding at any finite time. In such a case, without (5.9.10) the Lagrange multipliers for the money constraints (5.9.9) would all be zero even though the budget constraint (5.9.10) to which they all collapse is binding.

The Lagrangian for the household's optimization problem is given by

$$\begin{aligned}
L(t) &= U(\mathbf{c}(\cdot,t)) \\
&\quad -\int_t^\infty \beta(v,t)\left\{\int_0^\infty \mathbf{p}(\theta,v,t)\mathbf{z}(\theta,v,t)\,d\theta+\mathbf{w}(v,t)\mathbf{q}(v,t)+z_0(v,t)\right\}dv \\
&\quad -\int_t^\infty \boldsymbol{\lambda}(\theta,t)\left\{\mathbf{c}(\theta,t)+\mathbf{y}(\theta,t)-\boldsymbol{\phi}(\mathbf{y}(\cdot,t),\theta,t)\right. \\
&\qquad\qquad \left. -\bar{\mathbf{x}}(\theta,t)-\int_t^\theta \mathbf{z}(\theta,a,t)\,da\right\} \\
&\quad +\int_t^\infty\int_t^\theta \boldsymbol{\mu}(\theta,v,t)\left\{\bar{\mathbf{x}}(\theta,t)+\int_t^v \mathbf{z}(\theta,a,t)\,da+\boldsymbol{\phi}(\mathbf{y}(\cdot,t),\theta,t)\right. \\
&\qquad\qquad \left. -\mathbf{y}(\theta,t)-b_c\mathbf{c}(\theta,t)+\boldsymbol{\epsilon}(\theta,v,t)\right\}dv\,d\theta \\
&\quad +\int_t^\infty \mu_0(v,t)\left\{\bar{m}(t)+\int_t^v (z_0(a,t)+\mathbf{d}(a,t)\mathbf{k}(a,t))\,da\right\}dv \\
&\quad +\mu_0^*(t)\left\{\bar{m}(t)+\int_t^\infty (z_0(a,t)+\mathbf{d}(a,t)\mathbf{k}(a,t))\,da\right\} \\
&\quad +\int_t^\infty \boldsymbol{\alpha}(v,t)\{\mathbf{k}(v,t)-\boldsymbol{\kappa}(v,t)\}\,dv+\int_t^\infty \boldsymbol{\gamma}(v,t)\mathbf{y}(v,t)\,dv \\
&\quad +\int_t^\infty \boldsymbol{\delta}(v,t)\mathbf{c}(v,t)\,dv+\int_t^\infty \boldsymbol{\eta}(a,t)\left\{\bar{\mathbf{k}}(t)+\int_t^a \mathbf{q}(v,t)\,dv-\mathbf{k}(a,t)\right\}da
\end{aligned} \tag{5.9.11}$$

where $\boldsymbol{\lambda}(\cdot,t)$, $\boldsymbol{\mu}(\cdot,\cdot,t)$, $\boldsymbol{\alpha}(\cdot,t)$, $\boldsymbol{\gamma}(\cdot,t)$, $\boldsymbol{\delta}(\cdot,t)$, and $\boldsymbol{\eta}(\cdot,t)$ are vectors of Lagrange multiplier functions, $\beta(\cdot,t)$, and $\mu_0(\cdot,t)$ are scalar Lagrange multiplier functions, and $\mu_0^*(t)$ is a Lagrange multiplier. I have deliberately adopted a notation paralleling that used for firms, using the same symbols for the Lagrange multiplier functions corresponding to similar constraints in the two cases.

The first-order conditions for a maximum are (in addition to the constraints)[22]:

$$U_{\mathbf{c}(\theta,t)}(\mathbf{c}(\cdot,t))=\boldsymbol{\lambda}(\theta,t)-\boldsymbol{\delta}(\theta,t)+\mathbf{b}_z\int_t^{\theta}\boldsymbol{\mu}(\theta,a,t)\,da \quad \theta\geqslant t \tag{5.9.12}$$ [23]

$$\boldsymbol{\lambda}(v,t)+\int_t^{v}\boldsymbol{\mu}(v,a,t)\,da-\boldsymbol{\gamma}(v,t)$$
$$=\int_v^{\infty}\left\{\boldsymbol{\lambda}(\theta,t)+\int_t^{\theta}\boldsymbol{\mu}(\theta,a,t)\,da\right\}\boldsymbol{\phi}_{\mathbf{y}(v,t)}(\mathbf{y}(\cdot,t),\theta,t)\,d\theta \quad \theta\geqslant v\geqslant t \tag{5.9.13}$$

$$\boldsymbol{\lambda}(\theta,t)+\int_v^{\theta}\boldsymbol{\mu}(\theta,a,t)\,da=\beta(v,t)\mathbf{p}(\theta,v,t) \quad \theta\geqslant v\geqslant t \tag{5.9.14}$$

$$\beta(v,t)=\mu_0^*(t)+\int_v^{\infty}\mu_0(a,t)\,da \quad v\geqslant t \tag{5.9.15}$$

$$\beta(v,t)\mathbf{w}(v,t)=\int_v^{\infty}\boldsymbol{\eta}(a,t)\,da \quad v\geqslant t \tag{5.9.16}$$

and

$$\boldsymbol{\eta}(v,t)=\mathbf{d}(v,t)\left\{\mu_0^*(t)+\int_v^{\infty}\mu_0(a,t)\,da\right\}+\boldsymbol{\alpha}(v,t) \quad v\geqslant t \tag{5.9.17}$$

As discussed in Section 5.8, despite their complex appearance, these conditions have quite natural interpretations (which are rather richer than those for the firm). I begin with the ones which relate marginal utilities to prices.

Theorem 5.9.1. (A) If consumption is counted in the short constraints,

$$U_{\mathbf{c}(\theta,t)}\leqq\beta(t,t)\mathbf{p}(\theta,t,t) \tag{5.9.18}$$

with the equality holding for those commodities which the household plans actually to consume at θ.

[22] Differentiation is in the following order: $\mathbf{c},\mathbf{y},\mathbf{z},z_0,\mathbf{q}$, and $\mathbf{k}$.
[23] See footnote 15 above.

(B) If consumption is not counted in the short constraints,

$$U_{\mathbf{c}(\theta,t)} \leqq \beta(\theta,t)\mathbf{p}(\theta,\theta,t) \tag{5.9.19}$$

with the equality holding under the same conditions as before.

Proof. (A) In this case, $b_c=1$. Set $v=t$ in (5.9.14) and substitute the result into (5.9.12). The desired result now follows from the fact that $\delta(\theta,t)\geqq 0$ with equality holding for those commodities for which planned consumption is actually positive.

(B) In this case, $b_c=0$. Evaluate (5.9.14) at $v=\theta$ and substitute the result into (5.9.12). The desired result follows as before.

Note that (5.9.15) gives the interpretation of the factor of proportionality, $\beta(v,t)$. It is the opportunity cost of money at v, its full marginal utility in an optimal program.

Corollary 5.9.1. Consider two dates, v and v', with $t\leqslant v<v'$. Suppose that at no time in the interval $[v,v')$ is the money constraint binding. This implies that for any commodity which the household plans to consume at any date in that interval, the instantaneous marginal utility of consumption is proportional to the discounted price obtaining at the instant of consumption, with the *same* factor of proportionality holding at all such dates. (This is true regardless of whether or not consumption is counted in the short constraints.)

Proof. This follows from Theorem 5.9.1, equation (5.9.15) and the fact that $\mu_0(a,t)\geqq 0$ is the Lagrange multiplier associated with the money constraint at a.

A construct quite similar to $\beta(v,t)$ for households appeared in the theory of the firm as $J(v,t)$, defined in equation (5.6.15).[24] Indeed, using $\beta(v,t)$ in place of $J(v,t)$ in the proof of Theorem 5.6.1 above immediately yields:

Theorem 5.9.2.

$$\int_v^\infty \mathbf{p}(\theta,t,t)\phi_{\mathbf{y}(v,t)}\,d\theta \leqq \mathbf{p}(v,t,t) \tag{5.9.20}$$

with the equality holding for those commodities which the household actually plans to use as inputs to storage at v.

[24] The principal difference stems from the different units in which the objectives of the household and firms are measured. Note that the unit element in $J(v,t)$ comes from the fact that the firm maximizes profits; it corresponds to the element $\mu_0^*(t)$ in $\beta(v,t)$ coming from the imposition of the constraint that the household does not plan to hold money forever.

This proposition states that the household runs its storage activity exactly as if it were a profit-maximizing firm, valuing inputs and outputs as of the time when plans are made.

It is similarly easy to show that the household also acts as does the firm in its decisions about speculation on the commodity markets. The proofs of Theorems 5.6.2, 5.6.3, and 5.6.4 apply directly to the household, since the first-order condition for the firm (5.6.12) is exactly the same as the first-order condition for the household (5.9.14) with $\beta(v,t)$ and $J(v,t)$ playing the same role. Corollaries 5.6.1 and 5.6.2 also hold and the latter applies to goods held either for consumption or for storage inputs. I shall not restate all these results explicitly.

The speculative behavior of the household is richer than that of the firm, however, because the household is allowed to deal on the securities markets. I begin with the condition for holding shares and its relation to the shadow prices of money.

Theorem 5.9.3. (A) Suppose that the household plans to buy or to hold shares in the fth firm at some date $v \geqslant t$ and to hold such shares until some $v' > v$. Then

$$\beta(v,t)\mathbf{w}_f(v,t) = \int_v^{v'} \beta(a,t)\mathbf{d}_f(a,t)\,da + \beta(v',t)\mathbf{w}_f(v',t) \tag{5.9.21}$$

(B) Moreover, it is always the case that

$$\beta(v,t)\mathbf{w}(v,t) \geqq \int_v^{\infty} \beta(a,t)\mathbf{d}(a,t)\,da \tag{5.9.22}$$

with equality holding for those firms whose shares the household plans to hold forever.

Proof. (A) From (5.9.16),

$$\beta(v,t)\mathbf{w}(v,t) = \int_v^{\infty} \eta(a,t)\,da = \int_v^{v'} \eta(a,t)\,da + \int_{v'}^{\infty} \eta(a,t)\,da$$

$$= \int_v^{v'} \eta(a,t)\,da + \beta(v',t)\mathbf{w}(v',t) \tag{5.9.23}$$

Now substitute (5.9.15) into (5.9.17), evaluate the result at a rather than v, and substitute it in the integral on the far right-hand side of (5.9.23), obtaining:

$$\beta(v,t)\mathbf{w}(v,t) = \int_v^{v'} \{\beta(a,t)\mathbf{d}(a,t) + \alpha(a,t)\}\,da + \beta(v',t)\mathbf{w}(v',t) \tag{5.9.24}$$

The desired result now follows on observing that $\boldsymbol{\alpha}(a, t)$ is the vector of Lagrange multipliers for the short constraints on securities at a and is zero in its fth component for all a in the interval $[v, v')$.

(B) As before, substitute (5.9.15) into (5.9.17), evaluate the result at a and substitute it this time directly into (5.9.16). The desired result follows as before, since $\boldsymbol{\alpha}(a, t) \geqq 0$.

Turning to speculation in shares, the following result parallels Theorem 5.6.3 for speculation in commodities.

Theorem 5.9.4. Consider the household's investment in the shares of a particular firm, f, and a time, $v^* \geqslant t$. Define[25]:

$$n_f(v,t) \equiv \frac{\partial w_f(v,t)}{\partial v} + d_f(v,t)$$

(A) If $n_f(v^*,t)<0$, then the short constraint for shares of f is binding at v^*.

(B) If, at v^*, the money constraint is not binding, but the short constraint for shares of f is binding, then $n_f(v^*,t)<0$.

(C) If $n_f(v^*,t)>0$, then the money constraint is binding at v^*.

(D) If, at v^*, the short constraint for shares of f is not binding, but the money constraint is binding, then $n_f(v^*, t)>0$.

(E) If, at v^*, neither the short constraint for shares of f nor the money constraint is binding, then $n_f(v^*,t)=0$.

Proof. Differentiate (5.9.24) with respect to v and rearrange terms, obtaining[26]:

$$n_f(v,t) = \frac{w_f(v,t)\mu_0(v,t) - \alpha_f(v,t)}{\beta(v,t)} \tag{5.9.25}$$

The desired results now follow from the nonnegativity of the Lagrange multipliers.

These results are most easily interpreted by considering what it means for n_f to be zero. Ownership of a share of stock is ownership of a future dividend stream. Hence, the natural zero for the rate of change of the stock price is for that price to decrease at precisely the rate at which dividends are paid out. Indeed, the instantaneous rate of return on stock held at v is not the rate of price increase alone, but rather $n_f(v,t)/w_f(v,t)$.

This magnitude also turns out to be the natural one for the parallel to Theorem (5.6.2) when shares are involved, which is

[25] $d_f(v,t)$ is the component of $\mathbf{d}(v,t)$ corresponding to firm f.

[26] Note the parallel to (5.6.19).

Theorem 5.9.5. Consider the shares of two firms, f and f', a commodity, i, with date θ, and a time v^*, $t \leqslant v^* < \theta$.

(A) If, at $v = v^*$, $\partial \log p_i(\theta, v, t)/\partial v < n_f(v^*, t)/w_f(v^*, t)$, then the short constraint for (i, θ) is binding at v^*. Conversely, if the short constraint for (i, θ) is binding at v^* but that for the shares of firm f is not, then the inequality just given must hold.

(B) If, at $v = v^*$, $\partial \log p_i(\theta, v, t)/\partial v > n_f(v^*, t)/w_f(v^*, t)$, then the short constraint for shares of f is binding at v^*. Conversely, if the short constraint for shares of f is binding at v^* but that for (i, θ) is not, then the inequality just given must hold.

(C) If $n_f(v^*, t)/w_f(v^*, t) < n_{f'}(v^*, t)/w_{f'}(v^*, t)$, then the short constraint for shares of f is binding at v^*. Conversely, if the short constraint for shares of f is binding at v^* but that for f' is not, the inequality just given must hold.

Proof. These results all follow from (5.9.25) and (5.6.19) with $\beta(v, t)$ replacing $J(v, t)$ in the latter equation. The details are left to the reader.

CHAPTER 6

Transaction difficulties, individual price offers, and monopoly power

6.1 Introduction

The analysis of the previous chapter proceeded as though agents always expect to be able to complete their planned transactions with no difficulty. This is hardly a reasonable assumption in a disequilibrium model where agents constantly find their plans thwarted. Further, given the absence of any subjective uncertainty, the fact that transactions of all sizes are assumed to be costlessly made leads the otherwise very sensible speculation results of the previous chapter to be of the "bang-bang" sort: agents rush discontinuously from one arbitrage opportunity to another, switching from buying to selling large amounts in pursuit of even very small speculative profits. It is plainly time to deal with such matters.

In fact, there is more than one matter to deal with here; there are three, and they are related in somewhat different ways.

The first issue is the analysis of transaction costs, that is, difficulties in transacting that prevent the "bang-bang" property just described from arising. Such costs may be thought of either as effort which must be expended in the search for trading partners or as a partial substitute for the effects of subjective uncertainty, which is otherwise conspicuously absent from the model. As we shall see, incorporating this kind of transaction difficulty into the analysis is easy to do; it has some interesting consequences, but it raises no very deep problems.

The situation is quite different with regard to the second issue with which we shall deal in this chapter. This issue involves the case in which agents regard themselves as absolutely limited in the amounts they can buy or sell at given prices. This case has received a great deal of attention in the literature under the name of "quantity constraints," with most of the discussion centering about the existence of nontrivial quantity-constrained, fixed-price equilibria.[1] I shall refer to it as the case of "transaction constraints" to avoid any danger of confusing the constraints with the short constraints on quantities already introduced.

Now, transaction constraints and transaction costs are formally related. One way of looking at transaction constraints is as transaction costs that go from zero to infinity at a particular size of transaction (or from a continuous function to infinity if transaction costs are also present). It is not surprising, therefore, to find some formal similarity in the way in which these two cases affect the theory of the individual agent, with the shadow prices of the transaction constraints entering in the same way as the derivatives of transaction costs properly interpreted. However, the resemblance ends here; the problems presented by transaction constraints are far deeper than those presented by transaction costs.

At one level, those problems are easy to state. They can be summarized in the question: When are transaction constraints binding? In particular, will such constraints be binding in equilibrium? This is a matter of substantial importance, since its answer determines whether or not equilibrium will be Walrasian in the sense that it is supported by prices.[2]

At a deeper level, these issues can be described as the question: Why should such perceived constraints *ever* be binding at all? Agents may in fact be unable to complete their transactions – this is a fundamental aspect of disequilibrium – but if they *expect* this to happen at given prices one might suppose that they would attempt to get round their transaction constraints by offering more attractive prices to potential trading partners.

This brings us to the third subject dealt with in this chapter, the question of individual price offers. It turns out to be possible to incorporate such offers into the analysis in great generality, thus laying to rest the hoary tradition of having prices adjusted in the direction of corresponding aggregate excess demands by a fictitious auctioneer. However, the very generality of the treatment – some of which emerges in later chapters – leaves an unsatisfying void. We can deal with individual price offers in disequilibrium under general assumptions, but we lack any precise theory as to how such offers get made. This is a matter of central importance to economic theory, for the adjustment path of the system

[1] Drazen (1980) presents a survey of the very extensive literature on this subject.

[2] As briefly discussed later, the importance of this question is somewhat diminished if there are also smooth transaction costs, since Walrasian equilibria are not generally also Pareto-optimal in that case.

and the time it takes to get to equilibrium (if it gets there at all) depend on how prices move.

In terms of the matters studied in the present chapter, the way in which price offers get made affects the nature of the equilibrium itself. As already mentioned, in this model the answer to the question of whether or not transaction constraints are binding in equilibrium determines whether or not that equilibrium will be in any sense Walrasian. We now see that this is the question of whether individual price offers will prevent such constraints from being binding in equilibrium. A little thought suggests that agents will only refrain from making price offers to get round transaction constraints if the demand or supply curves they perceive as facing them are such as to make it optimal to refrain from doing so.[3] The question of whether the system reaches a fixed-price, transaction-constrained equilibrium on the one hand or a competitive one on the other thus becomes the question as to whether perceived monopoly power disappears in the limit. If such monopoly power reflects the usual sources of monopoly, this is easy to answer. If it reflects the informational problems connected with disequilibrium, it is not easy to answer at all.

6.2 Smooth transaction costs

I begin, however, with the analysis of the easiest of these matters, the introduction of smooth transaction costs. As already indicated, the presence of such costs can be thought of in more than one way. One can consider such costs as simply reflecting the effort required to find trading partners or as simply a substitute for subjective uncertainty. It is not very helpful, however, to consider them as price premia which must be paid to induce others to transact; dealing with transaction difficulties in this way is done later on.

Accordingly, since it would be overly complex to set up an explicit transaction technology in an already very complicated model, I assume that smooth transaction costs take the form of expenditure of effort rather than of money. In the case of the firm, this can be represented by thinking of transaction costs as a subtraction from output as resources are diverted from production to the effecting of transactions. In the case

[3] One must be careful here, however. This statement (and the analysis below) assumes that agents act in their own narrowly defined self-interest and take no account of repercussions. Thus, prices may not be lowered to ease a transaction constraint, not because the agent is at a monopoly optimum given the prices of others, but because of oligopoly reactions. Workers or businessmen may not lower their wages or prices in hard times, because they view such actions as socially repugnant. Such matters are outside the scope of this analysis, however.

of the household, similar treatment involves a subtraction from the output of the household's storage activity; since the household's endowment is represented as such an output, this can be thought of as the expenditure of endowment - labor, in particular - to effect transactions. Alternatively, in the case of the household we can represent transaction costs as direct subtractions from utility, which makes them closer to a substitute for risk premia than does treating them as subtractions from output.

Whether transaction costs are treated as substitutes for risk premia or as expenditure of effort, however, it is tempting to treat them as continuous with marginal transaction costs increasing in the size of the transaction involved. I shall do so, but this is not a trivial assumption and is doubtless an unrealistic one. The placing of advertisements or the opening of a shop involves increasing returns to such activities at small transaction sizes. These are among the reasons that such activities are undertaken. However, I rule such possibilities out, although a proper treatment of the technology of transactions would certainly have to include them. Once this is done, the "bang-bang" nature of the results of the previous chapter can be assumed to disappear and optimal programs assumed appropriately smooth in the variables which agents take as given.

The exact way in which this happens is of interest. I give the discussion explicitly only for households. The results for the firm are the same as those for the household in the case in which transaction costs are treated as a subtraction from output. Since the theorems on optimal production for the firm are the same as the theorems on optimal storage activity for the household and the theorems on arbitrage in commodities and money are the same in both cases there is no need for separate treatments.

Consider first the case in which smooth transaction costs enter the utility of the household. In this case, all the results in the theory of the household of the previous chapter remain unaffected save that all money prices are altered by subtracting from them terms reflecting the marginal disutilities of the corresponding transactions translated into money terms by the appropriate marginal utility (opportunity cost) of money. Similarly, in the case in which transaction costs enter as subtractions from output, all prices must be corrected by subtracting terms reflecting the negative marginal products of the corresponding transactions converted into appropriate money equivalents. In either version, call the altered money prices "virtual prices"; all previous theorems then hold with virtual prices replacing money ones.

Some of the resulting interpretations deserve comment. First, it is no longer true that the marginal utility of planned consumption is proportional to money price; rather the marginal utility of planned consumption must offset its marginal cost both in terms of money price and in terms of transaction costs. This does not mean, however, that marginal utility must be greater than the shadow price of the good calculated using only the opportunity cost of money as in Chapter 5. If the optimal plan calls for selling rather than buying the good in question, then consumption means a *saving* of transaction costs.

In either case, the marginal transaction costs involved are those that correspond to the date of the money price involved; as we saw in the previous chapter that date is either the planning date t or the consumption date depending on how the short constraints are interpreted. These remain the relevant dates for valuing marginal transaction costs even if they are not the dates at which the optimal plan calls for transactions. As in the case of money prices, it is virtual prices at these relevant dates that reflect the true opportunity costs of consumption. Note that, in the case in which the relevant date is the consumption date, this means that marginal transaction costs are to be evaluated at zero transactions if planned consumption takes place entirely out of stocks already acquired. In the case in which the relevant date is the planning date, marginal transaction costs will be similarly evaluated at zero transactions if the optimal program calls for acquisition (or sale) at some other date. In both cases, the transaction costs of acquisition at some different date play no direct role; while such costs do help to determine when the optimal acquisition date is and may spread acquisition over different dates, they are sunk costs so far as the determination to consume rather than sell is concerned.

A similar result holds when considering the household's optimal operation of its storage activities or the firm's optimal production decisions. Here the marginal cost of an input and the marginal revenues received from the resulting outputs must be evaluated taking account of the effects on transaction costs involved. These transaction costs will be those of the planning time since it is transactions at that time which would just offset planned input use or output production even if actual input purchases or output sales are planned for some other time.

Transaction costs do, of course, affect the timing of transactions. This is readily seen by considering the effects of such costs on the results as to arbitrage. Previously, for example, we found that agents would not plan to hold any commodity whose discounted money price was expected to fall. Now that result becomes one in terms of virtual prices, so that transaction costs can prevent its being worthwhile selling all one can of a particular commodity even though its discounted money price is expected to fall. Similarly, the theorem that, with prices measured to take account of the shadow price of money, agents will buy, hold, and sell so that marginal revenue equals marginal acquisition cost is no longer true. Now agents will buy, hold, and sell not when the rise in discounted money price is expected to offset the decrease in the shadow price of money but when in addition it is sufficient to offset the transaction costs accompanying the purchase and sale.

One particular implication of this last result deserves special mention. Previously it was the case that commodities purchased and held for use as inputs (into storage or production) had to have constant shadow prices. This meant that if their discounted prices were expected to be constant and there was a profitable use for money beyond investment in instantaneous bonds, such inputs would not be purchased in advance but only at the last instant. Now this is changed, since it is no longer shadow prices which must be constant for the holding of commodities but shadow prices adjusted for transaction costs. This will generally not make it optimal to plan to acquire needed inputs at the last minute. Instead, the presence of transaction costs will generally spread such planned transactions over time. Note that such spreading will be true of other transactions as well, including the clearing of short positions.[4]

Now, since smooth transaction costs will generally spread the times of acquisition and sale, they can cause transactions to occur at times and money prices at which those transactions would not otherwise take place. It is worth noting, however, that there is a sense in which *smooth* transaction costs cannot prevent otherwise profitable arbitrage transactions from taking place at the times and prices that would have obtained in the absence of such costs, although smooth transaction costs can reduce the size of such a transaction, spreading it out to surrounding dates and prices. To see this, suppose that a particular set of arbitrage transactions would be profitable in the absence of smooth transaction costs *pertaining to those transactions.*[5] This means that such transactions would take place if virtual prices and money prices coincided for them. We know from the results of Chapter 5 on arbitrage that the transactions in question would not be small; they would proceed until stopped by a constraint. Now, since transaction costs are certainly zero if no transactions take place, virtual prices and money prices would coincide if the transactions in question were zero. Hence, if such transactions were zero it would be profitable to plan to engage in them, and it follows that the optimal plan for the agent is to do so until the effect of transaction costs on virtual prices makes it no longer profitable at the margin (assuming that

[4] It is simplest to continue the assumption that the government stands ready to deal in bonds of very short maturity and that there are never any transaction costs or transaction constraints in trading in such bonds.

[5] Transaction costs on other transactions can make the given set of transactions profitable; such "other" transaction costs are held constant in this discussion.

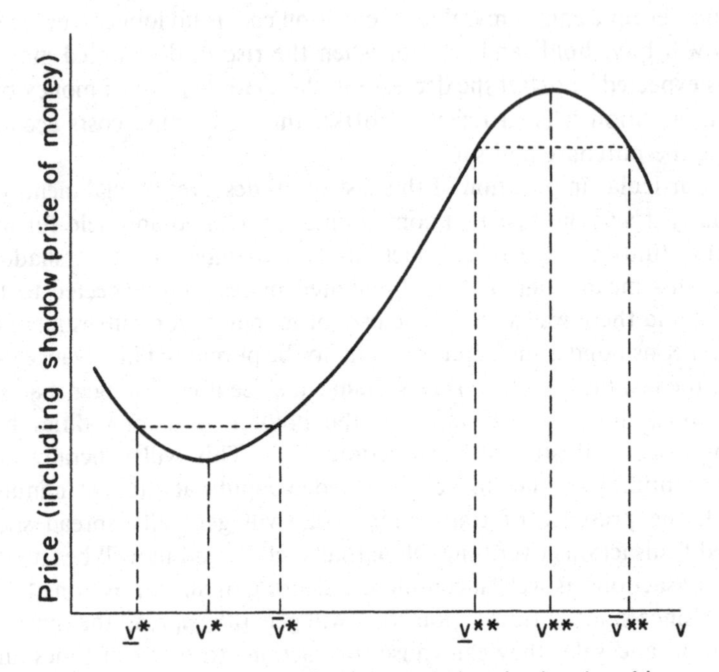

Figure 6.2.1. Discounted money and virtual prices in arbitrage.

constraints do not operate earlier.) Note that the continuity of transaction costs in transaction size is required here.

A picture may help to illustrate the effects of smooth transaction costs on the timing of transactions. Figure 6.2.1 depicts expected prices for some commodity as a function of future time. Since decisions are made taking the opportunity cost of money into account, the prices in question (discounted money prices or virtual prices) are measured in terms of that opportunity cost. Thus, for example, a flat segment of the curve for discounted money price does not correspond to a constant discounted price in money terms but to a discounted price which rises at a rate just sufficient to offset the fall in the shadow price of money which comes from the passing of opportunities. Over an interval in which the money constraint is not binding this would correspond to a constant discounted money price, but not otherwise. A similar statement holds for the depicting of virtual prices. The vertical axis is in utility units, not dollars.

Assume that the arbitrage opportunity reflected in the figure is the most attractive available over the relevant time interval. Discounted money price is represented by the solid curve. Without transaction costs, all purchases would be planned for v^* where discounted money price is lowest and all sales planned for v^{**} where discounted money price

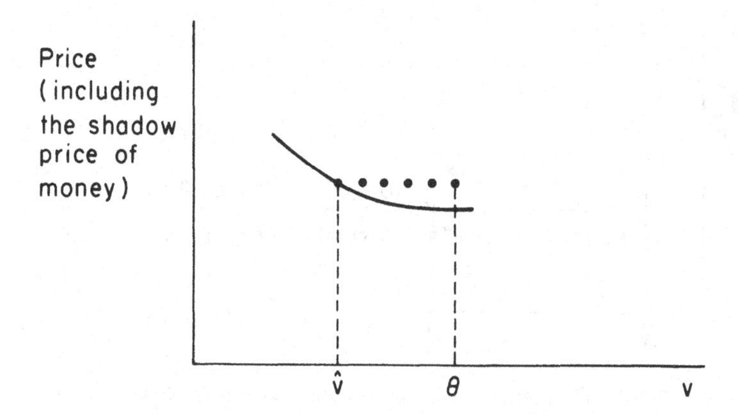

Figure 6.2.2. Discounted money and virtual prices for input purchase.

is highest.[6] When smooth transaction costs are present, the situation changes, for a policy of purchasing only at v^* would raise virtual price at v^* above that at surrounding points. Similarly, a policy of selling only at v^{**} would depress virtual price at v^{**} below that at surrounding points. Instead, the optimal policy involves spreading out purchases around v^*, say, on the interval $[\underline{v}^*, \bar{v}^*]$ and spreading out sales on an interval $[\underline{v}^{**}, \bar{v}^{**}]$ around v^{**}. (v^* and v^{**} need not be the midpoints of their respective intervals.)

The resulting effect on virtual prices is indicated by the dotted line segment. Before $\underline{v}^*$, where no transactions are planned, there are no transaction costs, and virtual price coincides with discounted shadow money price. Transactions begin at $\underline{v}^*$ and continue until $\bar{v}^*$ in such a way as to make virtual price, including the shadow price of money, a constant over that interval - that is, to make virtual price in dollars rise so as just to offset the decline in the shadow price of money. Between $\bar{v}^*$, where purchases end, and $\underline{v}^{**}$, where sales begin, virtual price again coincides with discounted shadow money price. Sales begin at $\underline{v}^{**}$ and continue to $\bar{v}^{**}$, with virtual price, including the shadow price of money, constant over that interval. Beyond $\bar{v}^{**}$, transactions cease and virtual price once more coincides with discounted shadow money price. Note that transactions do take place at both v^* and v^{**}, the points at which all transactions would be concentrated in the absence of transaction costs.

Similar diagrams illustrate cases in which a good is to be purchased for use as an input (either to consumption or for storage or production). In Figure 6.2.2, suppose that the agent plans to purchase a θ-dated good for

[6] Note that since the shadow price of money never increases (additional money earlier is never worth less than additional money later), the fact that discounted

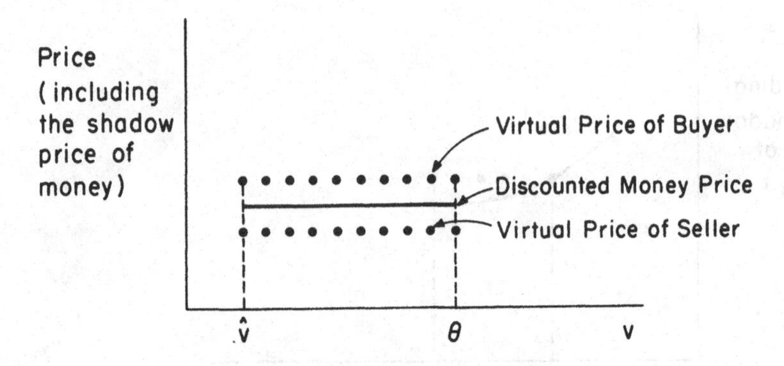

Figure 6.2.3. Discounted money and virtual prices for purchase and sale (Walrasian equilibrium).

use at θ. If his expectations as to discounted money price (including the shadow price of money) are as depicted by the solid curve, then, in the absence of transaction costs he will plan to buy only at θ. With smooth transaction costs, he plans to begin purchasing before that date, say, at $\hat{v}$, with constant virtual price (including the shadow price of money) above the corresponding discounted shadow money price from $\hat{v}$ to θ.

Finally, Figure 6.2.3 illustrates a case where both buyer and seller believe the discounted money price of a θ-dated good will be constant from $\hat{v}$ to θ. Again, this is the discounted money price including the shadow price of money, which may be different for the two agents. The situation depicted is not pathological, however. We shall see in the next chapter that constancy of actual and expected discounted money prices occurs in equilibrium and that money constraints are never binding (at finite times) in *Walrasian* equilibrium. Hence the solid line segment in Figure 6.2.3 can be taken to represent actual and expected discounted money prices for both the seller of an output *and* the buyer of that output in a Walrasian equilibrium with prices represented *either* in utility terms *or* in dollars.

Now, if there were no transaction costs, both agents would be indifferent as to the timing of their transactions over the interval shown. With smooth transaction costs, this is not the case; they will time their transactions so as to have constant virtual prices. The virtual price as seen by the buyer will be greater than discounted money price; that as seen by the seller will be less than discounted money price.

We thus see that the effect of introducing smooth transaction costs is

price is increasing from v^* to v^{**} is true whether or not the shadow price of money is taken into account.

quite helpful, so far. (Indeed, it may be thought that we have obtained quite a lot for a somewhat ad hoc assumption, which is an inadequate substitute for dealing with the real complexities of a transaction technology or of subjective uncertainty and risk aversion which would generate similar effects.) That the introduction of smooth transaction costs does not hurt is also apparent when we consider another aspect rather different from those already treated - the effect of smooth transaction costs on the nature of equilibrium.

As we have seen, when smooth transaction costs are introduced, virtual prices replace money ones in the theory of the individual agent. A fundamental property of Walrasian equilibrium, however, is the role played by market prices. It is market, not virtual, prices that support such an equilibrium. As we shall now see, there is a sense in which the introduction of smooth transaction costs does not change this, such difficulties being reserved for the case of transaction constraints considered below.

To see this, consider the household and the case in which transaction costs are in utility terms. Not surprisingly, it will turn out that, in equilibrium, the household expects constant discounted money prices for all its transactions, that is, it expects the current prices to rise at the (possibly varying) discount rate. Now consider the question of the optimal transaction path which the household plans to take to get from its current holdings to its desired consumption. In general, the choice of such a path involves two sets of considerations, the transaction costs in terms of utility loss and the discounted money cost of the transactions themselves. In equilibrium, however, the discounted money cost of *any* transaction path leading from current holdings to desired consumption will be the same, and this will be true independent of the particular values at which discounted money prices are expected to be constant. Hence, in equilibrium, the choice of an optimal transaction path will be independent of direct monetary considerations and will depend only on the utility lost to transaction costs.

Thus, in considering equilibria, we can take the optimal transaction path and its associated transaction costs as depending only on the household's current position and its desired consumption plan. Hence we can take utility as also depending only on these things. Since current positions are already determined, it is possible to show that we can treat the household in equilibrium as maximizing a "concentrated utility functional" in which transactions and transaction costs do not appear explicitly, their effects having already been taken into account. It turns out to be such concentrated utility maximization which will be supported by equilibrium money prices. At equilibrium, for example, marginal utility of consumption will be once more proportional to discounted money price, but such marginal utilities will include the disutility involved in getting to the consumption stream.[7]

The case in which transaction costs are treated as subtractions from output is handled similarly. Given an initial position of holdings, the discounted direct cost of every transaction path that leads to a particular program of inputs and outputs is the same in equilibrium and this is true independent of the constant level of discounted prices. Hence the optimal choice of such a transaction path depends only on initial holdings and the input and output plan to be achieved. With initial holdings given, we can absorb such dependence by substituting for transactions in the storage functional of the household or the production functional of the firm, obtaining a "concentrated" storage or production functional. The usual properties of equilibrium then apply to these so that, for example, it is true in discounted money prices rather than in virtual prices that marginal revenue product equals factor price, since the transaction effects have been absorbed into the definition of marginal product.

Note that such a treatment is not possible when discounted prices are expected to change. Note also that even though equilibria are supported by market prices in the sense described and can thus be called "Walrasian," they are not Pareto-optimal in any simple sense. This is because the initial endowments could have been distributed to avoid the losses due to transaction costs. I do not explore such matters further.

6.3* Smooth transaction costs: Formal treatment

I now briefly give the formal analysis corresponding to the previous discussion. Note that the notation of this section differs from that elsewhere in the book. In this section I give smooth transaction costs an explicit representation in utility, storage, and production functionals. Since it is burdensome to carry that notation explicitly throughout, I do not do so later in the book, although the presence of such smooth transaction costs is implicitly assumed henceforth.

The reason for that assumption has already been indicated. It is a matter of considerable technical convenience to be able to assume that the optimizing behavior of agents is unique and continuous in the prices.[8]

[7] The fact that utility so considered depends on the household's current holdings is not materially different from the general proposition that it depends on the household's past consumption history.

[8] Assuming continuity rather than upper semicontinuity in the prices (and hence strict quasi-concavity rather than just quasi-concavity in transaction costs) is largely a matter of convenience. Mostly what is needed is the existence of a solution to the differential equations of the system [and, for some purposes, the

I begin with the case in which transaction costs enter the household's utility functional. Expand the arguments of that utility functional so that it becomes $U(\mathbf{c}(\cdot, t), \mathbf{z}(\cdot, \cdot, t), \mathbf{q}(\cdot, t))$. I shall assume that this is strictly quasi-concave,[9] and Fréchet differentiable in all arguments. With regard to the Fréchet derivatives with respect to transactions, I shall assume

$$U_{z_i(\theta, v, t)} z_i(\theta, v, t) \leqslant 0; \quad U_{q_f(v, t)} q_f(v, t) \leqslant 0 \qquad (6.3.1)^{10}$$

It is easy to see what the introduction of transaction costs in this way does to the optimizing behavior of the household. Basically, transaction costs get added to the costs of buying and selling and must now be taken into account. More specifically, the first-order conditions which are affected are (5.9.14) and (5.9.16). The former equation has a term of $U_{\mathbf{z}(\theta, v, t)}$ subtracted from its right-hand side; the latter one has a term of $U_{\mathbf{q}(v, t)}$ subtracted from its left-hand side. Define

$$\mathbf{p}'(\theta, v, t) \equiv \mathbf{p}(\theta, v, t) - \frac{U_{\mathbf{z}(\theta, v, t)}}{\beta(v, t)} \qquad (6.3.2)$$

$$\mathbf{w}'(v, t) \equiv \mathbf{w}(v, t) - \frac{U_{\mathbf{q}(v, t)}}{\beta(v, t)} \qquad (6.3.3)$$

Then $\mathbf{p}'(\theta, v, t)$ and $\mathbf{w}'(v, t)$ are the "virtual prices," which include the monetary equivalent of the marginal transaction disutilities. Thus the first-order conditions for the household which are used in deriving the theorems of the household theory of the preceding chapter remain the same with the exception of the substitution of virtual prices for discounted money prices. It follows that those theorems continue to hold with these virtual prices replacing the actual ones.

The case is similar if transaction costs are treated as subtractions from output. I give the analysis explicitly only for the household, the case for the firm being essentially the same. Expand the arguments of the household's storage functional so that it becomes $\boldsymbol{\phi}(\mathbf{y}(\cdot, t), \mathbf{z}(\cdot, \cdot, t), \mathbf{q}(\cdot, t), \theta, t)$ with the obvious assumption that transactions at any one time cannot

continuity of that solution in the initial conditions (Champsaur, Drèze, and Henry, 1977)]. Note that, at least with transaction costs added (and to some extent without them), constant returns technologies can be accomodated (although the optimal storage plans of households may not be unique if such costs affect utility rather than the storage activity itself). A strengthening of the uniqueness assumption is required in a later chapter to ensure convergence to a point rather than to a set of equally optimal programs.

[9] This is where the absence of increasing returns in the technology of transactions is assumed. When transaction costs are treated as subtractions from output, that assumption is implicit in the assumption of concavity of the storage (production) functional.

[10] See footnote 15 of Chapter 5.

affect earlier outputs. Assume that this is concave and Fréchet differentiable in all arguments, with the equivalent of (6.3.1) holding when U is replaced by ϕ. In this case, virtual prices become:

$$\mathbf{p}'(\theta, v, t) \equiv \mathbf{p}(\theta, v, t) - \frac{\int_v^\infty \{\lambda(\theta, t) + \int_t^\theta \mu(\theta, a, t)\, da\} \phi_{\mathbf{z}(\theta, v, t)}\, d\theta}{\beta(v, t)} \tag{6.3.4}$$

and

$$\mathbf{w}'(v, t) \equiv \mathbf{w}(v, t) - \frac{\int_v^\infty \{\lambda(\theta, t) + \int_t^\theta \mu(\theta, a, t)\, da\} \phi_{\mathbf{q}(v, t)}\, d\theta}{\beta(v, t)} \tag{6.3.5}$$

and the first-order conditions for the household hold as before with such virtual prices replacing the corresponding discounted money ones. (The complex nature of the virtual prices in (6.3.4) and (6.3.5) stems from the fact that marginal effects on outputs affect the short constraints from t forward as discussed in Chapter 5.)

There is only one other point in the previous section which requires explicit formal discussion. This concerns the use of a "concentrated" utility, storage, or production functional in dealing with equilibrium. Indeed, the only point that needs further elaboration concerns the case in which smooth transaction costs enter the utility functional, since we had better show that the "concentrated" utility functional derived is strictly quasi-concave. This is easy to do. For any set of constant discounted prices, let

$$\mathbf{z}(\cdot, \cdot, t) = \mathbf{F}(\mathbf{c}(\cdot, t)); \quad \mathbf{q}(\cdot, t) = \mathbf{G}(\mathbf{c}(\cdot, t)) \tag{6.3.6}$$

be the utility maximizing transaction paths where dependence on current holdings has been suppressed. Define the "concentrated utility functional," $V(\mathbf{c}(\cdot, t))$ as the functional obtained when (6.3.6) is substituted into $U(\cdot, \cdot, \cdot)$. It is obvious that (still at equilibrium), the household acts to maximize $V(\cdot)$ given the prices (and the various constraints).

Lemma 6.3.1. The concentrated utility functional $V(\cdot)$ is strictly quasi-concave.

Proof. Choose any scalar a with $0<a<1$ and let $\mathbf{c}(\cdot, t)$ and $\mathbf{c}'(\cdot, t)$ be any two different consumption programs with $V(\mathbf{c}) = V(\mathbf{c}')$.[11] Let $\mathbf{c}'' = a\mathbf{c} + (1-a)\mathbf{c}'$. Let $\mathbf{z} = \mathbf{F}(\mathbf{c})$, $\mathbf{z}' = \mathbf{F}(\mathbf{c}')$, $\mathbf{z}'' = \mathbf{F}(\mathbf{c}'')$ and similarly for $\mathbf{q}$, $\mathbf{q}'$, and $\mathbf{q}''$. Then

$$V(\mathbf{c}'') = U(\mathbf{c}'', \mathbf{z}'', \mathbf{q}'') \geqslant U(\mathbf{c}'', a\mathbf{z} + (1-a)\mathbf{z}', a\mathbf{q} + (1-a)\mathbf{q}')$$
$$> U(\mathbf{c}, \mathbf{z}, \mathbf{q}) = V(\mathbf{c}) \tag{6.3.7}$$

[11] I omit the arguments of $\mathbf{c}(\cdot, t)$ where they are merely burdensome.

where the first inequality follows because $(\mathbf{z}'', \mathbf{q}'')$ is the utility-maximizing transactions path with which to achieve $\mathbf{c}''$ while that consumption program can certainly be achieved by using the transactions path given by $(a\mathbf{z}+(1-a)\mathbf{z}', a\mathbf{q}+(1-a)\mathbf{q}')$. The second inequality follows because $U(\mathbf{c}, \mathbf{z}, \mathbf{q})$ is strictly quasi-concave.

I now drop the explicit transactions arguments from the utility functional although I shall interpret later results to include them and shall assume them present, so that uniqueness and smooth behavior of optimal solutions is maintained as already discussed.

6.4 Transaction constraints and individual price offers

I now turn to the deeper questions involved when agents perceive themselves as unable to complete all their desired transactions regardless of the effort they expend. Of course, for this to make sense, it must mean that agents see themselves as constrained *at given prices*; hence this subject has received much attention in terms of "fixed-price equilibria." Hence, we shall also have to deal with the relations of such transaction constraints to prices.

At first, however, the theory of perceived transaction constraints presents no very great difficulty. If agents perceive such constraints they will take them into account in their optimizing problems. This means that the shadow prices of those constraints will enter the first-order conditions for optimizing behavior. Such entry is of a rather natural sort. The shadow prices of transaction constraints play a role isomorphic to that played by the marginal effects of transactions on smooth transaction costs in our earlier analysis. Indeed, if we adjust the discounted money price of any transaction by a term incorporating the money equivalent of the shadow price of the corresponding transaction constraint, we find, as in the case of smooth transaction costs, that all earlier theorems hold with the resulting "virtual prices" replacing discounted money ones. This is a natural result and will be important later on.

The resemblance to the case of smooth transaction costs and the easy incorporation of transaction constraints into the theory ends here, however. In particular, where smooth transaction costs could be substituted away at equilibrium, and equilibrium thus remain in some sense Walrasian in the presence of such costs, this is certainly not the case with transaction constraints. If such constraints remain binding in equilibrium, the nature of that equilibrium is fundamentally different from the case in which they are not so binding.

This is a relatively deep question. Before approaching it directly, there is one matter which should be disposed of. It is a trivial sort of fixed-price equilibrium which occurs because nobody believes he can transact *anything* and hence does not try. We shall assume this does not happen. Whether more generally it is appropriate to assume that not both buyers *and* sellers of a particular commodity at a particular moment in time perceive themselves as encountering binding transaction constraints is a more delicate matter. In the fixed-price literature it is customary to make this assumption and to refer to it as one of "orderly markets," referring to the Hahn Process assumption that there are not both unsatisfied buyers and unsatisfied sellers at the same time. The Hahn Process-Orderly Markets assumption, however, is *not* the same as the assumption that transaction constraints are not simultaneously binding for both buyers and sellers. Such constraints are *perceived* constraints; they are the constraints that agents take into account in forming their plans. The Orderly Markets assumption, on the other hand, has to do with what happens *when agents attempt to realize those plans.* This is not the same thing. It may or may not be reasonable to suppose that in a world of orderly markets agents realize that only one side will be constrained; it is quite another to suppose that they always know in advance which side that is. Out of equilibrium, such a supposition seems particularly unwarranted.

I return in later chapters to the formulation of the Hahn Process-Orderly Markets assumption for an economy with individual prices. Here I merely observe that such an assumption is not much help in considering the question of whether perceived transaction constraints are found binding by agents *before* transactions are attempted.

Indeed, even if we could assume that transaction constraints will not be binding on both sides of a market, this would not tell us whether they will be binding on one. There are two possible approaches to this problem (which we can formally absorb into one). The first approach is to assume that agents take transaction constraints as exogenously given bounds which they cannot affect through their own actions. In this interpretation, agents can be wrong about transaction constraints and they can change their view of where the constraints lie as time and experience progress, but they cannot deliberately attempt to get around the constraints.[12]

The other, more appealing view is that agents see transaction constraints as operating at given prices. An agent who believes that he is unable to sell as much as he would like at a high price can attempt to sell more by offering a lower price and moving to a lower point on the demand curve he perceives as facing him, and similarly for buyers and supply curves. (The case of immutable perceived constraints is the case of

[12] Since there is no subjective uncertainty, agents will never deliberately test a constraint to see if it is binding.

perceived demand and supply curves all perfectly inelastic.) Plainly, it is impossible to deal with such natural behavior while maintaining the inconvenient fiction of the Walrasian auctioneer who moves prices in the direction of excess demands. Hence we must drop that fiction, jettisoning the impersonal price-adjustment assumption (2.2.1) which has dogged the stability literature since the days of tâtonnement.

This turns out to be easy to do in the context of the present model whose driving feature, as explained in Chapter 4, is the assumption of No Favorable Surprise. As we shall see in Chapter 8, the fact that we wish to prove that the model is stable given no new favorable opportunities permits us a very general view of individual price adjustment; in particular, agents who perceive transaction constraints to be worse than they had previously supposed can register that fact either by reducing the size of their planned transactions or by revising their plans so that those transactions are expected to take place at less favorable prices than had earlier been anticipated. For the present, I wish to concentrate on the question of the relation of price offers to transaction constraints and the incorporation of individual prices into the analysis as so far developed.

Interestingly enough, individual price offers can readily be incorporated into the analysis of the preceding chapter despite the fact that agents, in that analysis, take prices as given. To do this, put aside for the moment the fact that agents are attempting to influence their transaction constraints by price offers and consider the mechanics of adapting the analysis so far given.

In the first place, agents planning for the future do so with expected prices. Those prices are already individualized. To individualize prices, therefore, we must consider the past and the present. This is easy to do. We drop the convention that agents encounter the same actual prices for the same commodity - that property may hold in equilibrium, but it can hardly be expected to hold out of it if agents make their own price offers. Instead, we individualize the actual prices encountered by agents. The actual prices relevant for any given agent are the ones at which that agent traded (or offered to trade). They need not have been the same for all agents.

Whether or not prices for the same commodity are the same in equilibrium depends largely on how one extends the view that markets are orderly. This is done in Chapter 8. Here we are concerned with the question of how the effect of price on transaction constraints is taken into account by agents; that is, we must now consider the fact that agents will *not* take their own prices as given.

To fix ideas, consider a selling agent who believes he faces a transaction constraint at a given price. This means that such an agent perceives the demand he faces at that price to be limited. Ignore for the moment the fact that such an agent can change his price. As already explained, the effect of introducing the transaction constraint in the agent's optimal program is to alter the discounted money price of the good to be sold by subtracting from it the shadow price of the constraint, obtaining a new "virtual price." If we assume, for simplicity, that there are no transaction constraints on the agent's acquisition of the good, optimal behavior requires that this virtual price equal marginal cost.[13]

When we consider how the agent sets his selling price, however, this optimizing condition turns out to have a very familiar interpretation. The shadow price of the transaction constraint is the amount which the seller would just be willing to give up in order to be able to sell an additional unit. If the seller lowers his price by an amount Δp in order to sell such an additional unit, he will in fact have to give up an amount of revenue equal to Δp times the sales he would otherwise have made.[14] If this amount is less than the shadow price of the perceived constraint, it will be worth lowering the price; if it is greater, it will be worth raising the price. Hence, price will be set so that the shadow price of the constraint just equals the amount described - the difference between price and marginal revenue. When this is done, the optimizing condition that virtual price (price less constraint shadow price) equal marginal cost is seen to be the familiar monopoly condition that marginal revenue equal marginal cost. When prices are optimally set to take account of their perceived effects on transaction constraints, the agent acts on his perceived demand curve to take advantage of his perceived monopoly power. At the price he sets the position of the perceived demand curve becomes the constraint.

Since a similar analysis holds for transaction-constrained buyers, it is evident that the analysis of the preceding chapter, with discounted money prices replaced by virtual prices as described, needs no formal attention. We can deal with transaction constraints and individual price offers by supposing agents set prices and then behave as if prices were given but that they face transaction constraints. It is not necessary to reformulate the theory.

Far more important than this convenience, however, is the substantive

[13] Even if there are transaction constraints on that acquisition, virtual price will have to equal marginal cost where marginal cost includes the shadow prices of those transaction constraints.

[14] Notice that all such sales are prospective when considering price setting. The prices and sales at issue are those which will apply at a particular time. The possibility of discriminating among customers by gradually lowering prices through time is not ruled out, but it is not relevant to the present discussion.

question of whether or not transaction constraints remain binding in equilibrium. Earlier we described this as determining whether or not equilibrium was Walrasian. Now we see that this issue turns on whether or not the monopoly and monopsony power perceived by agents vanishes in equilibrium. Departure from competitive Walrasian equilibrium does not take two separate forms: one the presence of transaction constraints and the other the presence of monopoly elements. We now see that these are the same. Thus, for example, if individuals can make price and wage offers, the relevance of quantity-constrained underemployment equlibria rests on the persistence of perceived monopoly or monopsony power.[15]

The question of whether or not such effects disappear in equilibrium is not an easy one. In the first place, it depends on how perceptions of demand and supply curves are formed. If we do not impose any conditions on the formation of such perceptions, there is no reason that agents cannot all find themselves transaction-constrained at equilibrium – or, what we now know to be the same thing, that they all believe their demand or supply curves are so steep and their monopoly power so great as to not make it worth changing prices.

Even where we impose some restrictions on the perceived demand and supply curves of agents, however, it is by no means clear that we can rule out such effects. Hahn (1978) shows that such transaction-constrained, monopoly element equilibria can exist even if agents' conjectures about their demand curves are not unreasonable, given the equilibrium point at which the economy is.

I believe that it is not possible to answer this important question by studying equilibrium alone. The answer depends on the perceptions of agents and these, in turn, are formed as a result of experience. Since the perception of a demand curve is the perception of what would happen under differing circumstances, it is not fruitful to model the learning process which leads to these perceptions by considering equilibrium alone or even by considering static experiments, which depart from equilibrium. If such experiments are to be more than *gedanken* experiments on the part of agents, they will reflect the true dynamic behavior that occurs when equilibrium is disturbed. More generally, the perceptions of agents at equilibrium will reflect the experience involved in getting there. Since Hahn's work shows that it is not foolish for agents to have binding transaction constraints in equilibrium, we cannot beg this question by assuming rational expectations.

Having said this, I wish I could go on to a satisfactory answer to the question of whether the experience acquired by agents during the

[15] But see footnote 3 above.

adjustment process is likely to retain or remove the transaction-constrained, monopolistically competitive elements which can characterize disequilibrium. Unfortunately, I cannot do so. While the analysis of the present model shows stability, it is silent on the question of whether or not the equilibrium asymptotically attained is Walrasian. Indeed, the present analysis shows stability even when there are monopoly or monopolistically competitive elements which stem from causes other than conjectured demand curves and lack of information so that the basic structure is not competitive. Even with an underlying competitive structure, however, resolution of the important question of when equilibrium will itself be competitive requires a more detailed set of assumptions on the adjustment process than I use here. It is a major issue for further work.[16]

6.5* Transaction constraints: Formal analysis

As in the case of smooth transaction costs I give the analysis of transaction constraints explicitly for the case of households, the treatment of firms being essentially the same. Suppose that at time t, the household planning its transactions in θ-dated goods at v believes that it is constrained by

$$-\mathbf{s}(\theta, v, t) \leqq \mathbf{z}(\theta, v, t) \leqq \mathbf{b}(\theta, v, t) \tag{6.5.1}$$

These constraints add two new terms to the Lagrangian (5.9.11), namely,

$$\int_t^{\infty}\int_t^{\theta} \boldsymbol{\zeta}(\theta, v, t)\{\mathbf{z}(\theta, v, t)+\mathbf{s}(\theta, v, t)\}\, dv\, d\theta$$
$$+\int_t^{\infty}\int_t^{\theta} \boldsymbol{\xi}(\theta, v, t)\{\mathbf{b}(\theta, v, t)-\mathbf{z}(\theta, v, t)\}\, dv\, d\theta \tag{6.5.2}$$

where the Greek letters denote vectors of Lagrange multiplier functions. Obviously at most one of $\zeta_i(\theta, v, t)$ and $\xi_i(\theta, v, t)$ will be nonzero, for given (i, θ, v, t).

Similarly, suppose that there are constraints on transactions in shares

$$-\mathbf{s}'(v, t) \leqq \mathbf{q}(v, t) \leqq \mathbf{b}'(v, t) \tag{6.5.3}$$

with corresponding terms in the household's Lagrangian:

[16] In Fisher (1973), I attempted to examine this question in the context of a single market where monopoly elements appear because of imperfect information and search. The results of that paper suggest that it is possible that learning removes monopoly elements and produces convergence to competitive prices; but it appears to require quite strong assumptions to ensure this.

$$\int_t^\infty \tau(v,t)\{\mathbf{q}(v,t)+\mathbf{s}'(v,t)\}\,dv+\int_t^\infty \psi(v,t)\{\mathbf{b}'(v,t)-\mathbf{q}(v,t)\}\,dv \quad (6.5.4)$$

Only one of $\tau_f(v,t)$ and $\psi_f(v,t)$ will be nonzero, for given (f,v,t).

It is reasonable to assume $\mathbf{s}(\theta,v,t)$, $\mathbf{b}(\theta,v,t)$, $\mathbf{s}'(v,t)$ and $\mathbf{b}'(v,t)$ all continuous in v and I do so. Now consider the first-order conditions (5.9.12) through (5.9.17). The only ones affected (as in the case of smooth transaction costs, which may also be present) will be (5.9.14) and (5.9.16). The former equation will have $\{\xi(\theta,v,t)-\zeta(\theta,v,t)\}$ added to its right-hand side; the latter equation will have $\{\psi(v,t)-\tau(v,t)\}$ added to its left-hand side. Not surprisingly, these terms play the same respective roles as $-U_{\mathbf{z}(\theta,v,t)}$ and $-U_{\mathbf{q}(v,t)}$ did in the discussion of smooth transaction costs above; they are simply terms showing the marginal effects of transactions on utility. The remainder of the analysis of the effects on individual behavior in terms of virtual prices, as in (6.3.2) and (6.3.3), will not be repeated. (Note that the sign restrictions of (6.3.1) will be automatically obeyed by the new terms.)

Since the analysis of household (or firm) behavior given in the preceding chapter goes through with the use of such virtual prices and since we saw in that chapter that the usual marginal optimality conditions (properly interpreted) apply, the demonstration that optimal individual price setting leads to monopoly optimization need not be repeated. I thus simply proceed in later chapters by indexing all prices (and all other agent variables) with an agent superscript.[17]

[17] There is one small point involved in such indexing. In the discussion of the choice of numéraire it was assumed that all agents encountered the same actual prices for bonds of very short maturity, so that discount rates used to discount from t back to time 0 are the same for all agents. This will be true if all agents deal with the government. It is a matter of no substantive importance whether or not to maintain this assumption. To remove it is slightly inconvenient notationally, however, and I shall therefore retain it for simplicity.

CHAPTER 7

Walras' Law and the properties of equilibrium

7.1 Walras' Law

I now move closer to modeling the interaction of agents, building on the theory of the individual agent set forth in the previous two chapters. I begin with a consideration of Walras' Law. Certainly, one expects to find some version of Walras' Law holding for this economy, and, indeed, some version does hold; however, there are some points of special interest as to just what that version is.

Walras' Law in its usual form states that the total value of all excess demands is zero. Here, the excess demands involved will be those for commodities (including bonds), shares, and money. But it is not so clear precisely how the result will turn out. To begin with, demands in this model are distinguished by the dates at which agents expect to exercise them; they are not static. Will Walras' Law hold as a statement about the demands planned for any future moment or only as a statement about the value of all future plans? In fact, the result applies to either case; this is because agents expect at every instant to exchange commodities or shares for money of equal value.

Second, Walras' Law requires that we value all excess demands. In more primitive models, this is straightforward. Such valuation simply uses the common prices. In the present model, however, individuals can have different prices for the same commodity. Even without the individual price offers considered in the preceding chapter, this is true of the prices which agents expect. Not surprisingly, therefore, Walras' Law requires us to value each agent's excess demands at the prices at which that agent personally expects to (or actually does) act on them.

Even this use of individual prices, however, does not itself result in a total value of excess demands equal to zero. The reason for this is not hard to find. In models with households only, Walras' Law comes simply from summing the budget constraints. Firms, unlike households, have no budget constraints but they do have balance sheets. Hence Walras' Law in models with firms requires us to use the fact that the profits of firms ultimately belong to their shareholders. The way in which such profits are transmitted to shareholders is through dividend payments. Where firms and shareholders both have the same view of those dividend payments, we obtain Walras' Law in its usual form. In the present model, however, this is not guaranteed (out of equilibrium). The dividends which firms expect to pay may not be the same as those which households expect to receive. This drives a wedge into the usual accounting calculations involved in obtaining Walras' Law. Hence it is not surprising that we find the statement of the Law in the present case to be that, valued at individual prices, the total value of excess demands for any moment in time equals the difference between the dividend flows which households expect to receive at that moment and the dividend flows which firms expects to pay.

Plainly, such different expectations as to dividend flows ought not to persist in equilibrium. Just what the properties of equilibrium in this model are I explore after the formal analysis of Walras' Law.

7.2* Walras' Law: Formal treatment

As always, the derivation of Walras' Law starts with the budget constraints of households. Denoting households by h (and, later, firms by f) the instantaneous budget constraint (5.9.7) implies for $v \geqslant t$

$$\{z_0^h(v,t)+\mathbf{d}^h(v,t)\mathbf{k}^h(v,t)\}+\int_v^\infty \mathbf{p}^h(\theta,v,t)\mathbf{z}^h(\theta,v,t)\,d\theta + \mathbf{w}^h(v,t)\mathbf{q}^h(v,t)=\mathbf{d}^h(v,t)\mathbf{k}^h(v,t) \tag{7.2.1}$$

which states that the household's demand for money inflow at v plus the value of its demand for inflow of ordinary commodities at v plus the value of its demand for inflow of shares at v must equal the value of the dividends which the household expects to take in at v, where all values are in the individual prices at which the household expects to transact at v.[1]

Now consider firms. We can write $g^f(v, t)$, the rate at which firm, f, expects to pay dividends at $v \geqslant t$ as the firm's expected money inflow

[1] Recall that $z_0^h(v,t)$ is the household's demand for money inflow through trade only – not its total demand for money inflow. Dividends are treated separately. A similar remark applies to (7.2.2) below.

through trade less the expected change in retained earnings at v. This is equivalent to

$$\left\{-\int_v^\infty \mathbf{p}^f(\theta, v, t)\mathbf{z}^f(\theta, v, t)\, d\theta - g^f(v, t)\right\}$$

$$+\int_v^\infty \mathbf{p}^f(\theta, v, t)\mathbf{z}^f(\theta, v, t)\, d\theta = -g^f(v, t) \tag{7.2.2}$$

which can be read as saying that the firm's demand for net money inflow at v plus the value (at its own expected prices) of its demand for inflow of ordinary commodities at v must be the negative of the dividends it expects to pay at v. Again individual prices are involved.

Now, sum (7.2.1) over households and (7.2.2) over firms and add the results. We obtain:

> *Theorem 7.2.1 (Generalized Walras' Law).* For every $v \geq t$, value each agent's demands (the ones which will be current at v) at the prices which that agent expects to offer or encounter at v. The total over all agents of the value of demands for inflows of money, ordinary commodities, and shares equals the difference between the total amount of dividends which households expect to receive at v and the total amount of dividends which firms expect to pay at v.

Since this holds for every $v \geq t$, a similar statement will hold for the total value of all excess demands integrated from t to infinity. Note that Theorem 7.2.1 holds whether or not there are binding transaction constraints.

7.3 Momentary personal equilibrium

I now consider the properties of equilibrium in this model. Some such properties are largely definitional; they are also the ones which will make equilibria the rest points of the dynamic process described in the next chapter. Other properties can be proved under various assumptions.

The simplest way to consider equilibrium in this model is from the point of view of the individual agent. I first consider what it means for an individual agent to be in what I shall term "momentary personal equilibrium" at t. Essentially, this is a state in which the agent's optimal program does not change because his plans and expectations are fulfilled. Equilibrium for the system as a whole is then said to be attained at T if all agents are always in momentary personal equilibrium for all later times $t \geq T$, with a Walrasian equilibrium being defined as one with no binding transaction constraints (save for free-good disposal).[2] I thus begin by discussing momentary personal equilibrium.

Plainly, the first requirement for momentary personal equilibrium at t must be that the agent in question finds that he can complete his planned transactions at t.[3] There is the usual exception to this; the agent may not be able to dispose of free goods. Note that, as discussed in the previous chapter, the question of whether or not agents can complete their transactions is *not* the same as the question of whether they face binding transaction constraints. Transaction constraints are perceived by agents and taken into account in formulating their desired transactions. What is at issue here is whether or not those desired transactions, which *already* take account of transaction constraints, in fact become real ones.

Obviously, agents who fail to complete an expected transaction will realize they were wrong about their ability to transact. However, agents' perceptions of their constraints and their expectations or plans about prices and dividends may change even if their transactions go through. If nothing else, they may find actual prices set by others or dividends to be different from expected; more generally, they may observe the experience of others as well as their own and change their beliefs in consequence.[4] Since expectations play a large role in the present model, it is plain that any equilibrium definition will have to include the property that expectations do not change.

It would be too strong, however, to require that none of an agent's expectations change in momentary personal equilibrium. This is because not all his expectations are relevant to his actions. Where a change in expectations does not affect the optimal program, and thus is irrelevant to the agent's actions, it will have no effect outside the agent. It would be unreasonable to require of an equilibrium definition that such irrelevant expectations do not change.

We must thus distinguish between "relevant" and "irrelevant" expectations. A particular parameter or function taken by the agent as given in forming his plans is *relevant* if some *ceteris paribus* small change in it would cause the agent to change his behavior. Such a parameter or function is *strongly relevant* if *any ceteris paribus* small change would cause the agent to change his behavior. (The distinction is needed to take care of the case in which a change in one direction would keep the agent

[2] As discussed in Chapter 6 such "Walrasian" equilibria need not be Pareto-optimal in the presence of transaction costs.

[3] These are not all of his planned transactions; some transactions are planned for future dates.

[4] This sort of learning is ruled out in Hahn (1978), as Maskin has remarked. See Hahn (1978, pp. 7–8).

doing the same thing as before while a change in another would matter.) Where a change in expectations changes behavior, I shall call the change itself "relevant."

Notice that any change which alters the value of an agent's objective (utility for households, profits for firms) is necessarily relevant. In the case of the household, this is because anticipated utility cannot change unless the household changes its consumption plan. In the case of the firm, anticipated profits can change even though production plans do not, but a change in anticipated profits produces a change in dividend policy since we have assumed that the firm plans eventually to pay out all its profits. Relevant expectations can change without affecting the value of the agent's optimand, however.

It is important to realize that any price at which an agent expects to transact is strongly relevant to that agent. In the case of firms this is obvious since, *ceteris paribus,* a change in such a price affects profits. In the case of households it follows if for no other reason because a *ceteris paribus* change in such a price affects the money constraints.[5]

Now, it is expectations as to relevant parameters that are either fulfilled or constant in momentary personal equilibrium. To be more precise, no change in relevant expectations occurs.[6] One special case of this is the agent's expectations as to transaction constraints (or perceived supply or demand curves); an agent who is unable to complete his transactions must perforce change his views of the constraints he in fact faces, and he will alter his behavior.

More important than this is the fact that equilibrium for the system as a whole will have the property that all agents expect all *relevant* discounted commodity prices to be unchanging with current prices rising at the foreseen interest rates on instantaneous bonds (money). A similar statement is true of all *relevant* share prices after adjustment for dividends which are also correctly foreseen. Hence the question of what makes prices relevant or irrelevant is a matter of some interest. We have already seen that prices corresponding to planned transactions are strongly relevant, now we consider other prices.

To begin with, neglect smooth transaction costs. It follows from the

[5] I assume that agents are never so completely transaction-constrained that changes in the money constraint do not matter because they believe that there is nothing they can usefully buy.

[6] This implies slightly more than the property that plans do not change. It is conceivable that expectations of two or more strongly relevant parameters could change in just such a way as to leave the optimal program unaffected. Such cases are of measure zero and I shall assume them away. They would in any case be ruled out by some versions of the No Favorable Surprise assumption of the next chapter.

theorems on speculation (Theorems 5.6.3 and 5.9.4) that any agent who does *not* expect constant discounted (dividend-corrected) prices must be engaging in transactions in the corresponding commodities or shares until stopped by a constraint. That constraint can be a short constraint, a money constraint (I shall have more to say on this below), or a transaction constraint. In any case, such an agent must be at a corner solution. So long as his price expectations are such as to leave him at that corner, the exact expectations he holds will not affect his actions. We cannot expect to prove convergence of such irrelevant expectations, and it would be unreasonable to require specific irrelevant expectations in equilibrium. The case is rather similar to that of the desire to dispose of free goods and, indeed, the full equilibrium definition implies complementary slackness conditions.

The presence of smooth transaction costs does not materially change this. If there were fixed costs to engaging in transactions, then transactions would only be undertaken when their (discounted) money profit was sufficient to justify such fixed costs. In such a case, price expectations which were not such as to produce such action would not be relevant. Continuous transaction costs, however, do not produce corner solutions of this type. In particular, as we saw in Chapter 6, arbitrage transactions otherwise profitable will still take place to some extent with smooth transaction costs. Such transaction costs, by spreading out transactions, will tend to make more prices relevant to planning than would otherwise be the case.

In short, by definition, the price expectations which are relevant and hence unchanging in momentary personal equilibrium are those which affect the optimal program of the agent; these are just those prices at which nonzero transactions are planned. Changes in price expectations which leave a corner solution undisturbed are (locally) irrelevant.

Price expectations are not the only relevant ones, however. Households also have dividend expectations and a change in these affects action by affecting the money constraints. Obviously, however, the dividend expectations of households who do not plan to hold (or take a short position in) the shares of the firms involved are not relevant and such expectations are allowed to change in momentary personal equilibrium.

Beyond such monetary matters, agents have expectations as to transaction constraints. Where these perceptions are of binding constraints they are relevant. Where they are such as to make those constraints nonbinding, then they are free to change in momentary personal equilibrium.

At a different level, there are relevant matters which we have not so far assumed to be matters of perception. The short constraints, the nature of smooth transaction costs, and the technology of production are all in this class. All of these, because, in principle, they pertain to events at different times, are subject to change. In particular, this is true of the technology of production, which can perfectly well be different at different times. What matters here, however, is not whether such things themselves change, but rather whether agents' perceptions of them do so. Foreseen changes in technology, for example, are consistent with momentary personal equilibrium (they are already incorporated in the production or storage functionals); unforeseen changes are not so consistent, unless the change is perceived too late to affect the agent's optimal plan.

One final matter concerning the relevant–irrelevant distinction must be discussed before proceeding. An agent may be at a corner solution and be just indifferent as to whether he is there or not (first-order conditions holding with equality at the corner). In such a case, a change in parameters in one direction will move him from the corner, while a change in the opposite direction will not. The parameter involved is thus "weakly relevant." The important thing to notice, however, is that the property of being a *strongly* relevant parameter – a parameter a change in which in *any* direction would matter to the agent – has some of the characteristics of strong inequalities. Since I assume that expectations only move continuously (save for perceived constraints on transactions attempted at t), the set of times at which a future parameter is strongly relevant must be open. Equivalently, an agent experiencing a relevant change in expectations experiences such a relevant change on an open set of times.

To see what this means, suppose that an agent expects a future change in relative discounted prices and plans to take advantage of it through arbitrage. The magnitude of the expected change will surely be strongly relevant; even if he were to find the particular arbitrage opportunity attractive at slightly different expected price changes, the arbitrage profits to be made would be affected by such expectations and these would affect his ability to make other purchases. But if, at t, the price change in question matters to the agent in this way, and expectations change continuously, then the magnitude of the price change must surely still be strongly relevant a little after t and (what is more important below) a little before t. Only if the expected price change were weakly relevant could there be a first moment at which such relevance came to be.

This property is important in the treatment of prices and arbitrage in the next section; it is not needed otherwise.

7.4 Equilibrium: The behavior of prices

As already indicated, an equilibrium in this model is a state of the system at a time T, such that, from T onward all agents are always in momentary personal equilibrium. I now explore the properties of such equilibrium states.

In the first place, once equilibrium is reached, all agents will find they can fulfill their plans. They will also not change their relevant expectations. This has an important implication: Since we assume that agents know the actual values of relevant magnitudes when they occur, agents whose expectations of such magnitudes do not change must find their expectations fulfilled. Agents will transact at previously expected prices; they will find transaction constraints no more binding than they had expected; where they own shares they will correctly foresee the corresponding dividend flows. Technology and transaction costs will also be correctly foreseen where such foresight matters.

Since dividends are correctly foreseen by shareholders in equilibrium, the effect on Walras' Law which comes about through different dividend expectations of households and firms disappears in equilibrium. If it is also true that individual prices become the same in equilibrium, for agents planning corresponding transactions, then the extended version of Walras' Law reduces to the usual one in this model.

What can we say about the behavior of individual prices in equilibrium? This is an obviously important question, although we need not answer it in order to discuss stability. There are two somewhat related issues: the persistence of price differences over individual agents and the persistence of price differences over time.

To secure the property that individual prices for the same good are the same in equilibrium, we need only employ what appears (perhaps deceptively) to be a relatively weak assumption. Suppose that, at some time T there is some market with price dispersion. Then it seems reasonable to assume either that there is some agent who cannot complete his transactions or at least that some agent changes some relevant expectation. Note that such changes need not take place at T or even on the market with price dispersion. It is enough that the presence of price dispersion eventually causes a change. Plainly such an assumption is enough to ensure that price dispersion is inconsistent with the definition of equilibrium, since it means that there will come a time at which not all agents are in momentary personal equilibrium.

Why is such an assumption plausible? If buyers and sellers of a particular dated commodity (or share) know each others' prices and not all agents have the same price, then it is reasonable to suppose that they will not all be content. One possibility is that not all buyers attempting to buy from the seller with the lowest price will be able to do so; another is that not all sellers attempting to sell to buyers at the highest price will be able to do so.

Things need not happen in this way, of course. It is conceivable that different buyers offering different prices manage to strike bargains with different sellers setting different prices in just such a way as to allow each of them to transact as desired at the price he foresaw (although this seems most unlikely). Even if this happens, however, we would not expect all agents to be satisfied *after* the event. Where there is a buyer offering more than a seller is willing to sell for, an arbitrage opportunity has appeared. It does not seem unreasonable to suppose that the buyer or the seller or a third party attempts to take advantage of that opportunity *and* that this is not just a matter of third-party arbitrageurs acting on an opportunity they have previously foreseen while buyer and seller *also* maintain their previous expectations about prices.

It is crucial here, however, that price dispersion is known to the agents involved. This will certainly be true if all agents know all prices. (It may also be true if agents search for advantageous prices, although here price dispersion can persist if search is costly.) Where there is a systematic persistent partition of agents and prices in terms of information with prices in any given group of agents known only to that group, it makes some sense to consider the commodity (or share) involved as if it were two or more separate commodities (or shares) in two or more separate markets.

All of this has a good deal to do with what we *mean* by the term "market"; more specifically with how far we are willing to extend the Hahn Process notion that markets are "orderly" in the sense that buyers and sellers can find each other. (I shall have more to say about this in the next chapter.) It is not necessary, however, to impose strict assumptions here that *always* keep transactions from taking place at differing prices. If we wish to have individual price dispersion disappear at equilibrium, all we need do is make the assumption under discussion, assuming thereby that price dispersion leads some agent to change his views in a way that affects his planning. In a model in which agents are allowed to perceive and act on arbitrage opportunities, this seems a reasonable assumption to make.[7]

If we do ensure that individual prices are all the same in equilibrium, and known to agents then it can be shown that all discounted prices at which transactions ever take place in equilibrium must be unchanging. More precisely, it must be the case that the discounted money prices at which commodities are bought and sold will be constant. The current

[7] Note, however, that such an assumption would be more reasonable if we assumed such changes to be caused by *persistent* price dispersion rather than by temporary price dispersion. Weakening the assumption in this way would lead to a situation in which equilibrium could begin with a finite period of price dispersion. To do this explicitly seems unnecessary, however, and would further complicate the discussion that follows.

prices will change, moving upward by the (commonly foreseen) instantaneous interest rate – the rate of growth of the money supply (which need not be constant over time). The discounted prices of shares will also be constant once they are corrected for dividend payments.

The fact that it is prices discounted back to time zero and not current prices that converge in this model should come as no surprise. Future commodities are defined here (in part) by absolute dates rather than by term – "September wheat" rather than "three-month wheat," for example. As these dates come closer we should expect *current* prices to change even in equilibrium reflecting the fact that the relevant money flows are coming closer and that money bears interest in this model, with the instantaneous interest rate the rate of growth of the money supply.

The demonstration of the constancy of those discounted money prices at which actual transactions take place is in two parts. First I show that such prices are expected before they occur; thus, in this point expectations model, equilibrium is a rational expectations equilibrium. More precisely, concentrating on commodity prices for ease of exposition (as I shall often do in this chapter), I show that for every agent a who plans at t to transact in θ-dated commodity i at time v, $\theta \geqslant v \geqslant t$, the discounted price he expects to encounter at v, $p_i^a(\theta, v, t)$, is independent of t for $t \geqslant T$ the start of equilibrium. Since agents know actual prices when they occur this means that $p_i^a(\theta, v, t) = p_i^a(\theta, v, v) = P_i(\theta, v)$ the actual price for the commodity which does occur at v. Having established this, I then use it to show that, for $v \geqslant T$, $P_i(\theta, v)$ is in fact independent of v so that neither the actual nor expected relevant price for the commodity changes after equilibrium is reached.

To show that relevant prices must be expected before they occur once equilibrium is reached ($p_i^a(\theta, v, t)$ independent of t for $t \geqslant T$) note that, as we have seen, every agent who transacts at a given price at time v finds that price relevant – in fact, strongly relevant. Hence such transacting agents must have expected that price correctly before v. Indeed, such correct expectations must have been held by such agents at all times t after equilibrium was reached at which the price was relevant. Since the price in question is not only relevant but strongly relevant, and expectations change continuously, there is no way that such correct foresight can come about if expectations as to the price in question change after equilibrium is reached. For suppose that such expectations did so change. Then they must have changed before the price in question became relevant and there must have been such a time after equilibrium was reached. In that case, however, the agent at such a time must not have planned to make the transaction in question and this is not possible since plans do not change once equilibrium is reached. Thus trade at equilibrium not only takes place at foreseen prices but in fact takes place at prices foreseen at all times after equilibrium is reached, at all $t \geq T$.

With this result in hand, I now proceed to the principal point – the fact that relevant discounted prices are not only correctly foreseen in equilibrium but in fact are constant, that is, that $P_i(\theta, v)$ is independent of v for $v \geq T$.

Suppose that some discounted commodity price changes after equilibrium is reached. As we know from the results of earlier chapters, this creates an arbitrage opportunity either between commodities or between a commodity and money. To fix ideas, begin by supposing that the only opportunity perceived by any agent involves arbitrage between the commodity and money. For the moment, ignore transaction constraints and smooth transaction costs. Then, if the discounted price in question is going down as v goes up, every agent expecting this will wish to sell; if it is going up, every agent expecting it will wish to buy. But the derivative of price is obviously relevant to all agents transacting in the commodity; hence all must hold the correct expectations and they must all expect the same thing. It thus cannot be the case that such agents are able to complete their planned transactions; successful arbitrage requires differing expectations.

The case in which arbitrage opportunities between commodities are perceived by some agents is basically the same (as we should expect since transactions take place for money) but slightly more complex. The additional complexity arises because such arbitrage can involve selling a commodity whose discounted price is expected to *rise* in order to buy one whose discounted price is expected to rise even faster. Thus, while any commodity whose discounted price is falling will have sellers but no buyers, there is at least the possibility that a commodity whose discounted price is rising will have both buyers and sellers because the sellers anticipate other more favorable opportunities which are not perceived by the buyers and hence are never relevant to them. (We need not consider whether such irrelevance can be maintained in the face of facts in order to show that this is impossible.)

To see that this cannot happen, I use the fact that there are a finite number of agents. The principle involved is illustrated well enough by supposing that there are only three; more introduces nothing essential. Suppose then that agent A believes the price of bananas to be increasing faster than that of apples and wishes to take advantage of this. If he transacts in apples at all, we know from the results on arbitrage in Chapter 5 that it must be the case that he is using the proceeds to buy bananas simultaneously. Now the bananas must be bought from someone, say, agent B. Since B as well as A correctly forecasts the price rise in bananas, he will certainly not sell unless there is some other commodity, say, carrots, whose price he believes to be rising faster. For B to succeed in purchasing the carrots, there must be some other agent who sees carrot prices as rising less fast than the prices of something else, say, dates. This cannot be A, or A would not wish to buy bananas. It can only be the third agent, say, C. But C cannot then succeed in buying dates since, in equilibrium, any seller of dates must anticipate their price rise and neither A nor B can do so and be content with their transactions as described. Similarly, there is no one to whom A can sell his apples in the first place.

Thus, while it is not the case as with the direct exchange of commodities for money that no single arbitrage transaction can succeed, it cannot be true that all arbitrage transactions succeed. Either some agent must fail in one leg of a two-part transaction which justifies the other or some agent must be wrong as to relevant price changes. As with the simpler case of arbitrage between commodities and money, the discounted prices at which transactions actually take place must be constant and expected to be so from the time equilibrium is reached.

Now consider what happens if we reintroduce transaction difficulties. Consider first transaction constraints. If these were discontinuous in transaction dates, it might be the case that an arbitraging seller, expecting prices to fall, could nevertheless find a buyer with the same expectations who bought at a high price because he expected not to be able to buy at a lower one. With continuity, however, such a circumstance cannot arise. Waiting a little longer cannot reduce a nonzero ability to buy to a zero one. (Even without continuity, such a situation would be rather special if the arbitraging seller himself plans to buy later; it requires asymmetric perception of transaction constraints over agents.) Thus, in equilibrium, any agent transacting in a θ-dated commodity at time v must encounter a time interval including v during which the discounted price for that commodity is constant. The union of such intervals over all agents, however, need not be $[T, \theta]$ (where T is the time at which equilibrium begins). If not, there is at least the possibility that there are (at least) two disjoint intervals with the discounted price differing between them. Such a case would be possible only if every agent who buys at the high price believes himself transaction-constrained from buying at the low one and every agent who sells at the low price believes himself transaction-constrained from selling at the high one, even though transactions in fact take place at both prices. I shall assume that – as with other forms of individual price dispersion – this segmentation of the market in time does not occur in equilibrium, so that all discounted prices at which transactions take place are the same once equilibrium is reached. Indeed, it will simplify matters (and do no harm) to assume that there are enough agents and enough differences in transaction constraints to make the union of the intervals referred to above the entire interval $[T, \theta]$ and discounted prices constant in equilibrium.

Smooth transaction costs create no difficulty. It is true that the presence of such costs permits buying when discounted money prices are going down and selling when prices are going up (see Figure 6.2.1). However, a transaction that would be undertaken at a given time for arbitrage profit in the absence of transaction costs will still be undertaken in their presence, although possibly in reduced amount. To put it another way, if it is optimal to buy a given commodity at a time v^* and to sell it at a time v^{**} without transaction costs in that commodity, then it is still optimal to do so with such transaction costs, even though agents may wish also to transact at times that would otherwise have been suboptimal. Transaction costs in a commodity (or share) can never reverse the sign of a transaction that would have been undertaken in their absence. This is illustrated in Figure 6.2.1. Hence the argument made earlier in the absence of transaction costs still holds in their presence as regards the same times. At the times at which all transacting agents would have wished to buy (sell) if there were no transaction costs involved in so doing, they will still all wish to do so and they will fail.

Thus equilibrium necessarily involves a cessation of arbitrage if agents have enough information. Only where there is individual price dispersion can arbitrage be possible in equilibrium. If such arbitrage takes place, it is reasonable to suppose that it is observed and that expectations then change so that equilibrium is not in fact present. Where individual price dispersion persists *without* arbitrage it will be the case that there is a systematic division of agents into groups with knowledge of the prices set by agents in any group not held outside that group. In that case, it is unreasonable to suppose that prices between groups will come together, but it is then sensible to speak of more than one "market" with prices within each market the same and discounted prices constant in equilibrium.

The fact that discounted prices are constant in equilibrium has two consequences worth noting here. First, since, in equilibrium, discounted share prices change only because dividends are paid out, it is evident that discounted share prices are in fact equal to the integral of discounted future dividends. This is equivalent to the natural result that, in equilibrium, the *un*discounted price of any share at time t equals the integral of the future dividend payments associated with that share, with dividends discounted back to t rather than to 0. Since dividends and profits are correctly foreseen in equilibrium and firms plan to pay out all their profits to their shareholders, this makes the total market value of the shares of a firm at t equal to the then present value of its undistributed profits. Note that such results are only guaranteed to hold in equilibrium.

Second, since, as we have seen, in equilibrium, price dispersion disappears and relevant prices are expected correctly, all agents planning a transaction expect the same price for it. In addition, relevant dividends are correctly expected. But the differences between our generalized version of Walras' Law (Theorem 7.2.1) and the usual version all stemmed from individual prices or price expectations and disagreement about dividends. Hence it is apparent that in equilibrium the usual version of Walras' Law holds: The total over agents of the value of all excess demands for money, goods, and shares will be zero, values being in the common prices. Moreover, this will apply to demands to be exercised at every future date $v \geqslant t$ and thus to the integral of those values over all future dates.

7.5 The equilibrium role of money

I now take up the question of the role played by money in equilibrium. Since, in this model, transactions continue in equilibrium, taking place at foreseen prices, the transactions demand for money does not disappear so that we do not encounter the awkward problem that agents wish to dispose of money as fast as possible. This is reflected in part by the properties of the money constraints in equilibrium: the fact that, at least in Walrasian equilibrium, the constraint that planned money stocks must always be nonnegative is not binding for any finite future time. Rather, in such an equilibrium the only money constraint is a single one ("binding at infinity"), the usual overall budget constraint for households (Equation (5.9.10)) and the definition of profits for firms.

Consider this question in more detail. Suppose that a particular agent finds in equilibrium that the money constraint is binding at a finite future v. In that case, credit markets are sufficiently imperfect that, if the agent is a household, his budget constraint *in equilibrium* breaks down into a whole series of budget constraints because he cannot borrow against future sales. Similarly, if the agent is a firm, profits have to be reduced because the firm cannot borrow working capital against future profits. The constraints involved here are both transaction constraints and short constraints on bond and futures dealings (recall that money can always be transferred forward).

That such constraints should be binding is entirely appropriate out of equilibrium where there may be speculative opportunities as shown in Chapter 5 and where, in particular, the term structure of bond prices may be viewed differently by different agents. In equilibrium, however, this is less clearly appropriate, as such reasons disappear. Hence, we should not be surprised to find that, at least at a *Walrasian* equilibrium, no money constraint for finite v can ever be binding.

To see this, first ignore transaction costs. In equilibrium, agents will be indifferent to the timing of their transactions (but not the timing of their consumption or production), since discounted prices are constant and expected to be so, and there are no arbitrage profits to be made. Now suppose that an agent has a program that would be optimal except for a money constraint binding at some finite time, v. (To fix ideas, suppose that the agent is a household whose program satisfies its budget constraint out to infinity but who is hampered for lack of funds at v.) If the equilibrium is Walrasian, then the agent perceives no binding transaction constraints (save for free-good disposal). Further, the bounds on short positions in commodities of a given date do not become looser as the commodity date approaches (and similarly for shares). It follows that the agent can attain the same objective by rearranging his planned transactions to move all sales to the present and postpone all purchases to the last possible date. He will do so, alleviating the money constraint at v, until either that constraint is no longer binding or he perceives a binding transaction constraint. In either case, the original program with the binding money constraint and no binding transaction constraints cannot have been optimal.

Another way of seeing this is as follows: Since, in equilibrium, discounted prices are constant and expected to be so, the results on arbitrage of Chapter 5 show that the money constraint can be binding at v only if the short constraint is *also* binding for every commodity with a date later than v (and for all shares). But in this case, the agent has *already* sold everything he will ever sell and must be able to afford his purchases at v if his program is otherwise feasible. (The binding short constraints here correspond to the rearrangement of purchase times in the earlier explanation.)

So far this discussion has ignored transaction costs. The somewhat surprising fact is that smooth transaction costs do not change things here despite the fact that some of the argument involved rearranging the timing of transactions. This can be seen in two ways.

The first way is to observe that, in equilibrium, agents can be thought of as maximizing concentrated utility (or having concentrated storage or production) functionals as in Chapter 6. The results of Chapter 5 then apply with actual rather than virtual prices (the effects of transaction costs having been absorbed into the functionals rather than stated as correcting the prices). In that case, however, the argument given above that the short constraints must all be binding at v if the money constraint is so binding still applies.

The other way to think of it applies directly to the rearrangement of timing argument. There it was pointed out that, in the absence of transaction costs, it would always be possible costlessly to rearrange the timing of purchases *if there were something to be gained from doing so.* With transaction costs, however, and with constant discounted prices, the transaction-costs disadvantage of such rearrangement has already been absorbed into the concentrated utility (or production or storage) functional. It will still be true that rearrangements will be made without *monetary* cost if there is something to be gained by doing so, and these are the only costs that matter because the transaction costs themselves have been absorbed into the evaluation of possible gain from rearrangement.

This is all closely related to the not very surprising observation that, in Walrasian equilibrium with transaction costs, not only will the expected discounted money prices relevant to planned transactions be constant, but so will the corresponding expected virtual prices. With discounted money prices constant, and the money constraint not binding, purchases or sales will be arranged to make the marginal disutility of transactions in a particular commodity constant. Such a situation is depicted in Figure 6.2.3.

It is obvious that smooth transaction costs as used here can ensure the determinacy of transaction plans in Walrasian equilibrium, even though agents would otherwise be indifferent about transaction timing.[8] However, it is in another sense not generally true that transaction times would be indeterminate in Walrasian equilibrium even if transaction costs were absent. In general, out of equilibrium, agents are not indifferent as to timing and, if they are, we need only assume that they choose one of a set of equally optimal plans and do so continuously.[9] Equilibrium, however, does not spring into being from initial conditions but rather, given stability, is the limit of a path of converging disequilibrium states. The transaction plans of equilibrium are thus the limits of the determinate transaction plans of that path as seen more explicitly in Chapter 8.

What happens if agents attempt to choose a different equally optimal transaction path once equilibrium is reached? Aside from the fact that equilibrium is reached only asymptotically, it is not the case that agents can do this. For, while any single agent can rearrange his plans, he will not be able to fulfill those plans unless other agents do so as well, so that his rearranged timing of transactions coincides with theirs. An attempt to do so otherwise will destroy momentary personal equilibrium for the

[8] They can also yield such determinacy even *out* of equilibrium when a particular agent happens to expect constant discounted prices.

[9] Note that this is far weaker than the imposition of the Present Action Postulate discussed in Chapters 2 and 3.

attempting agent with the consequence that equilibrium as defined was not present in the first place. (That groups of agents can jointly rearrange their transactions seems uninteresting.)

Returning to the question of the money constraints, the fact that such constraints are not binding at finite times in Walrasian equilibrium means that, in such equilibrium, the budget constraints of households all reduce to one constraint (Equation (5.9.10)). Further, for both households and firms, the shadow price of money becomes the same at all finite times, so that all the results of Chapter 5 concerning the effects of different opportunity costs of money at different times disappear. In particular, marginal utilities are all proportional to discounted money prices, and households no longer care about the dividend streams of firms for liquidity purposes.

Note, however, that all of this occurs *only* in Walrasian equilibrium. In general, money constraints will be binding at finite times out of equilibrium and, as we shall now see, they can also be binding at non-Walrasian equilibria. Indeed, the proof given above of their nonbinding nature at finite time rested heavily on the property that the equilibrium considered is Walrasian. The situation in non-Walrasian equilibrium is quite different and quite interesting. To see what is involved, consider the two demonstrations given above that finite-time money constraints cannot be binding in Walrasian equilibrium.

The first such argument involved the rearrangement of transaction timing to secure needed cash by putting sales as early and purchases as late as possible. This could be done in Walrasian equilibrium because there were no transaction constraints and agents cared only about the discounted money costs of transactions, with such money costs being the same in equilibrium for all transaction paths that differ only as to transaction timing. The same argument went through with smooth transaction costs because we could, in equilibrium, absorb those costs into the analysis as described in Chapter 6. When the equilibrium is not Walrasian, transaction *constraints* are involved. These cannot be absorbed as can transaction costs and it is evident that an attempt to rearrange purchase timing for liquidity purposes may fail because agents believe that early sales and late purchases are limited in amount.

A deeper insight than this can be obtained by considering the second demonstration given for the Walrasian case. There we observed that constant discounted money prices together with a binding money constraint at v implied a binding short constraint at v so that all sales which would *ever* be made had been made before v. As before, transaction costs did not affect this result. When transaction constraints are present, however, we must consider not the behavior of discounted money prices themselves, but the behavior of virtual prices - here discounted money prices adjusted for the shadow prices of the corresponding transaction constraints. Although in Walrasian equilibrium smooth transaction costs will be adjusted so as to make virtual as well as discounted money prices constant (another way of seeing that the arbitrage results imply short constraints all binding at v if the money constraint is), this is not true of virtual prices when transaction constraints are involved. There is no reason that some virtual prices cannot be rising in equilibrium in such a case even though discounted money prices are constant, so the binding nature of the money constraint does not imply that the short constraints are also binding.

What does it mean for virtual prices to be rising in such a situation? Consider first commodities which the agent wishes to sell. We saw in Chapter 6 that agents will plan to set prices taking their perceived demand curves into account so that the shadow price of the transaction constraint for a seller is the difference between price and marginal revenue. This makes virtual price equal to marginal revenue. Now, marginal revenue, as is well known, is given (in a notation used only in this section) by $P(1+1/\eta)$, where P is price and η is the perceived demand elasticity at the optimal point. Since P is constant in equilibrium, marginal revenue (virtual price) will be rising if and only if demand elasticity is perceived to be falling algebraically, that is, if and only if perceived demand curves are becoming more elastic at the constant price P. In such a situation, it is natural to find sellers reluctant to alter things by transferring sales toward the present. Too many sales early will affect the price by too much, while sales later on are more easily made. To take full advantage of their perceived monopoly power may thus require sellers to refrain from rearranging their sales toward the present even though this means putting up with cash problems.

A similar analysis applies to the timing of purchases. Here agents must set their price offers taking account of the *supply* curves they perceive as facing them. Evidently, this means that the shadow price of a purchase will be the difference between the marginal cost of the commodity and its price, taking account of the monopsony power perceived by the agent. This makes virtual price equal to that marginal cost itself which we can once again write as $P(1+1/\eta)$ where η this time denotes the perceived elasticity of *supply*. Since P is constant in equilibrium, marginal cost (virtual price) will be rising if and only if the (positive) elasticity of supply at P is falling so that the perceived supply curve is becoming more and more *in*elastic. In such a situation, it is natural to find buyers reluctant to change things by transferring purchases toward the future. Too many purchases late will affect the price by too much, while purchases early are more easily made. To take full advantage of their perceived monopsony power may thus require buyers to refrain from rearranging their purchases toward the future even though this means putting up with cash problems.

Such effects can plainly cause the money constraints to be binding for at least some agents at some finite times, not because agents all wish to get rid of money as fast as possible but because agents' perceptions of their own changing monopoly or monopsony positions are such as to make it suboptimal to take those actions which would alleviate their cash problems. (Note that if such perceptions are *not* changing then such cash problems cannot exist.) Whether an injection of money through monetary policy would make such effects disappear and whether this would be desirable in a welfare sense are interesting questions for further work.

7.6* Equilibrium: Formal statement

I now summarize some of the discussion of this chapter in a more formal manner. Since that discussion provides proofs of the propositions involved, I only give definitions and statements of results.

> *Definition 7.6.1.* An agent is in *momentary personal equilibrium* at t if he can complete his transactions at t (except possibly for the disposal of free goods) and if his optimal program is unchanging at t. (The optimal program for a firm is to be understood to include its dividend policy; this is true throughout.)
>
> *Definition 7.6.2.* A parameter (or function), α, with particular value α^* at t is *relevant* to an agent if, with all other exogenous parameters (or functions) constant at their values at t, every open neighborhood of α^* contains some value, $\hat{\alpha}$, such that the agent's optimal program at $\hat{\alpha}$ differs from his optimal program at α^*. If there exists an open neighborhood of α^* such that at *all* points of that neighborhood (other than α^*) the agent's optimal program differs from his optimal program at α^*, then α is called *strongly relevant* to that agent. A parameter *change* is called relevant to an agent if it changes his optimal program.
>
> *Lemma 7.6.1.* If a parameter change alters the value of an agent's objective function(al) it is relevant to him.

Note that, in particular, the price at which an agent expects to transact is strongly relevant to him. So is the level of any binding constraint and the dividend expectation for any share which the agent plans to hold in a nonzero amount.

Definition 7.6.3. The economy is in *equilibrium* at T if every agent is in momentary personal equilibrium at all $t \geqslant T$. If for all such t no agent encounters a binding transaction constraint (except for free-good disposal), the equilibrium is *Walrasian.*

As remarked in Chapter 6, in the presence of smooth transaction costs, equilibria which are Walrasian in this sense need not be Pareto-optimal.

Assumption 7.6.1. If there are different individual prices for the same commodity or share at t, then there exists a $t' \geqslant t$ such that either some agent fails to complete his transactions at t' or else some agent experiences a relevant parameter change at t'.

Theorem 7.6.1. In equilibrium, the prices at which transactions actually take place in any commodity or share at a given time are the same for all transacting agents.

Theorem 7.6.2. In equilibrium, all discounted commodity prices at which transactions take place are constant and expected to be so by all agents to whom they are relevant. Specifically, if $p_i^a(\theta, v, t)$ is relevant to a, for any $t \geqslant T$, the start of equilibrium, then $p_i^a(\theta, v, t)$ is independent of t for all t, $\theta \geqslant v \geqslant t > T$. Thus, in this point-expectations model, equilibrium is a rational-expectations equilibrium. Hence $p_i^a(\theta, v, t) = P_i(\theta, v)$ for all such t. Further, $P_i(\theta, v)$ is in fact independent of v as well for all such v. Hence, in equilibrium, we can write $p_i^a(\theta, v, t) = P_i(\theta, v) = P_i(\theta)$. Current prices increase at the rate of growth of the money supply. Similar results apply to all relevant discounted share prices corrected for dividends. Finally all relevant dividend expectations are correct.

Corollary 7.6.1. In equilibrium, the undiscounted price of any share at t is the integral of the future dividend payments associated with that share, discounted back to t. The market value of the shares of any firm at t is the then present value of its undistributed profits.

Corollary 7.6.2 (Walras' Law). In equilibrium, at every t, the total value over all agents of all demands for money, commodities and shares is zero for every future moment of time and for all future moments together.

Theorem 7.6.3. If an equilibrium is Walrasian, the money constraint for any agent is binding only at infinity. The budget constraints of each household reduce to a single overall budget constraint, and all agents find the shadow price of money constant. Further, virtual as well as discounted money prices which correspond to actual transactions are constant and expected to be so by the transacting agents. In a non-Walrasian equilibrium, the money constraint for an agent can be binding at finite time and virtual prices need not be constant. The presence or absence of such phenomena depends on the agent's view of how his monopoly or monopsony power is changing.

The existence of equilibria in this model is not examined directly but follows as an obvious consequence of the quasi-stability and global stability results of the next chapter.

CHAPTER 8

Dynamics and stability

8.1 Introduction

I come now to an examination of the dynamics of the system, the way the variables move out of equilibrium. The main assumptions used to secure stability are those of No Favorable Surprise as discussed in Chapter 4. These are the assumptions that ensure that new opportunities neither arise nor are perceived to do so. However, there are other properties of the motion of the system which it seems reasonable to assume. Since the proof of stability is not the only end of dynamic analysis and since the class of adjustment processes which are consistent with No Favorable Surprise needs to be studied, I discuss such properties as well in the hopes that such discussion will prove useful for further work.

To put it another way, given No Favorable Surprise, the class of models for which the stability result holds is quite general. On the other hand, that very generality means that we do not gain a great deal of information from that result about the workings of the model. To the extent that additional assumptions seem reasonably calculated to restrict the behavior of the model in directions that real economies may be supposed to take, it is useful to discuss such assumptions even though this book will not itself go beyond the proof of stability under No Favorable Surprise.

There is another reason for proceeding in this way. Were I to stop with a discussion of No Favorable Surprise, there would remain some question as to whether models with sensible dynamic assumptions could in fact be fitted into the framework used. By discussing such questions as individual price adjustment, orderly markets, and the problems of non-delivery within the context of the model I show that this is not an issue.

Such a discussion, I hope, will prove useful in the extensions of the present analysis discussed in Chapter 9, particularly in the study of what adjustment processes, given an *exogenous* favorable surprise then react in a way consistent with No Favorable Surprise as assumed here.

8.2 No Favorable Surprise

As we shall see, the analysis of No Favorable Surprise in the case of the firm presents one complication not present in the case of the household. Hence I begin by explicit consideration of the household case, postponing the complication raised by the firm until after a general discussion applicable to both.

We saw in Chapter 4 that the most basic stability result which it is important to prove as a foundation for equilibrium analysis is that the economy is stable provided new opportunities, real or imagined, do not keep on arising. One way of modeling such a circumstance is to assume that the feasible set of programs for the agent never expands to include new possibilities. As it happens, this is considerably stronger than necessary. There is no reason to preclude new opportunities from arising if those opportunities are not sufficiently attractive to be chosen. Indeed, we can allow new opportunities to arise which *are* eventually chosen so long as they are not chosen immediately.

For the household, it is sufficient to assume that the program which is optimal at any time t, was in the feasible set for some time interval $[t-\Delta^*, t]$ for some fixed $\Delta^* > 0$ (with the actual history on that interval included as part of the feasible program). This will be satisfied if new opportunities never arise, but it provides a more general result in which they do not arise and become chosen too fast. Note that Δ^* can be *very* small. (As we shall see, even this is somewhat stronger than necessary for our results.)

It is apparent what the immediate consequence of this assumption is for the household. All the constraints the household faces: short constraints, money constraints, instantaneous budget constraints, and transaction constraints, plus the convexity of its storage technology restrict the household's choice of programs: consumption, transactions, storage inputs, and share ownership, to a convex set. If two programs are feasible for the household then so is every convex combination of them. But the household's utility functional is strictly quasi-concave. Thus, if the utility of the optimal program chosen at t were greater than or even equal to the utility of the program chosen at $t-\Delta^*$, the latter could not have been optimal, for with both these programs in the feasible set at $t-\Delta^*$ the household could have chosen some strictly convex combination of them and done better than it did. It follows that, under No Favorable Surprise, the household must never have its utility increase and, indeed, must always experience a utility decrease except where its optimal program does not change, that is, except at points of momentary personal equilibrium, where all nonfree transactions are completed and no relevant parameter changes. All changes in relevant expectations must be in a pessimistic direction - hence the name "No Favorable Surprise."

This is the principal point, but it is worth going into the matter in more detail to see what is involved in the assumption that newly optimal programs were previously feasible. In so doing, it must be kept in mind that there is no contention that No Favorable Surprise is an assumption that plausibly characterizes real economies. New opportunities do arise and economies react to them. Rather, what is involved here, as explained in Chapter 4, is a proof that *without* such continued disturbances economies tend toward equilibrium; this is the minimum one can demand of stability analysis if equilibrium economics is to be soundly based. It is the first necessary step toward a demonstration that a cessation of *exogenous* shocks leads to convergence. I discuss the details of No Favorable Surprise so as to be able to see just what is involved rather than to contend for its realism. I return to this below.

The assumption that optimal programs were previously feasible means, in essence, that the environment in which the agent acts is not becoming more favorable in any very useful way. His technological opportunities in production, storage, or transactions cannot be expanding in unforeseen ways of which he instantaneously takes advantage. Further, the binding constraints under which he operates are not becoming looser. Those constraints are the short constraints, the money constraints, and the transaction constraints. I begin by discussing transaction constraints.

It is important to note that, quite generally, No Favorable Surprise is consistent with perfect foresight which, in a world of only point expectations, makes it consistent with rational expectations. This is because perfect foresight implies momentary personal equilibrium. However, as this suggests, if *all* agents always have perfect foresight, then the economy is automatically in equilibrium from the beginning. This is not an interesting case in an analysis which hopes to explain how economies reach equilibrium if they do not start out there. It is true that, in equilibrium, agents all have perfect foresight, but it is their learning experience on the way to equilibrium that brings this about. To analyze how agents learn of and take advantage of arbitrage opportunities and thus make them disappear is interesting and realistic; to assume that all agents always know everything and that such opportunities have hence never existed is to beg the question.

This view has particular force when we consider transaction constraints. Suppose that agents all have perfect foresight concerning transaction constraints. This can only mean that if agents optimize subject to their perceived transaction constraints, they all find themselves able to carry out their transactions. Further, since transaction constraints stem from perceived demand or supply curves, if those curves are perceived correctly, agents will also have perfect foresight as to prices. Even where it is only the transaction constraint at a given price and not the entire curve which is perceived correctly, agents, completing their expected transactions and observing that all other agents do so as well will have little reason to suppose that prices will change or to make new price offers. In short, mistakes as to the ability to transact provide the central feature of disequilibrium. To assume that all agents have perfect foresight about transaction constraints is to assume that all markets always clear, given the demands which agents attempt to exercise. This is not terribly interesting in an analysis which wishes to show how such market-clearing situations come about. To examine the consequence of No Favorable Surprise is interesting; to assume no surprise of any kind is not.

Now, if transaction constraints are occasionally found to be tighter than had previously been supposed, agents may very well revise their expectations of future transaction constraints to reflect this. (This is, of course, quite consistent with No Favorable Surprise. What would not be so consistent would be the optimistic revision of perceived transaction constraints in ways which appear to provide new opportunities advantageous to the agent.) Moreover, tighter transaction constraints may very well go with revised expectations as to short constraints and as to prices.

I shall be brief concerning short constraints. If such constraints are legal ones, imposed from outside, there is no reason, in general, to suppose that they change, although, as discussed later on, they may become tighter for agents who fail to deliver promised goods on time reflecting a lessened ability of such agents to be trusted or to obtain credit. Where short constraints are self-imposed, however, they reflect the realization that transactions may not be able to be completed in a short time and provide some substitute for the subjective uncertainty missing from the model. Where agents find transaction constraints tighter than they had thought, they may very well also reduce the amount they will allow themselves to go short, particularly if there are penalties for nondelivery as discussed in a later section.

As already indicated, agents' perceptions of prices are also linked – indeed closely linked – with their perceptions of transaction constraints. Expected and actual prices enter the analysis of No Favorable Surprise because of the money constraints; a favorable change in the prices at which an agent expects to transact (*relevant* prices) provides him with additional (expected) cash given his planned transactions. This enables him to take advantage of opportunities he would otherwise have had to pass up. Note that this is true even where money constraints are not binding at a finite time. In such a case, given more money, households can nevertheless increase their purchases, for their overall budget constraints (5.9.10) are surely binding. Firms that have more cash than they expected, if they do nothing else, will revise their dividend policies to pass on the increase in profits to their shareholders. Hence No Favorable Surprise implies no unexpected favorable price changes alleviating the money constraints or providing greater profits. As opposed to the Hahn Process, however, it is not necessary that *every* unexpected price change be unfavorable - only that all unexpected changes be unfavorable on balance.

As with transaction constraints, perfect foresight as to prices is consistent with No Favorable Surprise. Here, however, the question of whether such an assumption begs the disequilibrium question is a bit more subtle. If we suppose that agents encountering unexpectedly severe transaction constraints make price offers (for *later* transactions) to get around them, then it is hard to avoid the view that perfect foresight about prices implies perfect foresight about an agent's own transaction constraints. For if an agent will offer a different price if he encounters a transaction constraint than if he does not, then, if he knows what prices he will offer he also knows what constraints he will meet. If all agents know such things we are back in the uninteresting case of perfect foresight as to transaction constraints and no disequilibrium ever.

Such a view may not be totally persuasive, however. Whether one accepts it may depend on the institutional structure one has in mind as to how price offers get made. Thus, suppose that in a particular market it is customary for sellers to set prices and buyers to accept or reject such prices, possibly searching over sellers to find the lowest price or, more simply, with a single monopoly seller. In such a case, with buyers not themselves making price offers, it seems possible for the buyers to have perfect foresight as to the prices they will find without having perfect foresight as to their ability to buy at those prices. The matter does not end here, however. Suppose (for simplicity) that there is a single monopoly seller. We must suppose that *his* perfect foresight about the prices he will charge implies perfect foresight as to whether he will unexpectedly run into a transaction constraint, that is, that he knows the demand curve facing him well enough never to overestimate the amount which he can sell given his price. He might *underestimate* that amount, however, for this depends on whether unsatisfied buyers make themselves known to him. In any event, it is plausible that such a seller will alter his price if he is mistaken as to demand at that price in either direction and hence that perfect foresight about prices implies perfect foresight as to demand at those prices. If this is the case, there will certainly be no unsatisfied buyers willing to buy at the seller's price, so the buyers will not *in fact* encounter a transaction constraint they did not expect. While it is true that such buyers may change their minds about expected transaction constraints before they occur, so that their perfect foresight need not involve long-term predictions, there is still relatively little interest in such a case.

The moral seems clear. Perfect foresight for all agents as to prices when individuals set prices is not an interesting disequilibrium assumption. Perfect foresight for all agents as to prices appears interesting only if we do not delve too deeply into the process by which prices change.

It is important to realize, however, that this conclusion holds because we have assumed agents to have point expectations. If the model were extended to allow subjective uncertainty, then the extension of the perfect foresight case would be a more general case of rational expectations. The conclusion that perfect foresight is uninteresting would not, I think, apply in such a model since individual mistakes would then be possible. Certainly, rational expectations as to *prices* would not imply perfect foresight as to transaction constraints.

Putting perfect foresight for all agents aside, then,[1] what can be said concerning No Favorable Surprise with regard to prices. Here again unforeseen disequilibrium difficulties in completing transactions play a role. An agent who encounters such unforeseen difficulties may well change his expectations as to his future transactions. Such difficulties may reduce the extent of the transactions he expects to be able to complete at given prices; they may also cause him to expect that prices will be less favorable for given transactions than he had previously supposed.

This is, of course, strongly reminiscent of the Hahn Process assumption, under which everything an agent wishes to buy but cannot buy is going up in price, while everything an agent wishes to sell but cannot sell is going down in price. Indeed, such a reflection of transaction problems in expected prices makes most sense in an orderly market world where the transaction experiences of individual agents reflect overall conditions. Thus, where an agent can take his inability to sell as an indication that demand is generally lower than he supposed, it is plausible that he should expect further difficulties if he does not lower his price (or

[1] Note that perfect foresight for *some* agents is not ruled out.

expect to encounter lower prices if he himself is passive as regards the price in question). Where markets are not so orderly, on the other hand, an agent unable to sell may simply regard himself as unlucky. If he believes that there are others unable to buy, he may even revise his expectations in an optimistic manner. (I shall discuss orderly markets in more detail in a later section.)

Note that successful arbitrage is not ruled out by No Favorable Surprise. There is nothing to prevent an agent encountering expected prices (although, as we have seen, if this always happens for all agents the disequilibrium problem may become uninteresting). What is ruled out is the possibility that prices should be *more* favorable than expected so that windfall gains occur which loosen the money constraints in unanticipated ways.

Those constraints for households can also be affected even if prices and transaction amounts are foreseen. This is because households receive dividends from firms. Money constraints can be loosened if households receive dividends greater than they expect.[2] Note, however, that since firms are also subject to No Favorable Surprise, firms' estimates of their profits will be falling. Shareholders sharing those estimates will not find their expected dividends increasing. Those holding short positions in the shares will be pleased; however, this will be consistent with No Favorable Surprise if the expectation of such decreases in profit estimates and dividends were what caused them to take the short position in the first place.

This brings me to a related point. Even apart from the case of perfect foresight, a world of No Favorable Surprise is a world in which expectations are consistent in a sense with a strong rational expectations flavor. In a world in which new opportunities do not arise but changes are perceived as the result of the overestimation or disappearance of old opportunities, stability will hold. Hence in such a world old opportunities will in fact be arbitraged away and the expectation that this will happen is in harmony with the facts. The difference between this rather natural perception of the truth and the strong unrealism of the assumption of perfect foresight that a fully believing rational expectations economist might wish to impose on this model lies in the fact that the sensible perception that opportunities are disappearing is not the same as the unwarranted assumption that they have already disappeared. Systematic action on perceived arbitrage opportunities does indeed drive the economy to equilibrium – indeed, to a rational expectations equilibrium – if new opportunities do not arise. This is quite different from the question-begging position that this all happens instantaneously.

[2] In the case of households with short positions in shares, such loosening can occur if dividends are lower than expected.

There are two additional matters that need discussion before we proceed. The first of these is the extra complication that arises in the case of firms. The second and more important one has to do with the nature of the analysis being undertaken.

In the case of firms, the assumption that programs now optimal were previously feasible is not itself quite sufficient to ensure that profits decrease when the firm is not at a position of momentary personal equilibrium. This is because prices directly enter the objective function of the firm. Thus, while changes in other relevant parameters can only decrease profits (since we have assumed the profit-maximizing program to be unique) and while price changes cannot *increase* profits (since otherwise a money constraint would become looser or at least a more generous dividend program possible), there remains the possibility that expected prices might change in just such a way as to leave the profits expected from the new optimal program the same as those expected from the previous one, even though the price changes cause a change in plans. Consideration of what is involved in such a situation, however, reveals that this is a case of measure zero. Since, in addition, the firm's general experience with price and other changes under No Favorable Surprise will be unfavorable, it seems harmless to assume that such an anomalous situation, if it ever occurs, cannot persist forever, and this is all that is required. We shall therefore assume that unless a firm is in momentary personal equilibrium at t, there exists some $t^* > t$ at which its target profits are different from its target profits at t. In view of No Favorable Surprise such profits must decrease from t to t^*.

This brings me to the final matter in this section. The assumptions made are the heart of what ensures stability in the proofs below. But, while No Favorable Surprise is sufficient to justify the decline of target utilities and the ultimate decline of target profits out of equilibrium, it is obviously stronger than necessary. Utility and (ultimate) profit decline out of equilibrium does not require that newly optimal programs be previously feasible, nor does such decline require that all changes be adverse. Such decline merely requires that changes be adverse *on balance* with unfavorable surprise outweighing favorable surprise, so to speak.

It may be said, then, that No Favorable Surprise is too strong an assumption even for the proof of stability given below, for the stability results being proved plainly hold under more general conditions. Such increased generality is indeed welcome, but I do not explore it further here. This is because of the nature of the enterprise undertaken in this book. It is time to remind the reader about this and to add some additional remarks.

As discussed in Chapters 1 and 4, I am attempting to provide a foundation for the use of equilibrium analysis. Such a foundation requires a proof of stability. The stability theorem that one would like to prove is that an economy with rational arbitraging agents absorbs shocks, so that a cessation of new *exogenous* opportunities leads to convergence. Unfortunately, such a demonstration does not seem immediately possible. As a result, I prove a weaker, but still important, result: that the cessation of the appearance of *all* new opportunities, endogenous as well as exogenous, implies stability. As discussed in Chapter 4, this condition is very close to being necessary for stability and its sufficiency is not trivial.

Nevertheless, one cannot rest content with this result. If it is to be useful in the larger enterprise of showing that economies with rational, arbitraging agents absorb exogenous shocks, then we must learn what adjustment processes are consistent with No Favorable Surprise. It is true that adjustment processes that generate unfavorable surprises which outweigh favorable ones will also be stable, but this does not seem very helpful for further analysis, although I may well be mistaken. The fact that No Favorable Surprise leads to stability means that the appearance of new opportunities is necessary for *in*stability; this suggests that the question of what processes rule out such opportunities is an important one, and one more likely to be answered than the more general question of what processes generate surprises which are *on balance* not favorable.

What we know about processes which are consistent with No Favorable Surprise consists at this time of examples. One such example is that of the Hahn Process as analyzed in Chapter 3. A second is that of perfect foresight, which is uninteresting in the present, point-expectations context but becomes the very interesting case of rational expectations if we think in terms of extension to the more realistic case of subjective uncertainty.

It is clear that these two examples are not exhaustive. Consider the following. Suppose that some agents have perfect foresight and that these are buyers. Suppose that other agents – sellers – set prices and that these sellers begin by overestimating the demand facing them at their initial prices. In this situation, the sellers will find that they cannot sell as much as they expected; they will lower their prices. This will be an unfavorable surprise for them. Further, while such lower prices will be favorably viewed by the buyers, *they will not come as a surprise,* for we have assumed the buyers to have perfect foresight. No Favorable Surprise does not mean that things get worse; it merely implies that they do not turn out better than expected.

To take a more realistic case, consider a buyer and a seller bargaining with each other. If each agent makes an offer expecting the other to accept but finds that instead he must improve his own offer, we have an example of No Favorable Surprise.

Plainly, examples like this and more general than this are possible. Plainly also, we do not know enough about adjustment processes and expectations formation out of equilibrium to characterize such cases save as ones of No Favorable Surprise - a property which is not, as it were, a natural "primitive" idea to impose on adjustment mechanisms. It remains to be seen whether or not there are natural, more basic assumptions that lead to No Favorable Surprise. Certainly, rational expectations appears to be one such assumption, but it need not be the only one.

In any event, the study of No Favorable Surprise seems warranted, not because of its realism, but because it is a necessary step in the stability foundation for equilibrium economics.

8.3 Individual price adjustment and orderly markets

I now discuss other aspects of the dynamic behavior of the system; most of these have come up earlier.

Our previous discussion of individual price adjustment has been largely silent on just how such adjustment takes place. We have observed that it is sensible to suppose that price offers reflect perceived monopoly or monopsony power, taking into account the slope of the demand or supply curves which the agent perceives himself as facing. This moves the question of how prices change to that of how such perceptions change; beyond that, it does not advance us very far.

Some further indication of how prices adjust was given in considering No Favorable Surprise. There we said that relevant prices must not be seen to adjust favorably relative to expectations if new opportunities are to be ruled out. This suggests - but does not impose - the restriction that unfavorable transaction experiences should cause readjustment of anticipated or actual price offers. This restriction makes agents react to their own excess demands, so to speak; it is all that remains of the traditional but mysterious price-adjustment mechanism of tâtonnement days (2.2.1). The price-setting behavior involved differs from that of the traditional mechanism in two important respects, however. First, agents set prices and look at their own unsatisfied demands rather than aggregate excess demand; second, the change in an agent's price for a particular commodity does not necessarily have the same sign as the agent's unsatisfied demand for that commodity, although such a rule would not be implausible.[3]

[3] Note that since prices and demands are indexed as of a particular time, unsatisfied demand at t resulting from an unsuccessful trading attempt can only influence prices corresponding to later trades. It is harmless (and technically useful)

Indeed, agents may set prices taking into account the experience of others.[4]

Beyond this (and an assumption about price dispersion in equilibrium), I have said little to restrict price change. In one respect, of course, this is a great advantage. Given the strong restriction of No Favorable Surprise, it is not necessary to restrict price adjustment processes in other ways to secure stability. In another respect, it merely reveals our ignorance. Stability is not the only goal of the analysis of disequilibrium behavior. To take a leading example, it is important to know whether the equilibrium approached will be Walrasian or not. As we saw in Chapters 6 and 7, this depends on how perceptions of monopoly or monopsony power adjust, the question which underlies price adjustment. Without a more specific and restricted model of such adjustment, the question of the nature of equilibrium cannot be answered. Plainly, we know far too little about this topic - a topic which is central to the theory of value.

So far, this discussion has concerned how price offers get made. There is another question involved in price adjustment, however, that of how price offers get accepted. Here too I shall be general and vague, although such vagueness seems less important in this context.

I assume that institutions are such that some set of agents in each market explicitly set prices and the remaining agents, if any, decide which prices to accept. There is no need to be restrictive here. The active price-setting agents may be sellers, with the passive agents buyers, as in many retail markets; the active agents may be buyers and the passive ones sellers, as in many labor markets; there may be both buyers and sellers among the active agents, and, indeed, there need be no passive agents at all in the sense that all agents can offer prices with some institutional arrangements (such as a stock market specialist) deciding how buying and selling offers are matched. Within the quite general restrictions on price adjustment already given, there is no need to be more specific, save to assume that there are no problems caused by discontinuities as passive agents switch from one active agent to another.

As we have already seen in discussing equilibrium, however, there are some restrictions that are sensibly imposed on prices, which relate to transactions in the same market. These restrictions have to do with what we tend to mean by a "market," more specifically, with the extension of the Hahn Process assumption that buyers and sellers can find each other so that markets are "orderly," with at most one side unsatisfied after trade.

to assume that if excess demand for some good or share becomes unbounded if its price were zero, then price-setting agents are smart enough to demand a positive price for it.

[4] See Maskin's remark in Hahn (1978, pp. 7-8).

We saw in Chapter 6, but it is worth repeating here, that the question of who remains unsatisfied after trade is *not* the same as the somewhat related question of who encounters binding transaction constraints. The latter question is one of perception; the former is one of reality. In equilibrium, it is true that (by definition) agents never attempt to buy or sell more than they can. It is *also* true that they never (in equilibrium or out of it) attempt to violate a constraint they perceive as binding. Hence, it *may* be true that, in equilibrium, agents know the limits on their transactions correctly so that the assumption that at most one side perceives itself to be constrained coincides with the assumption that at most one side is unsatisfied after trade. Even this requires the (not very strong) assumption that agents who believe themselves more constrained than they in fact are eventually learn the truth about later transactions.

Out of equilibrium, however, there is no justification for supposing that the two assumptions coincide. We have already seen that mistakes about transaction constraints are the essence of disequilibrium. To assume perfect foresight of those constraints is to beg the entire disequilibrium question. Hence it is a mistake to suppose that the assumption that at most one side of the market perceives itself as constrained can be derived from the assumption that markets work well enough that at most one side of the market fails to satisfy the demands formulated with transaction constraints in mind. The latter assumption is reasonable; the former one is not.

What becomes of the orderly market assumption when there are individual prices? Plainly, we can no longer suppose that at most one side of the market is unable to complete its transactions.[5] There is nothing to prevent agents from mistakes as to what prices will be accepted. Hence, there may be buyers offering low prices and sellers offering high ones, both of whom can find no trading partners. What can be ruled out is the reverse: unsatisfied buyers offering high prices together with unsatisfied sellers offering low ones. Indeed, the natural extension of the Hahn Process assumption to the present context is twofold. In the first part, one assumes that among agents offering high prices only sellers are unsatisfied while among agents offering low prices only buyers are unsatisfied. In the second part, one assumes that, after trade, if any seller is unsatisfied so are all sellers who offered higher prices and that if any buyer is unsatisfied so are all buyers who offered lower prices. (The details are given later.)

Such assumptions are not needed for the stability proof (a much weaker version – Assumption 7.6.1 – was used to eliminate price dispersion in

[5] Unless we define markets by identifying the same physical commodity as different commodities if different agents set prices for it. See Fisher (1972b).

equilibrium), and fortunately so, for consideration of this matter reveals how strong such assumptions are (and, indeed, how strong the Hahn Process assumption is in its original form). For such extended orderly markets assumptions to hold, we must suppose either that information is perfect or that search is costless and instantaneous, for the plausibility of those assumptions plainly depends on the ability of agents to find out about prices as well as to find trading partners. Yet that process of information gathering may be very important in certain markets and, indeed, there is a large literature on search. Moreover, the questions of how search occurs and how efficient it is have a good deal to do with the important question of whether or not perceived monopoly power vanishes asymptotically, making equilibrium Walrasian.[6]

8.4 Nonperformance and bankruptcy

I now consider a different aspect of trade, the possibility that agents fail to redeem their promises. Such failure can take two forms. One of these is the failure to deliver goods previously sold as futures; the other is the failure to cover a short position in bonds or notes, that is, bankruptcy.[7] The object is to show that such matters can be modeled in a way consistent with No Favorable Surprise rather than to provide a fully realistic analysis.

When one agent fails to deliver to another as promised, there are two agents directly affected. What happens to them depends on the rules which society has for dealing with such situations. It seems reasonable to assume that such rules take the following form. The defaulting agent must pay a fine to the injured agent. That fine does not exceed the amount which would make the injured agent indifferent between receiving the promised goods and receiving the fine; the defaulter does not have to do more than make the injured agent "whole." Note that if the defaulter can make price offers, it must be the case that he prefers to default rather than raise his price sufficiently to buy back the commitment.

The injured agent is thus no better off than he would have been had delivery been made. This is consistent with No Favorable Surprise and

[6] See Fisher (1973) for a not very satisfactory treatment of this in a single market. Diamond (1971) shows that monopoly power can persist. A good survey of the early search literature is Rothschild (1973).

[7] I do not explicitly consider failure to cover short security positions. Delivery of securities does not affect consumption, production, or storage plans and was modeled in Chapter 5 only to be required asymptotically. If the law requires delivery in finite time, failure so to deliver can be handled along the lines about to be discussed.

the only problem which needs discussing with regard to the injured agent is that of continuity. We must ensure that the injured agent is not so suddenly surprised by the delivery failure that his behavior violates the smoothness conditions which lead to the existence and continuity of solutions to the differential equations of motion of the system. In essence, this means allowing the injured agent to become aware of the default in time to revise his plans. What must be ruled out is an attempt at the last instant to use the nondelivered commodity for consumption or input purposes.

This is easy to do. The simplest way to proceed is to assume that the injured agent, before the event, has expectations as to the amount of the commodity he will in fact receive and the resulting default penalty. As with all other expectations in this model, these are point expectations. They begin, well before the delivery date, at the full amount of his commitment holdings (although this is not necessary) and, consistent with No Favorable Surprise, never increase (save through purchase of additional commitments), converging to the true state of affairs as the commodity date is reached. It is obvious that such a treatment requires essentially no modification in the theory of earlier chapters; the agent anticipating his injury in this way continually revises his plans to take account of what seems to him shrinkage in his holdings of the particular future commodity in question.

It is, of course, not particularly appealing to have point expectations here (although whether the absence of subjective uncertainty is worse here than anywhere else in the model is open to question). To show that this is not crucial, I sketch a simple version in which uncertainty is allowed. Suppose, for simplicity only, that there is doubt about delivery of a particular portion of the agent's holdings and that such portion will either be delivered *in toto* or not delivered at all.[8] At any time, the potentially injured agent has a subjective probability, α, of nondelivery and receipt of fine. Note that No Favorable Surprise will require that α never fall; hence, the assumption of no new opportunities means that agents who receive delivery must have expected it with certainty. In any event, we assume that α goes to unity in the case of actual nondelivery. The potentially injured agent maximizes the expected value of his objective functional - more generally, firms as well as households are assumed to satisfy the von Neumann–Morgenstern axioms and maximize expected utility. It is obvious that such behavior is continuous in α so that no special problem as to the existence and continuity of solutions to the equations of motion is presented.

[8] More complex cases can be dealt with as combinations of simple ones like this.

I shall not follow this road very far, save to observe that if $\alpha > 0$, the agent in question will, quite naturally, value planned inputs, outputs, or consumption of the good in question *above* its market price, since inputs, outputs, and consumption changes represent sure changes in possessions, while purchases do not.[9] This kind of uncertainty happens to be fairly easy to model compared to price uncertainty in the context of equilibrium and No Favorable Surprise, but there seems no point in doing it explicitly in the present point-expectations model. The principal conclusions have already been demonstrated: Nondelivery can be accommodated within the model in a way consistent with appropriately smooth behavior on the part of the injured agent. Further, this is particularly easy in a No Favorable Surprise world, although here (as always) that assumption is a strong one.

There remains the analysis of the behavior of the defaulting agent. Here we can use the same device: point expectations as to the extent of the default and the resulting fine (or simple uncertainty as above). The defaulting agent too will have smooth behavior and there is nothing to prevent the situation from being consistent with No Favorable Surprise.

Note that such consistency is possible despite two phenomena. First, as already remarked, the defaulting agent would prefer default to a very high price offer; this merely puts a bound on the extent to which his expected utility or profit can decrease. Second, it is quite possible for *both* the injured agent and the defaulting agent to become worse off as default becomes more certain; this is because the fine will not do more than compensate the injured agent and there are limits to the closing price which defaulters are willing or able to pay. Note that there is nothing in No Favorable Surprise to prevent potentially injured agents from reaping large capital gains as potential defaulters attempt to buy back their commitments, as long as those gains are not *unexpectedly* large. Agents correctly foreseeing (or overestimating) such situations are permitted to take advantage of them, even with No Favorable Surprise.

The possibility that both the defaulting and the injured agent can be worse off as a result of default is enhanced if we consider other sanctions that society may impose on defaulters. It is reasonable to suppose that an agent who defaults will not be trusted again to the same extent. This can be represented in the model as an unfavorable change in a defaulting agent's short constraints with continuity being handled as before. Such changes represent costs to the defaulter which are not paid as compensation to the injured agent.

[9] Whether or not sales represent sure changes depends on the rules of liability – that is, whether an agent is liable for nondelivery if it occurs because of the nonperformance of his own supplier.

Such restrictions as to the extent to which a defaulting agent is thereafter allowed to go short are closely allied to the restrictions which, it is sensible to suppose, are imposed on agents who do not pay their debts - who default on notes or fail to cover short positions in bonds and become bankrupt.[10] The analysis given for the nondelivery case shows how to deal with this as well. We give creditors point expectations as to how much they will receive on the dollar. This can make their behavior continuous and consistent with No Favorable Surprise.[11] The debtor is also equipped with such expectations; however, the treatment of this behavior requires some elaboration.

The problem here arises because the bankrupt debtor cannot be supposed to pay a fine to the creditor (as in the parallel case of nondelivery). There must thus be some other sanction with which society attempts to prevent deliberate bankruptcy. One such sanction, readily accommodated in the current model, is the extent to which the bankrupt can borrow in the future. This involves the short constraints on notes and bonds and, presumably, on ordinary commodities as well. We can suppose that such penalties vary continuously with the amount of the defaulted debt.

Other sanctions require considerations not yet present in our model. Bankruptcy may involve social opprobrium and deliberate bankruptcy may involve prison terms. If the severity of such punishments is continuous in the size of the defaulted debt, the punishments can be accommodated as well, although it is a bit awkward to treat the matter in this way in the case of firms whose managers are not given noncorporate motivations in the present model.

In any event, we need not linger over these matters. Nondelivery and bankruptcy present some interesting problems but are basically side issues in our present analysis. They can both be assumed to be handled by institutional arrangements that make them unpleasant but leave the continuity of behavior unaffected. Both of them can be present in a world characterized by No Favorable Surprise, although, evidently they will not be present in equilibrium where all expectations are fulfilled and pessimistic as well as optimistic surprise comes to an end.

[10] The only other way for an agent to become bankrupt in this model is for him to be unable to pay a nondelivery fine. It is unnecesssary to treat this case explicitly; one can, if one wishes, treat the fine as paid in special very short-term notes (special so as not to interfere with the short constraints for ordinary notes) which then become subject to default.

[11] A similar device can be used to cover the case in which a firm, foreseeing bankruptcy if it continues in operation, winds up its affairs voluntarily, distributing its assets to its shareholders.

8.5 Other rules of motion

There are a few other assumptions that are reasonable to make concerning the motion of the system. These are partly matters of consistent accounting. Thus, the economy is closed so that the net actual transactions of firms must match the net transactions of the household sector in commodities and money. Similarly, total net trade in shares over households must be zero.

A more substantive assumption has to do with value paid and received in trade. As in the Hahn Process models of Chapter 3, it is sensible to impose a No Swindling assumption, which ensures that, in trading at constant prices, the value of the money received by the seller matches the value of the goods and shares received by the buyer. This ensures that wealth cannot change through trade at constant prices. It has already been imposed on agents with regard to *planned* transactions and is obviously sensible with regard to *actual* ones.

Such a No Swindling Assumption, however, is not needed directly below. This is because of the very direct form in which I have stated No Favorable Surprise - that currently optimal programs were previously feasible. If we were to weaken or look more deeply into that assumption and assume more directly that price expectations move so as to make planned purchases more expensive and planned sales less profitable, the No Swindling Assumption would play a larger role than it does below in establishing that actual transactions at constant prices need not be directly considered as they will not affect wealth.

8.6 The nature of stability

When the earlier sections of this chapter are formalized, we shall be in position to obtain the principal stability results of this book: That an economy with rational agents acting on perceived arbitrage opportunities is stable if such opportunities do not keep on arising - stable under No Favorable Surprise. The technical details are spelled out later in this chapter; in the present section I briefly discuss what the stability results turn out to be and take up some related matters.

I begin with quasi-stability. This, it will be recalled, is the property that every limit point of the time-path of the system is a rest point - rest points here being economic equilibria as defined in Chapter 7. To prove this one ordinarily finds a Lyapounov function, continuous, bounded below, and decreasing through time except at rest points. In Hahn Process models, the appropriate Lyapounov function turns out to be the sum of the target utilities which households expect to get if they complete their transactions. Out of equilibrium, these expectations are incompatibly high; as the system progresses, they are reduced through sad experience until they become compatible at equilibrium.

The situation in the present model is similar, as we should expect. No Favorable Surprise generates the same fall in target optimands as does the Hahn Process (which is a special case of No Favorable Surprise). However, there are two differences that are of some interest.

The first of these has to do with the role of firms. In the case of the Hahn Process, firms which are unable to complete their transactions find their target profits declining. The effect of such noncompletion on target profits is passed through directly to shareholders all of whom hold the same (naive) expectations as the firms as to the profits they will someday receive. Hence, personal disequilibrium for a firm is reflected in the target utilities of its shareholders and the sum of these utilities can serve as a Lyapounov function. In the present case, however, this is not necessarily so. Firms and their shareholders can have different expectations about future profits. Hence it is possible that a firm might not be in momentary personal equilibrium while its shareholders feel no effect on their target utilities. This is especially likely since the firm's failure to be in momentary personal equiibrium in the present model need not stem from a failure to complete transactions, but may only involve expectation revision - something which shareholders may simply have themselves anticipated.

The result of this is that the sum of target utilities alone will not do as a Lyapounov function. Such a sum can fail to decrease even if firms are not in momentary personal equilibria provided that households are all in such equilibria. Instead, we must include firms as equal personae, reflecting the fact that they have been given independent abilities to form expectations. This means taking as our Lyapounov function not the sum of target utilities but the sum of target utilities plus the sum of target *profits*.[12]

The second difference between the proof of quasi-stability in the present model and that in Hahn Process models also concerns expectations (which is not surprising). If, as just indicated, we take as our Lyapounov function the sum of target utilities and target profits, we

[12] The dimensionality difficulty with such a construct is only apparent. Any weighted sum of target utilities and profits or, indeed, any continuous function strictly monotonic in such target magnitudes (and bounded below) will do as well. Indeed, there is quite as much (or as little) meaning to adding utilities and profits as there is to adding utilities across agents. Both constructions are merely devices without direct economic content.

shall have a function which fails to decrease not only in equilibrium but also elsewhere. Such a function is constant whenever all agents are simultaneously in momentary personal equilibrium and this can occur even when the economy is not itself in equilibrium - a state in which all agents are always in momentary personal equilibrium *from then on*.

The problem arises because of the possibility that all agents can temporarily complete their transactions and find their near-term expectations as to prices and other relevant magnitudes fulfilled while some (or all) of them hold longer-term expectations that will not come true. In such a circumstance, the system - and the proposed Lyapounov function - will stop moving, but only temporarily. Eventually, agents will either change their expectations or find that they cannot go on completing their transactions.

Such temporary halts can occur in this system because of the relatively sensible nature of equilibrium which permits ongoing trade rather than ending the world after one great orgy of Arrow-Debreu market-clearing. Fortunately, it is not hard to take such possibilities into account by a related but different choice of Lyapounov function. That choice turns out to be the sum over agents of the average target utilities or profits which the agent will *ever* turn out to expect along the path of the system, and this does have the property that it stops moving only when all agents are *thenceforward* at momentary personal equilibria - an equilibrium for the economy.[13]

The model is thus quasi-stable. Unfortunately, however, that property does not have the direct importance which it has in other contexts. This is for a technical reason: The space in which the magnitudes of interest lie is quite complicated, since some of those magnitudes are themselves continuous functions. Hence it is not simple (or even possible in any obviously attractive way) to ensure that the time path of the system remains in a compact set, since boundedness and closure will no longer suffice. As a result, while quasi-stability assures us that every limit point of that time path is a rest point and hence an equilibrium, we do not know at this stage whether or not that time path *has* any limit points. This keeps quasi-stability from directly implying that the system actually converges

[13] The instantaneous sum of target utilities and target profits can also halt in the wrong place because of the measure zero possibility that a firm, not in momentary personal equilibrium, finds prices changing so as just to leave profits unchanged. I assumed above that such a circumstance did not persist forever and this is enough to handle the matter for the Lyapounov function actually used. Of course, had there been no other difficulty with the instantaneous sum of target utilities and profits as a Lyapounov function, I would have assumed that such anomalies *never* occur.

to the set of equilibria. Indeed, at this stage we do not even know whether or not any equilibria exist.

Fortunately, a stronger result than quasi-stability is available. Global stability of the dynamic system can be proved with some additional assumptions. This establishes that the system converges to a limit point and quasi-stability then implies that such a point is a rest point and hence an equilibrium. For the most part, the additional assumptions required for global stability are technical in nature and are designed to ensure that such things as strict quasi-concavity of utility functionals do not disappear asymptotically and that programs of firms which are bounded away from the profit maximizing program make discretely less profits than that program – a similar property. The details are left to the technical discussion.

There are two other assumptions involved that merit brief discussion here, however. The first of these is the boundedness of the time path of the system. While, given boundedness of prices, the boundedness of production, production plans, and quantities generally might be derived from more basic considerations concerning the finite supply of the primary resources of the planet, boundedness of prices would have to be assumed directly. The methods used to derive it in simpler contexts break down. While the assumption that prices are bounded seems reasonable, the fact that it cannot be derived from other more basic assumptions reflects once more how general our price-adjustment assumptions are – which is the nice way of saying that it reflects how little we know about the way in which prices really adjust.

The second assumption that should be mentioned before proceeding is closely related to one already discussed in Chapter 3, namely, the assumption that only one set of prices is consistent with a given equilibrium. Essentially, what is ruled out here is the possibility that the economy decomposes into two (or more) subsets of agents and commodities with all the agents in one subset at corner solutions with regard to the holdings or planned holdings of commodities in the other. Were this to occur, the prices of commodities in each subset would be irrelevant to the agents in the other subset and there might be nothing to tie down the relative prices of commodities in two different subsets. In addition to this, the assumption under discussion rules out the possibility that (in equilibrium) there exists a commodity (or share) such that *every* agent is at a corner solution with respect to it. This could happen, for example, if every holder of such a commodity wants more but believes himself prevented by transaction constraints from buying more or if every holder wishes to sell but is prevented from doing so by transaction constraints.[14]

[14] Note that such cases fail to determine price in part because of the dependence of individual prices on perceived demand or supply curves.

Either case is consistent with orderly markets if other agents are not interested in transacting but either is also pretty extreme and it seems reasonable to make the indicated assumption.[15]

Proceeding in this way, it is possible to prove global stability of the dynamic process: the property that, for every initial condition, the model converges to some equilibrium which will, in general, depend on the initial conditions from which we start and on the path of the system. I now consider just what this property means in the present context.

Convergence in the present model takes place as follows. Prices and expected relevant prices converge to equilibrium prices in the sense that the supremum over goods and shares of the absolute difference between undiscounted prices and their equilibrium values goes to zero. Consumption, storage, production, transaction, shareholding, and dividend profiles also converge, except for the holdings of goods which are free at the asymptotic equilibrium prices. The convergence of such profiles occurs in the following sense. At any moment, there may be differences between a quantity profile stretching into the future and its equilibrium equivalent. The integral of the absolute value of such differences discounted back to the moment in question goes to zero, so that differences of any given size and extent, if they persist, get farther and farther away from the planning time and thus, because of discounting, asymptotically cease to have any effect.

Far more important than the details of convergence, however, is the overriding fact that the equilibrium to which the process converges, and, indeed, the entire equilibrium set, is itself changing through time. This occurs both because "endowments" in the form of actual possessions and commitment holdings change through trade as in every model outside the implausible world of tâtonnement and because of the effects of consumption and production out of equilibrium. As we have seen, production out of equilibrium changes the set of technologically feasible opportunities because of the effects of past, irreversible input decisions. Consumption similarly fixes some of the arguments of the consumer's utility functional, as it were, forcing him to optimize only with respect to decisions as to consumption yet to come. This can be considered either as changing his objective functional or as altering the constraints within which he operates. In any case, such effects make the equilibrium to which the system tends depend not only on the initial position from which it starts but on the historical development it goes through on the

[15] If the price assumption discussed is not made, convergence of quantities and quantity profiles still takes place, but only quasi-stability holds for prices - as we might expect, since equilibria for prices will not be locally isolated, in view of the corner solutions permitted.

way. As emphasized in Chapter 1, such hysteresis or path-dependent effects cannot be assumed away and their presence, if at all large, has serious implications for the use of comparative statics. The equilibrium to which the system gets is not that (or, more properly, not one of *those*) corresponding to its initial position in a static analysis.

8.7* Equations of motion

I now summarize the treatment of the dynamic behavior of the system. The state variables are each agents' profiles of: actual and expected discounted prices and dividends, inputs, consumption, transactions, and shareholdings. These are assumed to change according to differential equations which have solutions which are continuous in the initial conditions. Additional restrictions on these differential equations are given in earlier chapters or are listed below.

The first such restriction is

> *Assumption 8.7.1 (No Favorable Surprise).* There exists a $\Delta^* > 0$ such that, for every agent and every t, the program which is optimal for that agent at t was feasible at $t - \Delta$ for every Δ such that $0 \leqslant \Delta \leqslant \Delta^*$.

Note that it is to be understood that dividend policy is to be included as part of the optimal program for a firm. For firms we also add

> *Assumption 8.7.2 (No Constant Disequilibrium Profits).* For every firm and every t unless the firm is in momentary personal equilibrium at t, there exists a $t^* > t$ such that target profits at t^* differ from target profits at t.

Evidently, these assumptions imply:

> *Lemma 8.7.1.* (a) For all times, t, and households, h, target utility U^h is nonincreasing and is strictly declining unless h is in momentary personal equilibrium at t.
>
> (b) For all firms, f, and all times, t, target profits, π^f, are nonincreasing. Further, unless the firm is in momentary personal equilibrium at t, there exists a $t^* > t$ such that π^f is strictly less at t^* than it is at t.

I now formalize the fact that the economy is closed. Bars denote actual transactions and prices.

> *Assumption 8.7.3 (Closed Economy).* For all t,

(a) $$\sum_h \bar{\mathbf{z}}^h(\theta, t) + \sum_f \bar{\mathbf{z}}^f(\theta, t) = 0 \quad \theta \geqslant t$$

(b) $$\sum_h \bar{\mathbf{q}}^h(t) = 0$$

(c) $$\sum_h \bar{z}_0^h(t) + \sum_f \int_t^\infty \bar{\mathbf{p}}^f(\theta, t)\bar{\mathbf{z}}^f(\theta, t) = 0$$

(d) For all f, $\bar{g}^f = \sum_h \bar{d}_f^h(t)\bar{k}_f^h(t)$

The four parts of this assumption state, respectively, that net trade in commodities of the household sector is with the productive sector; that total trade in shares is among households; that money spent in trade by the household sector is received by firms; and that dividends paid by firms are received by their shareholders.

The remaining two assumptions in this section are not required for the stability proof but are of some interest. The first such assumption is quite reasonable and, indeed, supplements the Closed Economy assumption (Assumption 8.7.3).

Assumption 8.7.4 (No Swindling). For every t and every household, h,

$$\bar{z}_0^h(t) + \int_t^\infty \bar{\mathbf{p}}^h(\theta, t)\bar{\mathbf{z}}^h(\theta, t)\,d\theta + \bar{\mathbf{w}}^h(t)\bar{\mathbf{q}}^h(t) = 0 \tag{8.7.1}$$

The next assumption, by contrast, is hardly innocuous in seeking to understand how markets behave in disequilibrium. I give it explicitly only for commodity markets.

Assumption 8.7.5 (Extended Orderly Markets). For all t, $\theta \geq t$, commodities i, and agents a and a' (bars denote actual values as opposed to planned ones):

(a) There exists $\tilde{P}_i(\theta, t)$, $0 \leq \tilde{P}_i(\theta, t) \leq \infty$, such that

(i) $\bar{p}_i^a(\theta, t) < \tilde{P}_i(\theta, t)$ implies

$$\bar{z}_i^a(\theta, t) \leq z_i^a(\theta, t, t)$$

(ii) $\bar{p}_i^a(\theta, t) > \tilde{P}_i(\theta, t)$ implies

$$\bar{z}_i^a(\theta, t) \geq z_i^a(\theta, t, t)$$

(iii) $\bar{p}_i^a(\theta, t) = \bar{p}_i^{a'}(\theta, t) = \tilde{P}_i(\theta, t)$ implies

$$(z_i^a(\theta, t) - \bar{z}_i^a(\theta, t, t))(z_i^{a'}(\theta, t) - \bar{z}_i^{a'}(\theta, t, t)) \geq 0$$

(b) If either: (i) $z_i^a(\theta, t, t) > 0$ and $z_i^{a'}(\theta, t, t) > 0$ and $\bar{p}_i^a(\theta, t) > \bar{p}_i^{a'}(\theta, t)$, or (ii) $z_i^a(\theta, t, t) < 0$ and $z_i^{a'}(\theta, t, t) < 0$ and $\bar{p}_i^a(\theta, t) < \bar{p}_i^{a'}(\theta, t)$, then $\bar{z}_i^{a'}(\theta, t) = z_i^{a'}(\theta, t)$ implies $\bar{z}_i^a(\theta, t) = z_i^a(\theta, t)$.

Part (a) of this assumption ensures that at high prices it is only sellers and at low prices only buyers who are unsatisfied. Part (b) ensures that high-priced sellers do not sell out unless low-priced ones do also and that low-priced buyers do not satisfy their demands unless high-priced ones do. Obviously both parts (which are independent) assume considerable information on the part of agents.

The discussion of the various ways to handle nonperformance will not be formalized further.

8.8* Quasi-stability

I assume target profits and target utilities bounded below. In a notation restricted to this chapter, let $A^a(t+\Delta)$ for all $\Delta \geqslant 0$, denote the value of the optimand for agent a (utilities for households, profits for firms) which a will turn out to expect at time $t+\Delta$ given the time path of the system. Since the solution of the system is continuous in its initial conditions, this is a continuous function of the state variables at time t.

Define

$$v^a(t) \equiv \rho \int_0^\infty e^{-\rho\Delta} A^a(t+\Delta)\, d\Delta \tag{8.8.1}$$

so that $v^a(t)$ is an exponentially weighted average of the values of the optimand which a will come to expect.[16] In view of Lemma 8.7.1, it is obvious that:

> *Lemma 8.8.1.* For all agents, a, and all times, T, $\dot{v}^a(T) \leqslant 0$ and $\dot{v}^a(T) < 0$ unless a is in momentary personal equilibrium for all $t \geqslant T$.

Evidently, we can use $V(t) \equiv \sum_a v^a(t)$ as a Lyapounov function, obtaining:

> *Theorem 8.8.1.* The system is quasi-stable; that is, every limit point of the time-path of the system is a rest point.

Rest points and equilibria coincide in this model.

8.9* Boundedness

Unfortunately, we do not yet know that there are any limit points to the time path of the system. The device of assuring such existence by means

[16] Any positively weighted average (with weights independent of t) will do; it seems neatest to use (8.8.1) with the discount rate, ρ, which defines the norm of commodity profiles.

of compactness does not seem available, since boundedness and closure are not here sufficient. Nevertheless, boundedness does need to be considered. As indicated, I shall assume boundedness where needed, but some discussion of the issues involved seems appropriate. To a large extent this is a discussion of why the methods used to establish boundedness in simpler models break down here.

I begin with prices. Here, it will be recalled, the norm in question will be bounded if the supremum of the undiscounted prices ($\sup_{\{\theta\}} \hat{p}_i^a(\theta, t)$ for actual prices, $\sup_{\{\theta\}} \hat{p}_i^a(\theta, v, t)$ for expected ones) is. Why should this be so?

In Chapter 3 there were essentially two ways of establishing boundedness of prices. The first of these was to assume that if the relative price of money goes to zero there will be excess demand for money. If the price-adjustment processes were specialized in form (they had to lie below some ray in the appropriate space), Walras' Law was used to show that the sum of squares of the prices remains bounded.

This is not a useful way to proceed in the present analysis. Apart from technical details and the fact that price changes no longer depend on aggregate excess demands, the conclusion that could be reached is not the required one. That conclusion would bound the integral of the squared undiscounted prices, whereas what is required is a bound on their supremum and these are not equivalent.

The other way of going about it given in Chapter 3 is rather more promising, although still not entirely satisfactory. This was to assume, since we are dealing with relative prices, that if some set of prices gets relatively high enough the commodity (or share) with the highest price has nonpositive excess demand, having been "priced out of the market," so to speak. Unfortunately, the proof of boundedness in Chapter 3 requires a finite number of prices, which we do not have here.

Nevertheless, it does not seem unreasonable to assume relevant prices and price expectations bounded. This amounts to assuming that price-setters do not find it optimal to set unbounded prices in terms of current money. Since money is needed for transaction purposes such an assumption is consonant with the view that goods or shares will not be demanded at too high relative prices. In fact, the assumption that prices are bounded is not needed directly; it merely serves to make the later (needed) assumption of bounded quantity profiles more plausible.[17]

[17] There is a potential confusion here which it is well to avoid. In equilibrium, undiscounted commodity prices increase at the interest rate – the rate of growth of the money supply. Nevertheless, it is not contradictory to assume that they are bounded. Commodities in this model are dated and prices are only quoted until the relevant dates are passed. What boundedness means is that $\sup_{\{\theta\}} \hat{p}_i^a(\theta, t)$

For all the quantity profiles (input, output, storage, consumption, and purchase), the relevant concept is the boundedness of their discounted integrals (their discounted values at unitary prices) with the discounting always being back to time t so that what is being measured is the "tail" of the profile yet to come. What might make this plausible?

We have already assumed that the solution to each agent's optimum problem is continuous in the prices. Suppose that we were to strengthen this assumption to one of weak* continuity, which does not seem particularly implausible. If prices are bounded, we can take prices to lie in a closed set, whereupon they will lie in a weak* compact set. It will then follow that, for any t, the norm of the solution to any facet of an agent's optimum problem will be bounded. In other words, faced with bounded prices, agents will not make unbounded plans.

This is not quite enough, however. The solution to the agent's optimum problem depends not only on prices but also on his own past history (consumption and storage decisions in the case of households, production decisions in the case of firms). Even though plans at any moment may be bounded, changes in experience may lead that bound to increase without limit.

Nevertheless, boundedness seems plausible, particularly if production requires primary resources, directly or indirectly, and I shall assume it henceforth.

> *Assumption 8.9.1 (Boundedness).* All price, dividend, and quantity profiles are bounded.

In fact, boundedness of prices is not needed directly. Note that dividends will be bounded if prices and quantities are since firms do not pay out more than their profits.

8.10* Limiting assumptions

Unfortunately, boundedness and closure (which it would be innocuous to assume) do not guarantee compactness for the set of commodity profiles (although they would guarantee weak* compactness for prices). Accordingly, it is necessary to make some additional assumptions in

is bounded in t. This is neither contradicted by the fact that $\hat{\hat{p}}_i^a(\theta, t)$ rises at the interest rate in equilibrium until $t=\theta$ nor guaranteed by the fact that $\hat{\hat{p}}_i^a(\theta, t) = p_i^a(t, t)$ for $t \geqslant \theta$. In the case of shares, which are not dated, it is the dividend-corrected undiscounted price which rises at the interest rate in equilibrium; the undiscounted price itself reflects the present value of undistributed profits (Corollary 7.6.1). There is nothing unreasonable about assuming boundedness here.

order to prove stability. Such assumptions would be unnecessary in the presence of compactness; they often amount to assuming that certain properties which have already been assumed to hold at every finite point hold asymptotically as well. This often amounts to a uniformity assumption. Note that Assumption 8.7.1 (No Favorable Surprise) has already been given such a uniformity property.

To provide the needed uniformity, it is essential to have a measure of the distance that an agent a is at time t from momentary personal equilibrium. It is convenient to do this by directly measuring the extent of his uncompleted transactions or change in relevant expectations. Accordingly, let $N_1^{*a}(t)$ denote the supremum of the absolute values of a's uncompleted transactions in nonfree goods and shares at t. Let $N_2^{*a}(t)$ denote the supremum of the absolute values of the rates of change of a's relevant expectations at t. Let $N^{*a}(t) \equiv \max\{N_1^{*a}(t), N_2^{*a}(t)\}$.

Thus, $N^{*a}(t)$ is a measure of how far a is from personal equilibrium.[18] Note, however, that $N^{*a}(t)$ can go to zero for all agents without it being true that the state variables of the system approach a *particular* point at which all agents are in momentary personal equilibrium. We begin to ensure that this does not occur by making No Favorable Surprise depend on $N^{*a}(t)$ directly.

> *Assumption 8.10.1 (Asymptotic No Favorable Surprise).* For every $\delta > 0$, every agent a, all times T, and every bounded set of states of the system, there exists an $\epsilon > 0$ and a time $t^* > T$ such that $N^{*a}(t) > \delta$ for some $t \geqslant T$ implies $A^a(T) - A^a(t^*) > \epsilon$.[19]

The next assumption in this line is both more basic and more complicated to state than that just given. We have assumed that utility functionals are strictly quasi-concave. Now it is necessary to ensure that such strict quasi-concavity does not disappear in the limit. For purposes of this assumption, let the arguments of the utility functional (consumptions and transaction costs) be denoted by $\mathbf{Q}$. Let $N(\mathbf{Q}, \mathbf{Q}')$ be the supremum of the norms of the components of $(\mathbf{Q} - \mathbf{Q}')$.[20]

> *Assumption 8.10.2 (Asymptotic Strict Quasi-Concavity).* For any household, and any $\delta > 0$, let $\{\mathbf{Q}_\lambda\}$ and $\{\mathbf{Q}'_\lambda\}$ be any two bounded sequences such that $\lim_{\lambda \to \infty} U(\mathbf{Q}_\lambda) = \lim_{\lambda \to \infty} U(\mathbf{Q}'_\lambda)$ and $N(\mathbf{Q}_\lambda, \mathbf{Q}'_\lambda) > \delta$ for all λ. For any α, such that $0 < \alpha < 1$,

[18] It would be possible to define $N^{*a}(t)$ to take account of the fact that not all relevant prices are equally relevant, so to speak. This would make Assumption 8.10.1 below more natural but at the expense of added complexity.

[19] As earlier in this chapter, $A^a(t)$ denotes the value of the agent's optimand at t.

[20] The supremum is involved because continuous dating leads to a continuum of commodities.

there exists an $\epsilon > 0$ such that, for λ sufficiently large, $U(\alpha \mathbf{Q}_\lambda + (1-\alpha)\mathbf{Q}'_\lambda) - U(\mathbf{Q}_\lambda) > \epsilon$.

In effect, what this says is that indifference curves do not flatten out along bounded infinite sequences.[21] Another way of looking at it is to observe that since, in this model, norms are always being taken by redefining the time origin to count only the future, the utility functional has to remain strictly quasi-concave as agents pay more and more attention to later-dated consumption and transactions.[22]

Now, as with strict quasi-concavity itself, it does not really make sense to assume asymptotic strict quasi-concavity when differences only involve goods whose marginal utility is zero along some relevant path. It is simplest to ignore this for the present and to take care of it in the next section when discussing the treatment of free goods. (A similar remark applies to Assumption 8.10.3 below.)

It is possible to use Assumption 8.10.2 to show that the consequence of strict quasi-concavity that the optimal choice is uniquely expenditure-minimizing, *ceteris paribus,*[23] is preserved asymptotically, but this will not be needed. The parallel property for profit maximization will be assumed directly and is somewhat simpler. For a firm, let $\mathbf{Q}$ denote the choice variables in its optimization program (input profiles, output profiles, and sales profiles). Consider $\pi(\mathbf{Q})$ as the target profits which the firm expects to make by choosing $\mathbf{Q}$. Let $N(\mathbf{Q}, \mathbf{Q}')$ be the supremum of the norms of the components of $(\mathbf{Q} - \mathbf{Q}')$.

Assumption 8.10.3 (Asymptotic Uniqueness of Profit-Maximizing Program). For any firm and any $\delta > 0$, let $\{\mathbf{Q}_\lambda\}$ be a bounded

[21] Note that this only makes sense along bounded sequences. (Hence the discussion of boundedness above.) I am indebted to Abigail S. Fisher for pointing this out to me.

[22] Note that if consumption and transactions converge then input and output programs must converge also, since outputs are given from past decisions and current inputs are determined if outputs, transactions and consumption are (see equation (5.9.3)). Hence, there is no need to extend Assumption 8.10.2 (or Assumption 8.10.3 below) to include inputs and outputs explicitly.

[23] Since the money constraint can be binding for finite times in non-Walrasian equilibrium and can certainly be so binding out of equilibrium, utility-maximizing choices are not automatically expenditure-minimizing without regard for such constraints. A similar statement holds for profit maximization for firms. Among other effects, this prevents the use of the rather pretty device employed in the Hahn Process models of Chapter 3 of showing that all limit points are the same by combining expenditure minimization and profit maximization together with the closed nature of the economy. In the present case, such an argument would have to be carefully employed *near* limit points and finite-time money constraints can be binding in such neighborhoods. This model takes place in real time and (necessarily) not in an Arrow–Debreu world.

sequence of optimally chosen points. Let $\{\mathbf{Q}'_\lambda\}$ be any corresponding bounded sequence of feasible points such that $N(\mathbf{Q}_\lambda, \mathbf{Q}'_\lambda) > \delta$. There exists an $\epsilon > 0$ such that for all $\lambda, \pi(\mathbf{Q}_\lambda) - \pi(\mathbf{Q}'_\lambda) > \epsilon$, where $\pi(\mathbf{Q}'_\lambda)$ is evaluated at the price expectations at which $\mathbf{Q}_\lambda$ was chosen.

In effect, this prevents the profit functional from flattening out and ensures that the uniqueness of the profit-maximizing choice is preserved asymptotically. This could be accomplished by restrictions on isoquants comparable to those that Assumption 8.10.2 places on indifference curves, so to speak, but it seems simplest to assume it directly although it is quite strong.

8.11* The treatment of free goods and the indecomposability of equilibrium

As already remarked, Assumptions 8.10.2 and 8.10.3 just given do not make sense unless all prices are positive. Further, we cannot hope to show the convergence of the holdings of goods or shares which are free asymptotically (unless agents wish to acquire such goods or shares and are kept from doing so by perceived transaction constraints). Hence we must deal with free goods explicitly. We do this along the lines already followed in Chapter 3.

Definition 8.11.1. In comparing two points, a difference in an agent's commodity or share holdings is called *inessential* relative to a system of relevant prices if (a) the commodity or share is free at those prices; and, (b) at the point with the lower amount of that commodity or share the transaction constraints on purchasing more of it are never binding.

Definition 8.11.2. The *essential norm* of the difference between two quantity profiles relative to a given system of relevant prices is the norm of that difference disregarding the norm of any inessential differences relative to that price system.

In other words, excess holdings of free goods or shares don't count. The reason for this is that it really does not make sense to have Assumption 8.10.2 for households or Assumption 8.10.3 for firms apply when the differences involved are all inessential. Such differences involve zero marginal utilities for households and zero marginal revenue products for both firms and households. (For shares they involve zero-priced shares with no return ever expected.) Accordingly, Assumptions 8.10.2 and 8.10.3 should be interpreted with $N(\mathbf{Q}_\lambda, \mathbf{Q}'_\lambda)$ a supremum of essential norms relative to the price expectations at which $\mathbf{Q}_\lambda$ was chosen.

Since it is tedious and distracting to have to repeat things for free shares that hold for free goods, the remainder of the chapter speaks in terms of free goods only, the natural extension being understood.

As these definitions remind us, just as we cannot expect to prove convergence of free good holdings because of corner solutions in quantities, so also we cannot hope to prove convergence of irrelevant prices or price expectations because of corner solutions in prices.[24] We thus define:

> *Definition 8.11.3.* The system is called *essentially globally stable* if and only if for every set of initial conditions the system converges to equilibrium, relevant prices and relevant price and dividend expectations converging in norm and quantity profiles converging in essential norm relative to the limiting relevant price system.

As already indicated, convergence of relevant prices requires us to assume that there is only one set of relevant prices which are consistent with a given equilibrium. This is largely a matter of assuming that corner solutions do not combine at equilibrium to split the economy into decomposable sets as discussed above. Such a condition can be derived from more specific assumptions about first-order conditions holding with equality, as was done in Chapter 3, but the conditions involved are complex enough that it is simpler to assume it directly.

Further, given the possible noncompactness of the space in which we are working, it is not quite enough even to assume such uniqueness. We shall therefore assume that if quantity profiles converge save for goods which are asymptotically free and if $N^{*a}(t)$ goes to zero for every agent so that all transactions are nearly completed and all relevant price changes are approaching zero, then relevant prices converge as well. (We shall also assume that relevant dividend expectations of households converge in such circumstances; dividend policies of firms must do so.) While convergence of relevant prices in such a case does not require uniqueness of the relevant prices supporting the asymptotic equilibrium, such convergence is most plausible with such uniqueness which, with quasi-stability, would guarantee convergence in the presence of compactness.[25] Essentially what is ruled out is the possibility that some sequence of relevant prices does *not* converge to the unique equilibrium relevant prices but is nevertheless "almost" compatible with the unique equilibrium quantities.

[24] Since, in principle, agents can quote prices at which they do not expect to transact, prices as well as price expectations can be irrelevant.

[25] See the Appendix. Note that weak* convergence of relevant prices is guaranteed by uniqueness under such circumstances since boundedness and closure (which it is trivial to assume) guarantee weak* compactness.

Assumption 8.11.1 (Indecomposability and Convergence of Relevant Prices). If (a) for every $\delta > 0$, as t goes to infinity, all quantity profiles converge in essential norm relative to every system of relevant prices and relevant price expectations which has as free goods or goods expected to be free only those goods corresponding to actual or expected relevant prices which are less than δ at t, and (b) for every agent a, $\lim_{t \to \infty} N^{*a}(t) = 0$, then relevant prices and relevant price and dividend expectations converge.[26]

As this section suggests, the stability proof below would be considerably simpler if we could be sure that all prices remained positive.

8.12* Proof of essential global stability

I shall prove the following theorem:

Theorem 8.12.1. The model is essentially globally stable. That is, from any initial position it converges to some equilibrium (which need not be Walrasian if there are transaction constraints). Convergence of prices is in norm and convergence of all quantity profiles is in essential norm relative to the limiting prices.

The plan of the proof is as follows: First we observe that convergence of utilities and profits, together with Assumption 8.10.1 (Asymptotic No Favorable Surprise), implies that the system *must* eventually have the property that, at every t, it is close to a momentary personal equilibrium for every agent. The remainder of the proof consists of showing that the various quantity profiles converge, so that the equilibria involved are the same for all agents and are constant over time. Convergence of relevant prices and of relevant price and dividend expectations is then handled with Assumption 8.11.1.

Lemma 8.12.1. For every agent, a, $\lim_{t \to \infty} N^{*a}(t) = 0$.

Proof. Since I have assumed utilities and profits bounded below, Lemma 8.7.1 ensures that they converge. By Assumption 8.10.1, such convergence cannot occur unless $N^{*a}(t)$ goes to zero for every a.

[26] Since, in equilibrium, share prices reflect the undistributed profits of firms (Corollary 7.6.1), it is tempting to suppose that share prices will automatically converge under the stated conditions if commodity prices and relevant commodity price and dividend expectations converge. It is not totally clear that this must be the case, however, because of the possibility of speculative expectations about share prices themselves. It seems best to avoid such matters here.

Thus every agent gets close to momentary personal equilibrium, with distance measured by $N^{*a}(t)$. This does not yet mean, however, that the system converges to a particular point at which all agents are in momentary personal equilibrium. To show that this in fact occurs, I now show the convergence of quantity (and then of relevant price) profiles.

For any agent, let $\mathbf{Q}(t)$ (agent superscript omitted) denote the profiles of the quantity variables in his maximization problem, chosen optimally as of t and with actual values before t. For any $\Delta>0$, define $\hat{N}(\Delta, t)$ as the essential norm of the difference between $\mathbf{Q}(t)$ and $\mathbf{Q}(t+\Delta)$ relative to price expectations at t (discounting back to t, of course). It is easy to prove:

> *Lemma 8.12.2.* For $\Delta^*>0$ as defined in Assumption 8.7.1 (No Favorable Surprise), any agent, any $\epsilon>0$, all Δ, $0 \leqslant \Delta \leqslant \Delta^*$, and large enough t, $\hat{N}(\Delta, t)<\epsilon$.

Proof. By Assumption 8.7.1, $\mathbf{Q}(t+\Delta)$, the optimal program at $t+\Delta$, was feasible at t. The desired result for firms follows immediately from Assumption 8.10.3 (Asymptotic Uniqueness of Profit-Maximizing Program). For households, it follows from Assumption 8.10.2 (Asymptotic Strict Quasi-Concavity) and the fact that the set of feasible programs is convex.[27]

Proof of Theorem 8.12.1. By Lemma 8.12.2, there exists a fixed $\Delta>0$ such that $\hat{N}(\Delta, t)$ approaches zero. By Lemma 8.12.1 the rates of change of actual and expected relevant prices are approaching zero. Thus, for large enough t, and any $\delta>0$, any actual or expected relevant price which is greater than δ at t will still be positive at $t+\Delta$. Suppose for a moment that all actual and expected relevant prices positive at t are still positive at $t+\Delta$. Then by the triangle inequality, $\hat{N}(2\Delta, t) \leqslant \hat{N}(\Delta, t)+\hat{N}(\Delta, t+\Delta)$, so that $\hat{N}(2\Delta, t)$ must also approach zero. Moreover, the same argument shows that $\hat{N}(b\Delta, t)$ approaches zero for fixed b if all positive actual and expected relevant prices at t are still positive at $t+b\Delta$. It follows that, for any $\delta>0$, $\mathbf{Q}(t+b\Delta)$ converges in essential norm relative to any price system which has as free goods or goods expected to be free only those

[27] The uniformity of the No Favorable Surprise assumption (the fixed nature of Δ^* in Assumption 8.7.1) is needed only to produce the comparable uniformity in the statement of Lemma 8.12.2. The latter result can be obtained by a different route in which the uniform nature of Δ^* in the former feasibility of currently optimal programs is retained so far as regards transaction constraints but dispensed with for money constraints, being replaced by the assumption that the agent's optimal program is uniformly continuous in his actual money stock on the bounded set of states of the system. There seems little point in giving the details, however.

goods corresponding to actual or expected relevant prices which are less than δ at t, and hence relative to the limit of actual and expected relevant prices, if such a limit exists.

Now, fix b and consider $\mathbf{Q}(t+f\Delta)$ where we shall let $f>b$ tend to infinity. Such a program is identical on the interval $[t, t+b\Delta]$ with $\mathbf{Q}(t+b\Delta)$. Moreover, the norm of any component of the difference between $\mathbf{Q}(t+f\Delta)$ and $\mathbf{Q}(t)$ consists of the discounted value of that difference over the interval $[t, t+b\Delta]$ plus the discounted value of the difference after $t+b\Delta$, discounting in both cases being taken back to t. But $\mathbf{Q}(t+b\Delta)$ approaches $\mathbf{Q}(t)$, so the first part of the difference goes to zero. Moreover, the second part is discounted for a time interval of b, and it is bounded. Since we can make b as large as we like, evidently $\mathbf{Q}(t+f\Delta)$ converges to $\mathbf{Q}(t)$ as both t and f go to infinity, convergence being in essential norm as before.

Thus, for every $\delta>0$, as t goes to infinity, quantity profiles converge in essential norm relative to any system of relevant actual and expected prices which has zero only those prices and price expectations which are less than δ at t. By Lemma 8.12.1, however, $\lim_{t\to\infty} N^{*a}(t)=0$ for every agent and convergence of relevant prices and relevant price and dividend expectations follows from Assumption 8.11.1. Since the system is quasi-stable (Theorem 8.8.1), the point to which all this convergence takes place must be an equilibrium, and the theorem is proved.

CHAPTER 9

Concluding thoughts

This investigation has come some distance from its origins in the traditional stability literature. Unfortunately, there is still a long way for further research to go before we have a sound foundation for equilibrium economics. I now review some of the road traveled and then consider the nature of the road ahead.

We now know that, under very general circumstances, in a world of rational agents who perceive and act upon a nonexpanding set of arbitrage opportunities cast up by disequilibrium, the economy will be driven to equilibrium as such opportunities disappear. This will occur if new opportunities in a wide sense do not continue to appear or to be perceived to appear. In fact, stability is achieved even with new opportunities, provided that such new opportunities do not appear as favorable surprises, seized by agents as optima the moment they appear. This result – while not nearly as helpful as would be a parallel result as to the effects of the nonappearance of new *exogenous* opportunities – is nevertheless a basic waystation. It holds both for competitive economies and for some economies including monopoly or monopolistically competitive elements.

This general (if weak) stability result is free of many of the problems which flawed the earlier literature. Consider first the tâtonnement literature. There, to obtain stability it was necessary to restrict excess demand functions very severely; no such restriction is required in the present context. Further, the entire setting of tâtonnement was unrealistic, requiring the absence of any disequilibrium activity save price adjustment with continual recontracting. That is plainly not the case here.

Indeed, the disequilibrium activity permitted in the present analysis is substantially greater than in its more immediate predecessors, the models of trading processes. In such models, the Edgeworth and Hahn Process models, time plays no real role. Adjustment takes place in an Arrow-Debreu world in which trade goes on out of equilibrium but no production or consumption takes place until equilibrium is reached. Some version of an arbitrary "Present Action Postulate" is required to fix the times of trade. Equilibrium in such models means a cessation of trade as all trading opportunities are exhausted and this remains true even when these models are adapted to permit disequilibrium production and consumption.[1] In the present model, by contrast, the timing of actions is optimally, not arbitrarily determined. We leave, as we must, the Arrow-Debreu world of prehistoric market clearing; economic activity of all sorts goes on in disequilibrium and does not cease when equilibrium is reached. Equilibrium in the present model involves continued trade at correctly foreseen prices and not the end of the economic system. As a result, agents have a reason to hold money in equilibrium in preference to other return-bearing assets or commodities.

These gains come about because the present model, unlike its predecessors, permits (indeed encourages) agents to perceive that the economy is in disequilibrium and to act upon the opportunities that such disequilibrium affords. It is such action that produces stability if those opportunities do not get wider. In allowing such disequilibrium consciousness we have advanced beyond analyses which assume that agents (like many economists) naively believe that the world is always in equilibrium.

In another respect as well, the present stability analysis is much more satisfactory than were its predecessors. It is no longer necessary - and certainly not desirable - to have price adjustment the province, not of self-interested agents, but of an impersonal and wholly fictitious auctioneer. The assumption that prices move mysteriously in the direction of the corresponding aggregate excess demands, an assumption which has dogged the literature since tâtonnement days, has been removed. In its stead, individuals are allowed to make price offers in their own interests, essentially restricting such offers only to be consistent with No Favorable Surprise - an admittedly strong restriction but the one which it is important to investigate.

There have been other gains as well. A good deal has been learned about the optimal arbitrage behavior of agents in disequilibrium. The connection between transaction constraints and conjectured monopoly power has been investigated, and the stability result turns out to hold when monopoly power is present - whether that power is real or merely perceived. We have seen how the perception of monopoly power is

[1] Fisher (1976a, 1977).

related to the nature of the money constraints in equilibrium. Further, we have seen how nonperformance problems can be handled and how the dated commodity problem disappears in a reasonable context of individual price-setting. As already remarked the (often hidden) Present Action Postulate is no longer needed or even relevant.

All of this is very pleasant. Unfortunately it is not nearly enough. Both in terms of stability analysis itself and in terms of other aspects of the analysis of disequilibrium there is a great deal more that needs to be done before we have a sound basis for equilibrium analysis. I now consider these matters in the hope that the present model can provide the framework for further research.

In terms of stability theory itself, the present analysis and its results require generalization or extension in two obvious directions. The first of these (and, I suspect, the easier of the two) is the introduction of subjective uncertainty. I have previously commented on how this might be done and shall therefore be brief here. The principal issues which must be faced - aside from the precise modeling of uncertainty itself when information as to prices comes in over time - are the nature of equilibrium and the precise statement of No Favorable Surprise. Equilibrium will have to be stochastic, of course; it seems very likely that it will continue to be a rational expectations equilibrium, but its precise properties need to be explored.

No Favorable Surprise needs to be given a stochastic statement. It will not do simply to assume that changes in subjective probability are automatically unfavorable; such unfavorable movement needs to be derived from or interpreted as assumptions about the nonappearance of new opportunities. On the other hand, merely ruling out such new opportunities from entering the support of agents' subjective probability distributions is not sufficient. It seems likely that the correct approach is to regard as a new opportunity in itself the realization that a previously rejected but still available alternative is in fact better than the alternative previously chosen. But the details, and indeed the full model, need working out.

The payoff from doing this seems fairly great. Generalization of the model to allow for subjective uncertainty permits greater realism. It seems likely to reduce the undue importance of smooth transaction costs in the present analysis. More important, such a generalization also permits proper handling of rational expectations, which, in the present model, have been represented only by perfect foresight. While it is interesting that equilibrium in the present model is a rational expectations equilibrium, the case of perfect foresight in disequilibrium turns out to be uninteresting. With subjective uncertainty permitted, the disequilibrium role of rational expectations can be properly studied. Whether that role is interesting, however, may depend on the nature of stochastic equilibrium in the extended model.

This is a matter of considerable importance for it bears on the second obvious need for extension of the present analysis - the study of the question of what assumptions on adjustment processes generate No Favorable Surprise in the absence of exogenous shocks. The case of rational expectations under subjective uncertainty is the obvious leading candidate here; studying that case is likely to produce a central example of stability under No *Exogenous* Favorable Surprise. This is particularly important because of the association of the rational expectations school with the view that markets always clear - a view that requires a stability proof as a minimal first step.

More generally, the present work has shown that No Favorable Surprise is sufficient for stability; the asymptotic disappearance of favorable surprise is obviously necessary. Hence the question of the derivation of No Favorable Surprise from more primitive assumptions may become a central focus for further work in this area. Apart from pointing to the case of rational expectations, however, I cannot now provide much guidance as to how such work is to be done.

This is for a reason that has consequences reaching beyond stability analysis to the study of all disequilibrium behavior and therefore to the foundations of equilibrium theory. The very generality of the result that shows stability under No Favorable Surprise with few other specific restrictions on disequilibrium behavior must not disguise the fact that such generality is attractive in part precisely because we know very little in the way of specifics about such behavior.

Perhaps the most important example of this fact lies in the area of price adjustment. This book was able to jettison the traditional assumption that prices move in the direction of the corresponding aggregate excess demands and replace it with a very general assumption about individual price adjustment. But in fact we know very little about how such adjustment takes place. The analysis of earlier chapters (aside from assuming No Favorable Surprise as required by the nature of the result to be proved) merely observes that prices will reflect perceived demand and supply curves, or, equivalently, the shadow prices of perceived transaction constraints. It says nothing about how such perceptions are formed.

This is far from a minor matter. The way in which prices are formed and the role which they play in the allocation of resources is the central topic of economic analysis. It is no small thing that we are uncertain as to how this takes place. In more specific terms, the answer to the question of how perceived demand and supply curves change - which, as we have seen, is also the question of how prices are set - determines whether or not equilibria will be Walrasian.[2] While our results can begin to give some very mild reassurance as to the appropriateness of analyzing equilibrium positions, it appears virtually certain that we cannot decide whether such positions are competitive or noncompetitive without a more detailed examination of the process of disequilibrium adjustment than has so far proved possible.

Nor is this a matter of only microeconomic interest. The question of whether the economy converges to a quantity-constrained equilibrium, possibly with underemployment à la Keynes, has been seen intimately to involve the question of how perceptions of demand and supply change. Such questions cannot be answered by looking only at the existence of such equilibria; they depend on the specifics of the adjustment process - specifics that are sadly lacking in the present state of the art.

We also know very little that seems of much help on another question which is crucial for the way in which economists do economic analysis. The generality of Lyapounov's Second Method and of our stability proof is such that we know nothing about speeds of adjustment. This means that we cannot be sure that the ability of the economy (as modeled) to absorb shocks means that it absorbs them very quickly - quickly enough that it spends most of its time between shocks near equilibrium rather than in a nonnegligible adjustment process. Real economies do have new opportunities and favorable surprises do occur. The fact that, absent such effects, one obtains asymptotic convergence does not justify analyzing economies as though they were in equilibrium without a showing that convergence is rapid.

There is a further issue here as well, to which I have several times referred. Even if speeds of adjustment are high enough that adjustment takes place quickly relative to the time between shocks, it may not be the case that equilibrium analysis is well founded. This is because of hysteresis - the path-dependent nature of the equilibrium reached in the adjustment processes studied. Economic change can happen out of equilibrium, and such change can affect the equilibrium reached. If comparative statics is to be useful, the adjustment process must not only be rapid and thus unimportant in terms of real time, it must also be unimportant in terms of its effects on equilibrium.

In the present state of our knowledge, there is no basis for the belief that this is the case. Our general stability result takes place in a context in which trade, production, consumption, and expectation revision all occur outside of equilibrium. While it is conceivable that expectation

[2] If smooth transaction costs were replaced by subjective uncertainty, such equilibria would once more be Pareto-optimal.

revision as revealed through price offers takes place consistent with No Favorable Surprise at a rate far faster than do trade, production, and consumption, we do not know that movements in quantities are unimportant in the time it takes to get to equilibrium. The setting in which price changes reflect No Favorable Surprise is most sensibly one of individual agent adjustment to experience as agents act on arbitrage opportunities. Such an assumption as to price adjustment is not appealing in the absence of such trading experience, and the lesson of the tâtonnement literature should make economists very wary of assuming that rapid price adjustment alone will produce stability.

Questions like these cannot be answered by assuming them away. If disequilibrium effects are in fact unimportant we need to prove that they are. If such effects are important, then the way in which we tend to think about the theory of value needs to be revised. Interest must then center not on equilibrium itself but on disequilibrium adjustment. Different economies cannot then be studied as though their future were determined solely by tastes, technology, and initial endowments with adjustment but a transient matter.

Moreover, if path dependence is important, there are consequences for normative as well as positive economics. While it is true that the theorems on the relation between Pareto-optimality and competitive equilibrium will remain relevant, welfare issues involving the distribution of income which start with given endowments will be affected. Further, even the relevance of the theorems on Pareto-optimality largely disappears if convergence takes place slowly or if the equilibria reached by a competitive system need not be Walrasian.

These are issues of great importance and I wish I could settle them. Instead, I can only offer the model of the present book as a starting point, a framework within which it may be possible to begin to analyze such questions. In addition to the two major extensions already discussed, here are some tentative suggestions as to how the model might be developed in possibly useful ways. I put them in the form of somewhat interrelated questions.

1. Is it possible to model the connection between trading experience and perceived monopoly power? How are price offers made and accepted? Are there fairly general restrictions on the adjustment process which imply that perceived monopoly power does or does not disappear in the limit so that the ultimate equilibrium is or is not Walrasian?

2. Can something sensible be said about the welfare properties of different classes of adjustment processes in the model? Is the absence of competition necessarily bad?

3. Under what circumstances does individual price dispersion persist in equilibrium? What role is played by information costs?

4. The model analyzed here assumes a fixed number of firms. But a crucial feature of disequilibrium in particular markets is the entry and exit of firms. While the entry of an established firm into a new area can be seen in the present model as an example of an agent acting on a profitable opportunity, there may be something to be learned from a consideration of the formation or dissolution of firms in disequilibrium.

5. The lack of an explicit transactions technology is unattractive. This is so partly because so much mileage is gotten from assuming smooth transaction costs as in Chapter 6 and partly because the way in which transactions take place is the basic stuff of disequilibrium. Any explicit treatment of a transactions technology should allow for increasing returns at low levels of transactions. Continuity problems are probably best left to the results of subjective uncertainty.

6. The government in this model has played almost no role. Yet there is some room in it for government policy. Fiscal policy involves the purchase of goods and services in exchange for bonds; monetary policy operates on the maturity structure of the bond market. Can such policies affect whether or not money constraints are binding at finite times in equilibrium? Is it desirable that such constraints not be binding? What policies affect the adjustment process? Can the welfare effect of such policies be assessed by looking only at equilibrium? Does the path-dependent nature of equilibrium lead to situations in which policies, effective only in disequilibrium, can nevertheless significantly influence the equilibrium reached? It may be that answering these questions requires a more specific model than the present one.

Work needs to be done on such matters. I believe that progress can be made in these directions and probably needs to be made before we can get very far with speeds of adjustment or the importance of path-dependent effects, but I am not certain.

What is certain is that work in this area must continue. The issues involved in disequilibrium analysis are too important to economics to be avoided. They must be faced head on rather than assumed away in the course of a desire to do what economists do best – analyze equilibrium without regard for the foundations on which such analysis must rest.

APPENDIX

Mathematics of stability

This Appendix is intended as an introduction for those unfamiliar with the subject. It is not a completely general treatment but provides the material necessary for the starred portions of the book. The notation is not that of the rest of the book.

A.1 Processes and rest points

Consider an autonomous differential equation *process:*

$$\dot{\mathbf{x}} = \mathbf{F}(\mathbf{x}) \tag{A.1.1}$$

where $\mathbf{x}$ is an n-vector and the dot denotes differentiation with respect to time. Let $\mathbf{x}_0$ be the value of $\mathbf{x}$ at time $t=0$. A solution to (A.1.1) is a function $\boldsymbol{\phi}(\cdot,\cdot)$ with $\mathbf{x}_0 = \boldsymbol{\phi}(0, \mathbf{x}_0)$, such that, if

$$\mathbf{x} = \boldsymbol{\phi}(t, \mathbf{x}_0) \tag{A.1.2}$$

then $\mathbf{x}$ satisfies (A.1.1). The processes with which we shall be concerned have solutions with the property that, for any t':

$$\boldsymbol{\phi}(t, \mathbf{x}_0) = \boldsymbol{\phi}(t-t', \boldsymbol{\phi}(t', \mathbf{x}_0)) \tag{A.1.3}$$

so that the value of $\mathbf{x}$ depends on initial conditions and the time elapsed since those initial conditions. There is thus nothing special about time 0 or the vector $\mathbf{x}_0$ in this regard; any other time t' and corresponding initial conditions $\mathbf{x}_{t'} = \boldsymbol{\phi}(t', \mathbf{x}_0)$ would do as well.

Further, we assume that $\boldsymbol{\phi}(\cdot,\cdot)$ is continuous, not only in t, which is trivial, but also in $\mathbf{x}_0$, the initial conditions. This will be true, for example, in finite dimensional spaces if $\mathbf{F}(\cdot)$ satisfies a Lipschitz Condition[1] or if

[1] $\mathbf{F}(\cdot)$ satisfies a Lipschitz Condition (everywhere) if there exists a finite scalar $M>0$ such that, for any two points, $\mathbf{x}$ and $\mathbf{x}' \neq \mathbf{x}$, $|\mathbf{F}(\mathbf{x}') - \mathbf{F}(\mathbf{x})|/|\mathbf{x}-\mathbf{x}'| < M$,

(as in (2.2.1)) it satisfies such a condition except for a restriction of $\mathbf{x}$ to the nonnegative orthant.[2] These properties of solutions are not needed everywhere below. I refer to the value of $\phi(t, \mathbf{x}_0)$ as t varies as the "time path of $\mathbf{x}$."

Definition A.1.1. A *rest point* of the process is a point $\mathbf{x}$ such that $\mathbf{F}(\mathbf{x})=0$.

A rest point of a dynamic process need not be the same as a competitive or other economic equilibrium. Naturally, however, in interesting economic stability models, these will coincide.

A.2 Global stability and quasi-stability

Definition A.2.1. Let $\mathbf{x}^*$ be a rest point of (A.1.1). $\mathbf{x}^*$ is said to be a *globally stable rest point* if and only if, for every $\mathbf{x}_0$, $\lim_{t\to\infty} \phi(t, \mathbf{x}_0)=\mathbf{x}^*$.

In other words, a rest point is globally stable if and only if the process converges to it *for every initial condition.* As shown in the text of Chapter 2, this is too strong a condition to be very interesting in economic stability analyses since, among other things, a rest point which is globally stable must also be unique and this is not the usual case for economic equilibria.

Definition A.2.2. The *process* (A.1.1) is called *globally stable* if and only if, for every initial vector, $\mathbf{x}_0$, there exists some rest point $\mathbf{x}^*(\mathbf{x}_0)$, such that $\lim_{t\to\infty} \phi(t, \mathbf{x}_0)=\mathbf{x}^*(\mathbf{x}_0)$.

The *process* is thus globally stable if and only if it always converges to *some* rest point. Which rest point it approaches, however, may depend on the initial conditions at which it starts.

This property is related to but stronger than the property of *quasi-stability* which is defined as follows:

Definition A.2.3. For any initial vector, $\mathbf{x}_0$, choose a sequence of times $\{t_\lambda\}\to\infty$. Choose a corresponding sequence of points $\{\mathbf{x}_\lambda\}$, where $\mathbf{x}_\lambda\equiv\phi(t_\lambda, \mathbf{x}_0)$. Suppose the sequence $\{\mathbf{x}_\lambda\}$ converges to a point $\mathbf{x}^*$. The process (A.1.1) is called *quasi-stable* if and only if every $\mathbf{x}^*$ constructed in this way is a rest point.

A shorter (and less precise) way to say this is that the process is stable if and only if every limit point of the time path of $\mathbf{x}$ is a rest point. Some

where $|\mathbf{x}-\mathbf{x}'|$ denotes the norm of $(\mathbf{x}-\mathbf{x}')$. The satisfaction of a Lipschitz Condition is a property stronger than continuity and weaker than differentiability.

[2] See Henry (1973a,b) and Champsaur, Drèze, and Henry (1977).

authors include a restriction of the time path of **x** to a compact set in the definition of quasi-stability. This assures that the definition will not be empty since it guarantees that the time path of **x** will have at least one limit point. Largely because Lyapounov's Second Method (below) proves quasi-stability as I have stated it, I prefer to treat compactness issues separately.

The fundamental difference between global stability and quasi-stability of a process lies in the fact that a process can be quasi-stable and have *many* limit points without converging to a single one of them. This is best understood by an example.

Let **x** have two components, u and v. It will be convenient to work in polar coordinates in the u-v plane, so let

$$u \equiv r \cos\theta; \quad v \equiv r \sin\theta \tag{A.2.1}$$

Further, define

$$w \equiv (r-1)^2 \tag{A.2.2}$$

and suppose that

$$\dot{w} = -w^2 \tag{A.2.3}$$

$$\dot{\theta} = w \tag{A.2.4}$$

(It is left to the reader to show that these are equivalent to differential equations in the original variables u and v in the form (A.1.1) – although rather messy ones.) Evidently, the rest points of this process are the points where $w=0$. In view of the definitions, these are all the points on the unit circle in the u-v plane.

Now, let w_0, θ_0 be the initial values of w and θ, respectively, and choose $w_0 \neq 0$, so that the process does not start (and hence remain) at a rest point. Then, by (A.2.2), $w_0 > 0$. Rewriting (A.2.3),

$$-\frac{dw}{w^2} = dt \tag{A.2.5}$$

so that

$$w = \frac{1}{t+C} \tag{A.2.6}$$

where C is a constant of integration. Substituting $t=0$, we see that

$$C = 1/w_0 > 0 \tag{A.2.7}$$

Now substitute from (A.2.6) into (A.2.4) obtaining:

$$d\theta = \frac{dt}{t+C} \tag{A.2.8}$$

Integrating, we obtain:

$$\theta = \log(t+C) + \log K \qquad \text{(A.2.9)}$$

where $\log K$ is a second constant of integration. Substituting $t=0$, we see that

$$K = \frac{e^{\theta_0}}{C} = w_0 e^{\theta_0} \qquad \text{(A.2.10)}$$

using (A.2.7). The full solution to (A.2.3) and (A.2.4) in the form (A.1.2) (in the variables w and θ) is thus:

$$w = \frac{w_0}{w_0 t + 1}; \quad \theta = \theta_0 + \log(w_0 t + 1) \qquad \text{(A.2.11)}$$

Note that the solution is continuous in the initial conditions (w_0, θ_0); in particular, it is continuous in w_0 at $w_0 = 0$ - a rest point.

Now, it is obvious from (A.2.11) that w approaches zero but that θ fails to converge. In terms of the original variables, u and v, what is happening is that the process approaches the unit circle (the rest point set) by spiraling toward it - outward if it begins inside the circle, inward if it begins outside the circle. While the speed at which the time path of u and v passes through a 360° revolution decreases, however, it does not decrease fast enough for the angle, θ, to converge, even though the radius, r, does. The process is thus not globally stable. On the other hand, it is obvious that the process is quasi-stable since every limit point of the time path of u and v must be on the unit circle. In effect, that time path approaches the entire rest point *set* without converging to any *particular* rest point. That this property is a general one for quasi-stable processes is shown by:

> *Theorem A.2.1.* Suppose that, for any initial vector $\mathbf{x}_0$, the time path of $\mathbf{x}$ remains in a compact set. Let $d(\mathbf{x})$ be the infimum of the distances from $\mathbf{x}$ to a rest point. If the process (A.1.1) is quasi-stable, then $\lim_{t\to\infty} d(\mathbf{x}) = 0$.

Proof. Suppose not. Then there is an infinite sequence of times $\{t_\lambda\}$ and a corresponding sequence $\{\mathbf{x}_\lambda\}$, $\mathbf{x}_\lambda \equiv \phi(t_\lambda, \mathbf{x}_0)$, such that $d(\mathbf{x}_\lambda) > \epsilon$ for some fixed $\epsilon > 0$. Since $\{\mathbf{x}_\lambda\}$ remains in a compact set it has a convergent subsequence. By quasi-stability, the limit of such a subsequence must be a rest point and this is impossible.[3]

It is not an accident that in the above example there is a continuum of rest points. More precisely, it is not an accident that the rest points are

[3] It is because of this result that it is tempting to include compactness in the definition of quasi-stability.

not locally isolated. That this is essential is shown by the following two theorems. I begin with the (slightly) simpler one, which makes no direct use of quasi-stability.

Theorem A.2.2. Suppose that, for any initial vector $\mathbf{x}_0$, the time path of $\mathbf{x}$ remains in a compact set. Suppose further that, given $\mathbf{x}_0$, that time path has at most one limit point, $\mathbf{x}^*(\mathbf{x}_0)$. Then the process (A.1.1) is globally stable.

Proof. Since $\mathbf{x}$ remains in a compact set, its time path starting from any $\mathbf{x}_0$ *has* a limit point, $\mathbf{x}^*(\mathbf{x}_0)$, which, by assumption, is the only one. Now suppose the process were not globally stable. Then there would exist at least one $\mathbf{x}_0$ and corresponding $\mathbf{x}^*(\mathbf{x}_0)$ such that $\lim_{t\to\infty} \phi(t, \mathbf{x}_0) \neq \mathbf{x}^*(\mathbf{x}_0)$. In that case, there would be some $\delta > 0$ and a ball of radius δ around $\mathbf{x}^*(\mathbf{x}_0)$ such that $\phi(t, \mathbf{x}_0)$ failed to always be inside that ball after some large enough time. Hence, we can choose a sequence of times $\{t_\lambda\} \to \infty$ such that the corresponding sequence $\{\mathbf{x}_\lambda\}$, $\mathbf{x}_\lambda \equiv \phi(t_\lambda, \mathbf{x}_0)$, has the property that the distance from $\mathbf{x}_\lambda$ to $\mathbf{x}^*(\mathbf{x}_0)$ is at least $\delta > 0$. The sequence $\{\mathbf{x}_\lambda\}$, however, lies in a compact set and must therefore have a convergent subsequence. Let the limit point of that convergent subsequence be $\mathbf{x}^{**}$. Plainly, $\mathbf{x}^{**} \neq \mathbf{x}^*(\mathbf{x}_0)$, but this is a contradiction, since $\mathbf{x}^*(\mathbf{x}_0)$ is the only limit point of the path starting from $\mathbf{x}_0$.

Quasi-stability plays no direct role in this result. In practice, however, the proof that all limit points starting from a given $\mathbf{x}_0$ are the same often proceeds by using the quasi-stability property that all limit points are rest points, the fact that rest points and economic equilibria coincide in the model being studied and the properties of equilibria.[4] The analysis of the Hahn Process in Chapter 3 exemplifies this; the fact that the rest points of the dynamic system are also Walrasian equilibria plays a crucial role.

The next (more general) theorem does use quasi-stability, although it too could be stated without that property by directly assuming limit points rather than rest points locally isolated.

Theorem A.2.3. Suppose that, for any initial vector $\mathbf{x}_0$, the time path of $\mathbf{x}$ remains in a compact set. Suppose further that the rest points of (A.1.1) are each locally isolated (that is, there is an open neighborhood of each rest point that contains no other rest point). Then, if the process (A.1.1) is quasi-stable, it is also globally stable.

[4] For certain tâtonnement cases such as gross substitutes which imply uniqueness of equilibrium, quasi-stability can be used to infer the uniqueness of the limit point. Such cases are very special and, of course, require the path independence of tâtonnement.

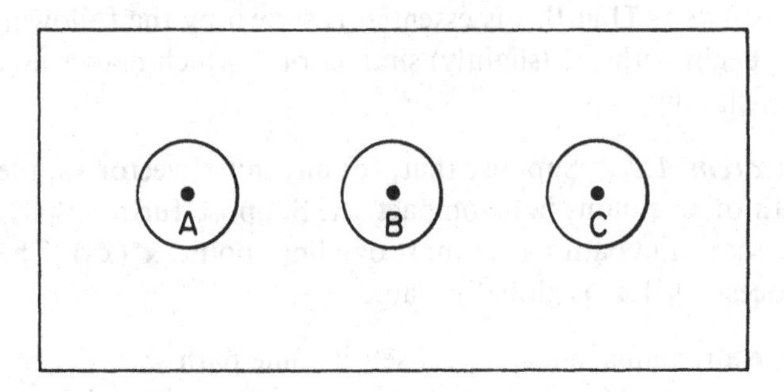

Figure A.2.1.

Proof. Fix $\mathbf{x}_0$. Consider the rest points of (A.1.1). Since these are all locally isolated, each rest point is in the center of a ball containing no other rest point, and the balls do not overlap. Such a situation is depicted in Figure A.2.1 for a case of three rest points. (There will be a finite number of rest points if $\mathbf{F}(\cdot)$ is continuous.) Here the set containing the time path is depicted as a rectangle. The three rest points are A, B, and C.

Now suppose that the process is not globally stable. Then, in view of Theorem A.2.2, there must be some $\mathbf{x}_0$ for which the time path of $\mathbf{x}$ must have more than one limit point, which, by quasi-stability must all be rest points of (A.1.1). Thus, there exist at least two nonoverlapping balls, constructed as above, such that the time path of $\mathbf{x}$ keeps on reentering them. That is, for any $\delta > 0$, there exist at least two rest points, say, $\mathbf{x}^*$ and $\mathbf{x}^{**}$, and two infinite sequences of time, $\{t_\lambda^*\} \to \infty$ and $\{t_\lambda^{**}\} \to \infty$ such that the corresponding sequences $\{\mathbf{x}_\lambda^*\}$ and $\{\mathbf{x}_\lambda^{**}\}(\mathbf{x}_\lambda^* \equiv \phi(t_\lambda^*, \mathbf{x}_0)$; $\mathbf{x}_\lambda^{**} \equiv \phi(t_\lambda^{**}, \mathbf{x}_0))$ have the property that the distances from $\mathbf{x}_\lambda^*$ to $\mathbf{x}^*$ and of $\mathbf{x}_\lambda^{**}$ from $\mathbf{x}^{**}$ are both less than δ. Further, $\phi(t, \mathbf{x}_0)$ is continuous in t. Hence the time path of $\mathbf{x}$ cannot get from the ball surrounding $\mathbf{x}^*$ to the ball surrounding $\mathbf{x}^{**}$ or back again without passing through points that lie outside *all* of the balls. Thus there exists an infinite sequence of times $\{t_\mu\} \to \infty$ and a corresponding sequence $\{\mathbf{x}_\mu\}$ defined in the obvious way such that $\{\mathbf{x}_\mu\}$ is outside the ball surrounding any rest point. However, $\{\mathbf{x}_\mu\}$ lies in a compact set and must have a convergent subsequence. Let the limit of that convergent subsequence be denoted by α. Then α is a limit point of the time path of $\mathbf{x}$. By construction, however, α is not a rest point of (A.1.1), and this contradicts quasi-stability, proving the theorem.

A.3 Lyapounov's Second Method

Quasi-stability is thus an important property. It is usually proved using Lyapounov's Second Method, to the details of which I now turn.

Definition A.3.1. Consider a real-valued function, $V(\cdot)$, whose domain is the set of possible values of $\mathbf{x}$ for all possible initial vectors $\mathbf{x}_0$. Suppose $V(\cdot)$ has the following properties:

(a) $V(\cdot)$ is continuous;

(b) For each initial vector, $\mathbf{x}_0$, the set of values taken on by $V(\cdot)$ is bounded below;

(c) $V(\mathbf{x})$ is decreasing through time unless $\mathbf{x}$ is a rest point of (A.1.1). That is, for all $t>0$,

$$V(\phi(t,\mathbf{x})) \leqslant V(\mathbf{x})$$

with equality holding only if $\mathbf{x}$ is a rest point of (A.1.1).

Then $V(\cdot)$ is called a *Lyapounov function* (for the process (A.1.1)).

In the example given above, w, defined in (A.2.2) is itself a Lyapounov function for the process given in (A.2.3) and (A.2.4). (Further examples appear in the body of the book.) That process, as already seen, is quasi-stable, which it must be, in view of:

Theorem A.3.1 (Lyapounov's Second Method). If the process (A.1.1) has a Lyapounov function, $V(\cdot)$, it is quasi-stable.

This is such a central theorem that I shall give two proofs. The first of these is easier to follow and quite illuminating but assumes that the Lyapounov function has a first derivative with respect to time that satisfies a Lipschitz Condition on the time interval $[0, \infty)$. It also requires that (c) of Definition A.3.1 be slightly strengthened to require $\dot{V}(\mathbf{x}) \leqslant 0$ and $\dot{V}(\mathbf{x})=0$ only for $\mathbf{x}$ a rest point.

Proof of Theorem A.3.1 when $V(\mathbf{x})$ is continuously differentiable. Since $V(\mathbf{x})$ is monotonically nonincreasing and is bounded below, it has a limit, say, $\bar{V}$ (which in general depends on $\mathbf{x}_0$). Thus it follows that

$$\lim_{t\to\infty} \dot{V}(\mathbf{x}(t))=0 \tag{A.3.1}$$

Let $\{t_\lambda\}\to\infty$ be an increasing infinite sequence of times with $\{\mathbf{x}_\lambda\}$ the corresponding sequence of values of $\mathbf{x}$. Suppose that $\{\mathbf{x}_\lambda\}$ converges to a point $\mathbf{x}^*$, that is,

$$\lim_{\lambda\to\infty} \mathbf{x}_\lambda=\mathbf{x}^* \tag{A.3.2}$$

We must prove that $\mathbf{x}^*$ is a rest point of (A.1.1).

Now,

$$\lim_{\lambda \to \infty} \dot{V}(\mathbf{x}_\lambda) = 0 \tag{A.3.3}$$

since (A.3.1) shows that $\dot{V}(\mathbf{x})$ converges to zero along *any* such infinite sequence of values in the time path of $\mathbf{x}$. By the continuity of $\dot{V}(\mathbf{x})$, then,

$$0 = \lim_{\lambda \to \infty} \dot{V}(\mathbf{x}_\lambda) = \dot{V}\left(\lim_{\lambda \to \infty} \mathbf{x}_\lambda\right) = \dot{V}(\mathbf{x}^*) \tag{A.3.4}$$

But $\dot{V}(\mathbf{x}) < 0$ unless $\mathbf{x}$ is a rest point of (A.1.1) so $\mathbf{x}^*$ must be such a rest point and the proof is complete.

The proof for the general case is similar in its ultimate structure, making use of first-differences instead of derivatives. However, there are some housekeeping details which are required first.

Proof of Theorem A.3.1 in the general case. As before, the fact that $V(\mathbf{x})$ is monotonically nonincreasing and bounded below means that it approaches a limit, say, $\bar{V}$. Consider an increasing infinite sequence of times $\{t_\lambda\} \to \infty$ and a corresponding sequence of values of $\mathbf{x}$, $\{\mathbf{x}_\lambda\}$ converging to a point $\mathbf{x}^*$ as in (A.3.2). Since both the sequence $\{t_\lambda\}$ and the sequence $\{\mathbf{x}_\lambda\}$ have an infinite number of members and the latter sequence converges, we will not change anything by deleting some members of the sequence (if necessary) by assuming:

$$t_{\lambda+1} \geqslant t_\lambda + 1 \tag{A.3.5}$$

$$\phi(t_\lambda + 1, \mathbf{x}_0) = \phi(1, \mathbf{x}_\lambda) \tag{A.3.6}$$

so that the value of $\mathbf{x}$ at time $(t_\lambda + 1)$ is a function, indeed, by earlier assumption, a *continuous* function of $\mathbf{x}_\lambda$. We can thus define

$$\Delta(\mathbf{x}_\lambda) \equiv V(\phi(t_\lambda + 1, \mathbf{x}_0)) - V(\mathbf{x}_\lambda) \tag{A.3.7}$$

a continuous function of $\mathbf{x}_\lambda$. Since $V(\mathbf{x})$ is decreasing out of equilibrium, it follows from (A.3.5) that

$$0 \geqslant \Delta(\mathbf{x}_\lambda) \geqslant V(\mathbf{x}_{\lambda+1}) - V(\mathbf{x}_\lambda) \tag{A.3.8}$$

Now, since $V(\mathbf{x})$ converges to $\bar{V}$ along any infinite sequence of values on the time path of $\mathbf{x}$, it must be true that

$$\lim_{\lambda \to \infty} \{V(\mathbf{x}_{\lambda+1}) - V(\mathbf{x}_\lambda)\} = 0 \tag{A.3.9}$$

whence

$$\lim_{\lambda \to \infty} \Delta(\mathbf{x}_\lambda) = 0 \tag{A.3.10}$$

Since $\Delta(\mathbf{x}_\lambda)$ is continuous, it follows that

$$0 = \lim_{\lambda \to \infty} \Delta(\mathbf{x}_\lambda) = \Delta\left(\lim_{\lambda \to \infty} \mathbf{x}_\lambda \right) = \Delta(\mathbf{x}^*) \tag{A.3.11}$$

However, $\Delta(\mathbf{x}) < 0$ unless $\mathbf{x}$ is a rest point of (A.1.1), whence $\mathbf{x}^*$ must be such a rest point and the theorem is proved.

References

Arrow, K. J. (1958). "Toward a Theory of Price Adjustment," in M. Abramovitz et al. (eds.), *The Allocation of Economic Resources: Essays in Honor of B. F. Haley*. Stanford: Stanford University Press.

Arrow, K. J., H. D. Block, and L. Hurwicz (1959). "On the Stability of the Competitive Equilibrium II," *Econometrica* 27, 82–109.

Arrow, K. J. and F. H. Hahn (1971). *General Competitive Analysis*. San Francisco: Holden-Day/Edinburgh: Oliver & Boyd.

Arrow, K. J. and L. Hurwicz (1958). "On the Stability of the Competitive Equilibrium I," *Econometrica* 26, 522–52.

Champsaur, P., J. Drèze, and C. Henry (1977). "Stability Theorems With Economic Applications," *Econometrica* 45, 273–94.

Clower, R. W. (1965). "The Keynesian Counterrevolution: a Theoretical Appraisal," in F. H. Hahn and F. P. R. Brechling (eds.), *The Theory of Interest Rates*. London: Macmillan/New York: St. Martin's Press.

Debreu, G. (1959). *Theory of Value: an Axiomatic Analysis of Economic Equilibrium*. New York: Wiley.

(1970). "Economies With a Finite Set of Equilibria," *Econometrica* 38, 387–92.

(1974). "Excess Demand Functions," *Journal of Mathematical Economics* 1, 15–21.

Diamond, P. A. (1971). "A Model of Price Adjustment," *Journal of Economic Theory* 3, 156–68.

Drazen, A. (1980). "Recent Developments in Macroeconomic Disequilibrium Theory," *Econometrica* 48, 283–306.

Fisher, F. M. (1961). "The Stability of the Cournot Oligopoly Solution: The Effects of Speeds of Adjustment and Increasing Marginal Costs," *Review of Economic Studies* 28, 125–35.

(1970). "Quasi-competitive Price Adjustment by Individual Firms: A Preliminary Paper," *Journal of Economic Theory* 2, 195–206.

(1972a). "Gross Substitutes and the Utility Function," *Journal of Economic Theory* 4, 82–7.

(1972b). "On Price Adjustment Without an Auctioneer," *Review of Economic Studies* 39, 1–15.

(1973). "Stability and Competitive Equilibrium in Two Models of Search and Individual Price Adjustment," *Journal of Economic Theory* 6, 446–70.

(1974). "The Hahn Process With Firms But No Production," *Econometrica* 42, 471–86.

(1976a). "A Non-Tâtonnement Model with Production and Consumption," *Econometrica* 44, 907–38.

(1976b). "The Stability of General Equilibrium: Results and Problems," in M. J. Artis and A. R. Nobay (eds.), *Essays in Economic Analysis (The Proceedings of the Association of University Teachers of Economics, Sheffield 1975)*. Cambridge University Press.

(1977). "Continuously Dated Commodities and Non-Tâtonnement with Production and Consumption," in A. S. Blinder and P. Friedman (eds.), *Natural Resources, Uncertainty, and General Equilibrium Systems: Essays in Memory of Rafael Lusky*. New York: Academic Press.

(1981). "Stability, Disequilibrium Awareness, and the Perception of New Opportunities," *Econometrica* 49, 279–318.

Fisher, F. M. and F. M. C. B. Saldanha (1982). "Stability, Disequilibrium Awareness, and the Perception of New Opportunities: Some Corrections," *Econometrica* 50, 781–83.

Goose, M. (n.d.) *Nursery Rhymes*. Various publishers.

Hahn, F. H. (1958). "Gross Substitutes and the Dynamic Stability of General Equilibrium," *Econometrica* 26, 169–70.

(1962a). "A Stable Adjustment Process for a Competitive Economy," *Review of Economic Studies* 29, 62–5.

(1962b). "On the Stability of Pure Exchange Equilibrium," *International Economic Review* 3, 206–13.

(1978). "On Non-Walrasian Equilibria," *Review of Economic Studies* 45, 1–18.

(1982). "Stability," in K. Arrow and M. Intrilligator (eds.), *Handbook of Mathematical Economics*. Amsterdam: North-Holland.

Hahn, F. H. and T. Negishi (1962). "A Theorem on Non-Tâtonnement Stability," *Econometrica* 30, 463–9.

Henry, C. (1973a). "An Existence Theorem for a Class of Differential Equations With Multivalued Right-Hand Side," *Journal of Mathematical Analysis and Applications* 41, 179–86.

(1973b). "Problèmes d'Existence et de Stabilité Pour des Processes Dynamiques Considerés en Economie Mathematique," Laboratoire d'Econometrie de l'Ecole Polytechnique.

Hicks, J. (1939). *Value and Capital*. New York: Oxford University Press (Clarendon Press).

Kagawa, A. and K. Kuga (1980). "On Professor Hahn's Tâtonnement Stability Theorem: Comment and Example," *Review of Economic Studies* 47, 813–16.

Keynes, J. M. (1936). *The General Theory of Employment, Interest, and Money*. New York: Harcourt, Brace.

Koopmans, T. C. (1957). *Three Essays on the State of Economic Science*. New York: McGraw-Hill.

Kurz, M. and R. W. Wilson (1974). "On the Structure of Trade," *Western Economic Journal* 12, 492–516.

Lucas, R. E. (1976). "Econometric Policy Evaluation: A Critique," in K. Brunner and A. H. Meltzer (eds.), *The Phillips Curve and Labor Markets*. (Carnegie–Rochester Conferences on Public Policy 1, supplement to *Journal of Monetary Economics*). Amsterdam, New York, Oxford: North-Holland.

(1977). "Understanding Business Cycles," in K. Brunner and A. H. Meltzer (eds.), *Stabilization of the Domestic and International Economy* (Carnegie-Rochester Conferences on Public Policy 5, supplement to *Journal of Monetary Economics*). Amsterdam, New York, Oxford: North-Holland.

Luenberger, D. G. (1969). *Optimization by Vector Space Methods*. New York: McGraw-Hill.

Lyapounov, A. (1907). "Problème Génèral de la Stabilité du Mouvement," *Annales de la Faculté des Sciences de l'Université de Toulouse* 9, 203–474.

McFadden, D. (1968). "On Hicksian Stability," in J. N. Wolfe (ed.), *Value, Capital, and Growth. Papers in Honour of Sir John Hicks*. Edinburgh: Edinburgh University Press.

Madden, P. (1978). "Why the Edgeworth Process Assumption Isn't That Bad," *Review of Economic Studies* 45, 279–84.

Mantel, R. (1976). "Homothetic Preferences and Community Excess Demand Functions," *Journal of Economic Theory* 12, 197–201.

Metzler, L. (1945). "The Stability of Multiple Markets: The Hicks Conditions," *Econometrica* 13, 277–92.

Negishi, T. (1958). "A Note on the Stability of an Economy Where All Goods Are Gross Substitutes," *Econometrica* 26, 445–7.

(1962). "The Stability of a Competitive Economy: A Survey Article," *Econometrica* 30, 635–69.

Patinkin, D. (1949). "The Indeterminacy of Absolute Prices in Classical Economic Theory," *Econometrica* 17, 1–27.

(1950). "A Reconsideration of the General Equilibrium Theory of Money," *Review of Economic Studies* 18, 42–61.

(1965). *Money, Interest and Prices* (second edition). New York: Harper & Row.

Saldanha, F. M. C. B. (1982). *Essays on Non-Tâtonnement Stability*. Unpublished doctoral dissertation, Massachusetts Institute of Technology.

Samuelson, P. A. (1941). "The Stability of Equilibrium," *Econometrica* 9, 97–120.

(1947). *Foundations of Economic Analysis*, Cambridge, Mass.: Harvard University Press.

Scarf, H. (1960). "Some Examples of Global Instability of the Competitive Equilibrium," *International Economic Review* 1, 157–72.

(1973). "The Computation of Economic Equilibria" (in collaboration with T. Hansen). New Haven: Yale University Press.

Schumpeter, J. (1939). *Business Cycles*. New York: McGraw-Hill.

(1951). *The Theory of Economic Development* (fourth printing). Cambridge, Mass.: Harvard University Press.

(1962). *Capitalism, Socialism and Democracy* (third edition). New York: Harper & Row.

Smale, S. (1976a). "A Convergent Process of Price Adjustment and Global Newton Methods," *Journal of Mathematical Economics* 3, 107–20.

(1976b). "Exchange Processes With Price Adjustment," *Journal of Mathematical Economics* 3, 211–26.

Sonnenschein, H. (1972). "Market Excess Demand Functions," *Econometrica* 40, 549–63.

(1973). "Do Walras' Identity and Continuity Characterize the Class of Community Excess Demand Functions?" *Journal of Economic Theory* 6, 345–54.

Theocharis, R. D. (1960). "On the Stability of the Cournot Oligopoly Solution," *Review of Economic Studies* 27, 133–4.

Uzawa, H. (1961). "The Stability of Dynamic Processes," *Econometrica* 29, 317–31.

(1962). "On the Stability of Edgeworth's Barter Process," *International Economic Review* 3, 218–32.

Index

Printed in the United States
By Bookmasters